Essential Arabic Vocabulary
Vocabulary
A handbook of core terms

Mourad Diouri

This edition published in 2015 by John Murray Learning

Copyright © Mourad Diouri 2015

The right of Mourad Diouri to be identified as the Author of the Work has been asserted by him in accordance with the Copyright, Designs and Patents Act 1988.

Database right Hodder & Stoughton (makers)

The *Teach Yourself* name is a registered trademark of Hachette UK.

British Library Cataloguing in Publication Data: a catalogue record for this title is available from the British Library.

ISBN: 9781473600591

eBook ISBN: 9781473600607

3

The publisher has used its best endeavours to ensure that any website addresses referred to in this book are correct and active at the time of going to press. However, the publisher and the author have no responsibility for the websites and can make no guarantee that a site will remain live or that the content will remain relevant, decent or appropriate.

The publisher has made every effort to mark as such all words which it believes to be trademarks. The publisher should also like to make it clear that the presence of a word in the book, whether marked or unmarked, in no way affects its legal status as a trademark.

Every reasonable effort has been made by the publisher to trace the copyright holders of material in this book. Any errors or omissions should be notified in writing to the publisher, who will endeavour to rectify the situation for any reprints and future editions.

Typeset by Datapage India (Pvt.) Ltd.

Printed and bound in Great Britain by CPI Group (UK) Ltd., Croydon, CR0 4YY.

John Murray Learning policy is to use papers that are natural, renewable and recyclable products and made from wood grown in sustainable forests. The logging and manufacturing processes are expected to conform to the environmental regulations of the country of origin.

John Murray Learning
Carmelite House
50 Victoria Embankment
London
EC4Y 0DZ

www.hodder.co.uk

Dedication

This book is dedicated in loving memory to my late grandmother

Lalla Rhimou El-Bazi (لالا ارحيمو البازي)

who played a huge role in my upbringing and was one of the strongest role models of strength, compassion and character.

Acknowledgements

Firstly, thanks to my beloved life companion, best friend and wife Umm-Taha (أم طه) for her continuous support and honest feedback since I started writing my first book.

I am grateful to my editor Frances Amrani and to Robert Williams for their continuous encouragement and patience during the process of writing and production. Their professionalism meant that the project was kept on track and achieved its major milestones in a timely manner.

Many thanks to Dr Muntasir Al-Hamad for his expert perspective on reviewing the vocabulary material.

I also would like to thank Salem Al-Mandhari for help with the meticulous vocalization of the Arabic text in the final stages of the project.

My particular thanks to all my colleagues and students who kindly volunteered to review the draft material and provide generous feedback: Abla Oudeh, Kevin Moore, Jona Fras, Thomas Finch, Suzana Brezinova, Pesha Magid, Lin Chih-lan, Liza Melms, Melanie Quintero, Gabrielle Roth and Isabel Lachenauer.

For the initial support and endorsement of the project idea, I would like to than Sarah Irving, Caitlin Simpson, Robert Smart and Tim Tabler.

شُكْرًا لَكُم وتَحيّاتي الحارّة للجَميع   Thank you and best wishes to you all.

Text credits

Unit 20
A frequency dictionary of Arabic, core vocabulary for learners
Tim Buckwalter, Dilworth Parkinson, Routledge, 2011

Photo Credits

Unit 10
Coats of arms: Wikipedia
Casablanca sign: © Mourad Diouri
Casablanca movie poster: Wikipedia

Unit 19
Maltese sign: Western Australian Museum

Contents

Meet the author

My name is Mourad Diouri. I am a native Arabic speaker, originally from Tangiers (طَنْجة), Morocco (المغرب). Currently, I am a teaching fellow and an e-learning instructor/developer in Arabic language studies at CASAW (Centre for the Advanced Study of the Arab World), University of Edinburgh.

This is my second book in the Teach Yourself series, following *Read and Write Arabic Script*. I very much look forward to being your guide on your journey of mastering the vocabulary of this beautiful language.

The idea of this book came about after I noticed that, while there are numerous instructional textbooks teaching Arabic at beginner, intermediate and advanced level, there are very few lexicons that could accompany these textbooks. Something extra was needed to help the committed language learner, such as yourself, to acquire vocabulary efficiently and improve their skill in reading Arabic texts.

The book grew out of a need and desire, shared by many, to create a comprehensive and compact theme-based guide to furnish and bring learners of Arabic up to speed with contemporary and commonly used vocabulary. This guide covers the essential terms every learner must possess from beginner up to advanced level.

Every effort has been made to ensure that this book is up to date at the time of compilation and that it includes the most common and current terms. However, I cannot claim that this book is exhaustive.

Also, since this is a human effort, mistakes might exist and constructive feedback, from students and teachers alike, would be most welcome. Whatever faults or shortcomings there are in the book, they remain mine and will be rectified in future editions.

If you have any suggestions, comments or just want to get in touch, please contact me via the portal: www.yaqut.org

Let's get started! لنبدأ على بركة الله

Welcome to *Essential Arabic Vocabulary*.

مَرْحَبًا بِكُم في كِتاب "عَلِّم نَفْسَك: الـمُفْرَدات العَرَبِيّة الأساسِيّة! التي تَحْتاج حَقاً إلى مَعْرِفَتِها".

مراد الديوري Mourad Diouri

Introduction

This new vocabulary guide has been designed for both beginners and those who have already embarked on learning Arabic.

It has been written particularly for learners studying on their own, although I am confident that it will be an essential study companion and vocabulary-building tool for classroom use.

The book contains over 10,000 vocabulary items arranged in easy-to-learn theme-based lists divided into 20 self-contained units, covering most aspects of everyday life. These range from everyday reference language to spoken Arabic, covering a wide range of generic themes such as *family and relations, education, work, food and drink, health, shopping, weather, arts and entertainment, sports, nature, travel, tourism, economics, politics* and many others.

Some contemporary and emerging themes have been covered, such as *environmental issues, science and technology, feminism, e-learning, social networking, digital identity, online activism* and *the Internet*.

However, in order to enhance cultural awareness, theme-based vocabulary specific to the Arab world and culture is also included, for instance: *popular Arab dishes and Arabic music genres, Arab currencies, language varieties in Arabic, national holidays* and *famous tourist sites in the Arab world*.

Also more importantly, to help you keep up to date with current affairs in the Arab world, specialized vocabulary sections have been included to address issues such as *the Arab Spring, human rights, the Arab–Israeli conflict, security and intelligence, political organizations, ethnic and religious groups and social issues*.

The theme-based vocabulary units, which make up the core of this guide, provide a comprehensive source of essential must-know words to help you understand the gist of important issues taught in Arabic language curricula across different educational settings around the world. This also includes students of GCSE (General Certificate of Secondary Education) Arabic.

TARGET AUDIENCE

This book has been compiled to meet the needs of anyone learning Arabic as a foreign language. It provides a concise, quick-fix guide to the most essential and commonly used vocabulary items.

t is primarily for English speakers who wish to master Arabic vocabulary
easily and speedily. However, the book is also valuable
to native Arabic speakers who are learning English as a foreign language.

Whatever reasons motivate you to learn Arabic vocabulary, you will find the
material in this guide particularly useful and comprehensive.

How this book works

STRUCTURE

Each unit has its own internal logic in terms of the way vocabulary is organized.
Units are divided into vocabulary groupings or families organized into sub-
themes with subtitles for ease of learning and searching. Most units contain

sections of *core vocabulary* (مُفْرَدات أساسيّة). Some units are also
grouped by meaning and word-origin.

The words listed have been meticulously selected because they are essential and
relevant to anyone studying Modern Standard Arabic (MSA).

The vocabulary items are listed in thematic groupings and subsections
within each unit, starting with basic words and ending with advanced words,
thus enabling you to develop a good mastery of the relevant topic.

You will notice that units vary slightly in length and extent of vocabulary
covered. For instance, Unit 16 (Politics and the military) contains more terms
than Unit 6 (At home) or Unit 7 (In town).

Alphabetical ordering of vocabulary has been avoided on purpose, since this can
be counterproductive to learning and memorization. This is also more complex
in Arabic since ordering is normally based on the root of a word rather than the
word itself.

All the vocabulary lists are structured logically and incorporate:

What will you learn: introducing the detailed contents of each unit.

As the Arabs say ... كَما قالتِ العَرَب

In each unit, you will be rewarded with plenty of opportunities to see Arabic
vocabulary contextualized, using popular Arabic. These quotes will expose you
to the poetic nature and cultural richness of Arabic and include proverbs, quotes,
poetry lines, Qur'anic verses and colloquial sayings. You are strongly advised to
study these quotes to enhance your spoken and written Arabic. In total, there
are 66 quotes, which have been recorded and are provided with a key to the
vocabulary. These are available at www.aas.yaqut.org

Insights: these are short author insights into language and grammar that
are useful to know.

4 **'You Already Speak Arabic' insights:** to familiarize yourself with commonly used Arabic loanwords that exist in English and other European languages.

5 **Study tips.**

PRONUNCIATION OF VOCABULARY

Phonetic transcription (or transliteration) of the Arabic script has been consciously avoided, as it can be an obstacle to learning rather than an aid.

However, to support correct pronunciation of Arabic vocabulary, the text is fully vocalized. This provides beginners with plenty of opportunity to practise reading Arabic.

NOTES ON PRESENTATION

Plural abbreviations

In the majority of cases, Arabic words are supplied in both the singular and plural using the following abbreviations:

(ج)   for all plurals (the letter ج stands for جمع i.e. plural)

ات-   for sound feminine plural

ون-   for sound masculine plural

For example:

تَقْليد (ج) تَقاليد   *tradition*   مُدَرِّس (ج) ون-   *teacher*

ثَقافة (ج) ات-   *culture*   جامِعة (ج) ات-   *university*

Synonyms

\	for Arabic synonyms
/ or ,	for English synonyms
(1), (2), (3)	synonyms are numbered between (1) and (3)
coll.	colloquial Arabic (unspecified or most dialects)
Egy.	Egyptian dialect
Fr.	French
Lev.	Levantine dialect
MSA	Modern Standard Arabic

Other abbreviations

ة   feminine ending Taa' Marbuta (e.g. جديدة)

adv.   adverb

adj.	adjective
e.g.	for example
f.	feminine
i.e.	that is
lit.	literally
m.	masculine
n.	noun
pl.	plural
st.	something
so.	someone
v.t.	transitive verb
v.i.	intransitive verb

Presentation of verbs

Verbs have been presented as the basic root (past tense masc. singular) followed by the present tense and then the verbal noun (Masdar).

For example: دَرَّس يُدَرِّس تَدْريس   to teach

NOTES ON VOCALIZATION (التَّشْكيل)

The Arabic text has been fully vocalized to ensure correct pronunciation. However, bear in mind the following exceptions:

Short vowels have been omitted, particularly when:

▶ a Fatha precedes a long Alif (ا) or a Taa' Marbuta (ة)

▶ a Kasra precedes a long Ya' (ي)

▶ a Damma precedes a long Waw (و)

In addition:

▶ Vowels of grammatical endings known as (التنوين) are not supplied since they are not generally pronounced and vary depending on grammatical structures. However, adverbs have been vocalized, e.g. أَحْيانًا

▶ There is no Kasra under Alif or Ya' with hamza below, e.g. مائدة الإسْلام or

▶ The Ya' of the relative adjective is vocalized with a Shadda, while the Kasra that precedes it is not supplied, e.g. عالَميّ

▶ The definite article ال is not vocalized. However, the sun and moon letters are fully vocalized to help with correct pronunciation, e.g. القَمَر and الشَّمْس

MAIN FEATURES OF THE BOOK

This book provides:

1 a handy concise reference guide to any unfamiliar Arabic term
2 a collection of the core and most commonly used terms and phrases
3 a logical format, which enables:

    a ease of reference (vocabulary organized into theme-based units instead of in alphabetical order)

    b the book to be easy to read and navigate

4 vocalization of each Arabic term (to aid pronunciation), followed by an equivalent in English (or the nearest meaning).

Learn to learn

There have been many studies carried out into the way we learn vocabulary. The Swiss, who are generally acknowledged as experts in multi-language learning, are also leaders in the understanding of the processes of language acquisition and some of their findings may be of interest to people wanting to broaden their vocabulary.

> **Studies have shown that the most successful way of learning vocabulary is when the student is able to relate the new word to a concept and to integrate it into a conceptual system. (Wokusch, 1997)[1]**

Put simply, this means that the most successful way of learning vocabulary is to put the new language into a context. When a child first learns a language they are learning the concepts at the same time as the language. If you give a child an ice cream and say 'ice cream', they are learning the word and the concept of ice cream. An adult has the advantage of already having the concept. An ice cream already conjures up other words: *cold, vanilla, strawberry, like/don't like, price,* etc.

Similarly, if you decide to learn about a computer or a car, you probably already know the parts or expressions you want to learn and can visualize them before you meet the word. In fact, you already have the concept and you can 'place' the new words within that concept. It is for this reason that the vocabulary in the book has been grouped in context rather than, as in a dictionary, in alphabetical order. The words chosen are those most likely to be useful or of interest to the learner.

HOW TO LEARN ARABIC VOCABULARY

Among the most fascinating aspects of the Arabic language is the richness of its vocabulary and its rhetorical devices. Vocabulary is considered by linguists to be one of the most essential tools that language learners require to construct meaning and communicate effectively. Good reading comprehension, as well as fluency in speaking, is fundamentally dependent on how robust and sophisticated our knowledge of vocabulary is.

Learning Arabic vocabulary is an extremely rewarding experience on your journey towards mastering the language. Yet, at the same time, 'the acquisition of vocabulary is the most important challenge that learners of Arabic face'[2].

Here are some successful tips and strategies to help you learn Arabic vocabulary efficiently.

BE A SUCCESSFUL LANGUAGE LEARNER

Everyone can succeed in learning a language – the key is knowing how.

Learning is more than just reading or memorizing vocabulary lists. It's about being an active learner, learning in real contexts, and, most importantly, using what you've learned in different situations.

Simply put, *if you figure it out for yourself*, you're more likely to understand it. And when you use what you've learned, you're more likely to remember it.

Make a habit out of learning

- Study a little every day, between 20 and 30 minutes if possible, rather than two to three hours in one session.
  Give yourself short-term goals, e.g. work out how long you'll spend on a particular unit and work within the time limit. This will help you to create a study habit, much as you would for a sport or music.
- You will need to concentrate, so try to create an environment conducive to learning, which is calm and quiet and free from distractions.
- As you study, do not worry about your mistakes or the things you can't remember or understand. Languages settle differently in our brains, but gradually the language will become clearer as your brain starts to make new connections. Just give yourself enough time and you will succeed.

Expand your language contact

As part of your study habit, try to take other opportunities to expose yourself to the language. As well as using this book, you could try listening to the radio and television, or reading articles and blogs. Perhaps you could find information in Arabic about a personal passion or hobby or even a news story that interests you. In time you'll find that your vocabulary and language recognition deepens and you'll become used to a range of writing and speaking styles.

Pronunciation

When organizing the study of pronunciation, keep a section of your notebook for pronunciation rules and practise those that trouble you. Repeat all the words you find difficult to pronounce. Listen to yourself and try to mimic what you hear.

- ► Record yourself and compare your pronunciation to that of a native speaker.
- ► Make a list of words that give you trouble and practise them.
- ► Study individual sounds, then full words.
- ► Don't forget, it's not just about pronouncing letters and words correctly but using the right intonation. So, when practising words and sentences, mimic the rising and falling intonation of native speakers.
- ► Listen to different Arabic dialects by watching movies or listening to national radio stations online.

4 Grammar

- ► To organize the study of Arabic grammar, write your own grammar glossary and add new information and examples as you go along.
- ► Experiment with grammar rules. Sit back and reflect on the rules you learn. See how they compare with your own language or other languages you may already speak.
- ► Try to find out some rules on your own and be ready to spot the exceptions. By doing this you'll remember the rules better and get a feel for the language.
- ► Try to find examples of grammar in conversations or other articles.
- ► Keep a 'pattern bank' that organizes examples that can be listed under the structures you've learned.
- ► Use old vocabulary to practise new grammar structures.
- ► When you learn a new verb form, write the conjugation of several different verbs you know that follow the same form.

5 Listening and reading

When listening to conversations and reading texts, you can go further by following some of these tips:

- ► Imagine the situation. When listening to or reading the conversations, try to imagine where the scene is taking place and who the main characters are. Let your experience of the world help you guess the meaning of the conversation, e.g. if a conversation takes place in a market you can predict the kind of vocabulary that will be used.
- ► Concentrate on the main part. When watching a foreign film, you usually get the meaning of the whole story from a few individual shots. Understanding an Arabic conversation or article is similar. Concentrate on the main parts to get the message and don't worry about individual words.
- ► Guess the key words; if you cannot, ask or look them up.
- ► When there are key words you don't understand, try to guess what they mean from the context.

6 Speaking

Rehearse in Arabic! As all language teachers will assure you, the successful learners are those students who overcome their inhibitions and get into situations where they must speak, write and listen to the foreign language.

Here are some useful tips to help you practise speaking Arabic:

► Hold a conversation with yourself (or, better, with a study partner).
► After you have conducted a transaction with a salesperson, clerk or waiter in your own language, pretend that you have to do it in Arabic, e.g. buying groceries, ordering food, drinks and so on.
► Look at people around you and try to describe them in detail.
► Keep talking! The best way to improve your fluency in Arabic is to talk every time you have the opportunity to do so.
► Keep the conversations flowing and don't worry about the mistakes.
► If you get stuck for a particular word, don't let the conversation stop; paraphrase or replace the unknown word with one you do know, even if you have to simplify what you want to say.
► As a last resort, use the word from your own language and pronounce it in the foreign accent.

7 Learn from your errors

► Don't let errors interfere with getting your message across. Making errors is part of any normal learning process, but some people get so worried that they won't say anything unless they are sure it is correct. This leads to a vicious circle as the less they say, the less practice they get and the more mistakes they make.
► Note the seriousness of errors. Many errors are not serious as they do not affect the meaning. So concentrate on getting your message across and learn from your mistakes.

8 Learn to cope with uncertainty

► Don't over-use your dictionary.
► When reading a text in Arabic, don't be tempted to look up every word you don't know. Underline the words you do not understand and read the passage several times, concentrating on trying to get the gist of the passage. If after the third time there are still words which prevent you from getting the general meaning of the passage, look them up in the dictionary.
► Don't panic if you don't understand.
► If at some point you feel you don't understand what you are told, don't panic or give up listening. Either try to guess what is being said and keep following the conversation or, if you cannot, isolate the expression or words you haven't understood and have them explained to you. The speaker might paraphrase them and the conversation will carry on.

MAKE LEARNING A LIST OF WORDS MORE INTERESTING

To make learning a list of words more interesting, follow these steps:

▶ First, decide the theme you are going to look at.
▶ See how many words you know already and tick them off.
▶ Choose the new words you want to learn – don't try too many at once!
▶ Say them aloud. Record yourself saying them in Arabic.
▶ Use them in a real context.
▶ Go online and search for a short article related to the theme selected. Read the article and look out for the words just learned.
▶ Take note of new or emerging words that are not covered in this book.

1   Wokusch, S (1997), *L'apprentissage du vocabulaire: que se passe-t-il dans nos têtes?*, UNIL/CHUV Switzerland.

2   Al-Batal, M. (2006) 'Playing with words: Teaching vocabulary in the Arabic curriculum *Handbook for Arabic Language Teaching Professionals in the 21st Century*, ed. K. Wahba, Z. Taha, L. England, Mahwah, NJ: Lawrence Erlbaum Associates Inc.

Toolbox: Essential grammar

Basic grammar structures and rules, mainly related to learning Arabic vocabulary, are summarized in this section. For detailed lessons on grammar, please refer to established grammar books.

Gender (الجنس)

Nouns in Arabic, be they human or non-human, are either masculine (مذكر) or feminine (مؤنث).

While masculine nouns are unmarked, feminine nouns are distinctively identified with the following feminine ending or suffix:

1 **Tied Taa'** (التاء المربوطة): ة\ـة

طالبة	طالب
جدة	جد
بنية	بني

2 **Shortened Alif** (الألف المقصورة): ى

مستشفى	*hospital*
دعوى	*lawsuit, invitation*
ليلى	*Laila (proper name)*

3 **Alif-Hamza** (ألف همزة): ـاء

صحراء	*desert, Sahara*
عذراء	*virgin*
حمراء	*red* (f. form of أحمر)
زرقاء	*blue* (f. form of أزرق)

Nouns

PLURAL SYSTEM نظام الجموع العربية

In Arabic, there are mainly two types of plural:

▶ Sound plural (الجمع السالم)

▶ Broken or irregular plural (جمع التكسير)

Throughout this book, the majority of plurals are provided alongside the singular indicated by the abbreviation (ج).

Sound plural (الجمع السالم)

Sound plurals are formed by simply adding a suffix to the singular noun. There are two types of suffix:

▶ ون- or ين- for the masculine sound plural (جمع المذكَّر السالم)

▶ ات- for the feminine sound plural (جمع المؤنَّث السالم)

For example:

Humans

معلمات	معلمون	معلم	teachers
مسلمات	مسلمون	مسلم	Muslims
مترجمات	مترجمون	مترجم	translators

Non-humans

كلمات	كلمة	words
سيارات	سيارة	cars
طاولات	طاولة	tables

Broken or irregular plural (جمع التكسير)

Broken plurals in Arabic are similar to the irregular plural in English (e.g. *mouse–mice*, *foot–feet*, etc.)

The pattern does not normally retain the structure of the singular noun and broken plurals are formed by applying a variety of patterns (وزن ج. أوزان) (about 30 in total).

When memorizing broken plurals, you should bear in mind the following:

▶ There is no one rule which governs the formation of the broken plural.

▶ Broken plurals are best learned by exposure and memorization alongside the singular.

▶ The broken plural occurs more frequently than the sound plural.

The following table contains some of the most common patterns.

Plural	Singular	English	Plural	Singular	English
(أَفْعُل)					
أَشْهُر	شَهْر	*month*			
أنفس	نفس	*soul, breath*			
أرجل	رجل	*feet*			
(أَفْعال)			These are the exception to the rule		
أولاد	وَلَد	*boy, son*	أخوات	أخت	*sister*
ألوان	لون	*colour*	آباء	أب	*father (fathers or parents)*
أخبار	خبر	*news (item)*	أمهات	أم	*mother*
(أَفْعِلة)			**(فُعُل)**		
أسئلة	سؤال	*question*	كُتب	كتاب	*book*
أطعمة	طعام	*food*	مدن	مَدينة	*city*
ألبسة	لباس	*dress, clothing*	أسر	أسرة	*family*
(فُعول)			**(فُعَل)**		
دُروس	دَرْس	*lesson*	غرف	غرفة	*room*
بيوت	بيت	*house*	صور	صورة	*picture*
علوم	علم	*science*	حجج	حجة	*proof, excuse*
(أَفْعِلاء)			**(فعال)**		
أصدقاء	صديق	*friend*	جبال	جبل	*mountain*
أغنياء	غني	*rich*	رجال	رَجُل	*man*
أنبياء	نَبِيّ	*prophet*	كلاب	كلب	*dog*

(فُعْلان)

	الجمع	المفرد	
country, land	بُلْدان	بلَد	
monk	رهبان	راهب	
shirt	قمصان	قميص	

(فُعَّال)

الجمع	المفرد	
طلاب	طالب	student
كتاب	كاتب	writer
تجار	تاجر	trader

(فُعَلاء)

الجمع	المفرد	
وُزَراء	وَزير	minister
فقراء	فقير	poor
سفراء	سفير	ambassador

(أفاعل)

الجمع	المفرد	
أماكن	مكان	place
أقارب	قريب	relative
أجانب	أجنبي	foreigner

(أفاعيل)

الجمع	المفرد	
أسابيع	أسبوع	week
أقاليم	إقليم	province
أساليب	أسلوب	method, way

(مَفاعل)

الجمع	المفرد	
مدارس	مَدْرَسَة	school
مكاتب	مكتب	office, desk
منازل	منزل	house

(مفاعيل)

الجمع	المفرد	
مفاتيح	مفتاح	key
سلاطين	سُلْطان	Sultan
مناديل	منديل	napkin

(فعاللة)

الجمع	المفرد	
تَلامِذَة	تِلْميذ	pupil
أساتذة	أستاذ	teacher
مغاربة	مغربي	Moroccan

(فعالل)

الجمع	المفرد	
تذاكر	تذكرة	ticket
تجارب	تجربة	experience
مطاعم	مطعم	restaurant

(فعلى)

الجمع	المفرد	
مرضى	مريض	patient
أسرى	أسير	prisoner
قتلى	قتيل	killed, fatality

In addition to the sound and broken plurals, you should also be aware that there are the 'collective nouns'. These nouns indicate a gathering in one unit or group, can refer to both humans and non-humans and are treated mostly as masculine singular.

For example:

عِنْدي أَرْبَعة شَجَرات في الحَديقة — I have four trees in the garden. (sound pl.)

عِنْدي أَشْجار كَثيرة في الحَديقة — I have many trees in the garden. (broken pl.)

هُناك شَجَر كَثير في الحَديقة — There are many trees in the garden. (collective nouns)

Further examples

Singular	Sound plural	Collective noun	Broken plural	English
دجاجة	دجاجات	دجاج	—	chicken
ليلة	ليلات	ليال	—	nights
سمكة	سمكات	سمك	أسماك	fish
تفاحة	تفاحات	تفاح	—	apples

● INSIGHT – HOW TO PLURALIZE ADJECTIVES

Sound plurals

Adjectives that modify masculine nouns end in ون-, whereas those that modify feminine nouns end in ات-.

جميلون جميلات جميل *beautiful*

فقيرون فقيرات فقير *poor*

Irregular plurals

كبار كبير *big*

صغار صغير *small*

For human nouns that have both masculine and feminine forms, often the feminine plural is regular while the masculine is irregular. For example:

أصدقاء	صديقات	friends
طلاب	طالبات	students
زملاء	زميلات	colleagues

NOUNS OF PLACE, TIME AND INSTRUMENT
(أسماء المكان والزمان والآلة)
Noun of place (اسم المكان)

Nouns of place indicate the place where the action of the corresponding verb took place. Arabic nouns of place (أسماء المكان) are easy to derive from any root word by adding the prefix مـ to the root according to the following three patterns: (مَفْعَلة), (مَفْعِل) or (مَفْعَل).

Their plural is broken and is formed following the patterns: مَفاعِل or مَفاعيل

> **STUDY TIP**
> As long as you are familiar with the basic meaning of common root verbs, it is extremely useful to learn the three patterns above. It will help you guess new nouns of place or time easily, which I am sure you will come across regularly in your reading practice.

Here are some common verbs with their derived nouns of place.

Pattern 1: (مَفْعَل)

Root verb		Noun of place	
كتب	to write	مكتب	office, desktop
دخل	to enter	مدخل	entry
خرج	to exit	مخرج	exit
طعم	to eat, taste	مطعم	restaurant

> ● **INSIGHT – YOU ALREADY SPEAK ARABIC!**
>
> The term مخازن, i.e. *storehouses*, is the plural of مخزن which is an Arabic loanword in the English language which eventually became *magazine*.

Pattern 2: (مَفْعِل)

جلس	to sit down	مجلس	seat, council
نزل	to reside, settle	منزل	residence
سجد	to prostrate	مسجد	mosque (lit. prostration place)

Pattern 3: (مَفْعَلة)

كتب	to write	مكتبة	library, bookshop
درس	to study	مدرسة	school
حكم	to rule, judge	محكمة	courthouse
خبز	to bake	مخبزة	bakery
زرع	to plant, sow	مزرعة	farm

Verbs that start with /أ/

أَكَل	to eat	مأكل	dining area

Verbs that have a long /ا/ in the middle

طار	to fly	مطار	airport
كان	to be	مكان	place
زار	to visit	مزار	pilgrim site, shrine
قال	to say	مقال\مقالة	speech, article

Verbs with the letter و

وقف	to stop	موقف (سيارات)	parking area
وصل	to arrive	موصل	connecting place

Adverbs of time and place that are derived from verbs with more than three letters are formed following different patterns. The following table summarizes all the patterns for each verb form.

Examples		Adverbs of time and place	Verb form (I–X)
مكتب\منزل\ مكتبة	desk, house, library	مَفْعَل\مَفْعِل\ مَفْعَلة	فَعِلَ فَعَلَ I
—		—	فَعَّلَ II
—		—	فاعَلَ III
—		—	أَفْعَلَ IV
—		—	تَفَعَّلَ V
—		—	تَفاعَلَ VI
منخفض	low	مُنْفَعَل	انْفَعَلَ VII
مفترق	crossroads	مُفْتَعَل	افْتَعَلَ VIII
—	—	—	افْعَلَّ IX
مُسْتَشْفى	hospital	مُسْتَفْعَل	اسْتَفْعَلَ X

Noun of time (اسم الزمان)

Nouns of time indicate the time when the action of the corresponding verb took place. They are formed by following the same patterns as discussed.

Examples:			
وعد	to promise	موعد	appointment
ولد	to give birth	مولد	birthdate or birthplace
غرب	to go westward	مغرب	time (or place) of sunrise
اسْتَقْبَل	to receive	مُسْتَقْبَل	future

Noun of instrument (اسم الآلة)

Instrumental nouns indicate the tool of the action corresponding to the root verb. They are formed only from verb form I by following the patterns (مِفْعَل), (مِفْعال) or (مِفْعَلة). For example:

8

فتح	to open	مفتاح	key
غسل	to wash	مغسلة	laundry
نشر	to saw	منشار	saw
حرث	to plough, cultivate	محراث	plough
كنس	to sweep	مكنسة	broom

VERBAL NOUNS (المصدر)

In Arabic, each verb has its own corresponding verbal noun, or Masdar, which is predominantly predictable and regular. This makes the Masdar extremely easy to derive by following a fixed pattern as in the table.

Verbal nouns simply indicate the action or act related to the verb. For instance, if the verb is to study (درس), the verbal noun is studying (دراسة), i.e. the act of studying.

Examples		Verbal noun	Verb form (I–X)	
		(المصدر)		
studying/ working	دراسة\عمل	فَعْل\فَعالة	فَعِلَ\فَعَلَ	I
teaching/ strengthening	تدريس\تقوية	تَفْعيل\تَفْعِلة	فَعَّلَ	II
correspondence/ dispute	مكاتبة\خصام	مُفاعَلة\فِعال	فاعَلَ	III
direction (film)	إخراج	إفْعال	أفْعَلَ	IV
graduation	تخرج	تَفَعُّل	تَفَعَّلَ	V
collaboration	تعاون	تَفاعُل	تَفاعَلَ	VI
withdrawal	انسحاب	انْفِعال	انْفَعَلَ	VII
meeting	اجتماع	افْتِعال	افْتَعَلَ	VIII
redness	احمرار	افْعِلال	افْعَلَّ	IX
independence	إستقلال	اسْتِفْعال	اسْتَفْعَلَ	X

PRONOUNS (الضمائر)

There are three types of pronoun in Arabic:

1 Possessive pronouns (attached) (ضمائر الملكية)

2 Subject pronouns (detached) (ضمائر الفاعل)

3 Object pronouns (detached) (ضمائر المفعول)

1 Possessive pronouns (attached) (ضمائر الملكية)

Possessive pronouns appear as attached suffixes at the end of nouns instead of separate words (as *my*, *his*, *her*, etc. in English)

Person	Singular		Dual		Plural	
1st person (المُتَكَلِم)	ي	*my*	نا	*our*	نا	*our*
2nd person (المُخاطب)	كَ	*your (m.)*	كُما	*your (m./f.)*	كُم	*your (m.)*
	كِ	*your (f.)*			كُنَّ	*your (f.)*
3rd person (الغائب)	ـه	*his, its*	هُما	*their (m./f.)*	هُم	*their (m.)*
	ها	*her, its*			هُنَّ	*their (f.)*

2 Subject pronouns (detached) (ضمائر الفاعل)

Subject pronouns are more or less similar to those in English and used to substitute nouns in order to avoid repetition.

Person	Singular		Dual		Plural	
1st person (المُتَكَلِم)	أَنا	*I*	نَحْنُ	*we*	نَحْنُ	*we*
2nd person (المُخاطب)	أَنْتَ	*you (m.)*	أَنْتُمَا	*you (m./f.)*	أَنْتُمْ	*you (m.)*
	أَنْتِ	*you (f.)*			أَنْتُنَّ	*you (f.)*
3rd person (الغائب)	هُوَ	*he, it*	هُما	*they (m./f.)*	هُمْ	*they (m.)*
	هِيَ	*she, it, they**			هُنَّ	*they (f.)*

* for non-human plural nouns

Object pronouns (detached) (ضَمائر المفعول)

Object pronouns appear as attached suffixes at the end of verbs in reference to the object of the verb. For instance:

درس + أنا = درس + ني = درسني — *he taught me*

ساعد + هو = ساعد + ه = ساعده — *he helped him*

● INSIGHT

Please note that the possessive pronouns and object pronouns are identical, with the exception of the first person. For example:

مدرستي — *my school* **درسني** — *he taught me*

---

erson	Singular		Dual		Plural	
st person (المُتَكَلِم)	ني	*me*	نا	*us (two)*	نا	*us*
nd person (المُخاطَب)	كَ	*you (m.)*	كُما	*you (m./f.)*	كُم	*you (m.)*
	كِ	*you (f.)*			كُنَّ	*you (f.)*
rd person (الغائِب)	ـه	*him, it*	هُما	*them (m./f.)*	هُم	*them (m.)*
	ها	*her, it, them*			هُنَّ	*them (f.)*

ARABIC QUESTION NOUNS (أدوات الاستفهام)

terrogative question nouns are used to form questions.

sential question nouns

أَ/هَل	yes/no questions	كَيفَ	*how*
ما	*what (in questions without a verb)*	كَمْ	*how many/how much?*
ماذا	*what (in questions using verbs)*	مَتى	*when*
لِماذا	*why (1)*	مَنْ	*who*
لِمَ	*why (2)*	أَيّ	*which (m.)*
أَينَ	*where*	أَيَّة	*which (f.)*

Interrogative nouns (with prepositions)

لِمَن	whose	مِن أي	from which
عَنْ ماذا	about what	مِن أَيْن	from where
عَنْ أَيّ	about which	مَعَ مَنْ	with whom
في أَيّ	in which		

Using these in context:

هَل هي انجليزية؟	Is she English?
أَأنت طالب؟	Are you a student?
ما اسمك؟	What's your name?
ما هذا؟	What's this? (m.)
ماذا تدرس في الجامعة؟	What do you study at the university?
لماذا تدرس اللغة العربية؟	Why are you studying Arabic?
لِمَ تدرس اللغة العربية؟	Why are you studying Arabic?
أَيْنَ تعمل؟	Where do you work?
كيف حالك؟	How are you?
كم عدد الطلاب في الفصل؟	How many students are there in the class?
مَتى تسافر اليوم؟	When are you travelling today?
مَنْ أنت؟	Who are you?
أي كتاب تريد؟	Which book do you want?
لِمَن هذا الكتاب؟	Whose book is this?
عَنْ ماذا تبحث؟	What are you looking for?
عَنْ أي موضوع تتكلم؟	Which subject are you talking about?
في أية جامعة تدرس؟	In which university do you study?
مِن أي جامعة تخرجت؟	From which university did you graduate?
مِن أَيْن أنت يا محمد؟	Where are you from, Muhammad?
مَعَ مَن تسكن؟	With whom do you live?

12

ARABIC NEGATION PRONOUNS (أَدَوَاتُ النَّفْي)

In Arabic, there are different ways to negate using a variety of pronouns. Here are some of the most essential to learn:

Using لا

Using لا to negate the present

To negate verbs in the present tense, لا must proceed the verb, as in:

لا أعرف	*I don't know.*
لا أفهم	*I don't understand.*
لا أدرس اللغة الألمانية	*I don't study German.*
لا أعرف كيف أقول book بالعربية	*I don't know how to say 'book' in Arabic.*

Using لا to negate the imperative

To negate verbs in the imperative, لا is placed before the verb, as in:

لا تقف أمام هذا البناء	*Don't stop in front of this building.*
ألا	*Don't you ...*
ألا تتذكر اسمي؟	*Don't you remember my name?*
ألا تعرف معنى هذه الكلمة؟	*Don't you know the meaning of this word?*

Using لا with the indefinite noun

لا أحد	*nobody*
لا شيء	*nothing*
لا إنساني	*inhuman*
لا بَأسَ بِه	*not bad, there is no objection*
لا داعِي	*there is no need*
لا ذنب له	*he is not guilty*
لا شك في ذلك	*there is no doubt about that*
لا مثيل له	*matchless, unrivalled*
لا مُبرر له	*unjustifiable*

Using لا with the definite noun

اللا-	*non-*
اللانظام	*the no-system*

نُقطَة اللاعَوْدَة	*point of no return*
اللامعقول	*absurdity, irrational*

5 Using لا with the preposition (ب)

بلا	*without*
بلا شروط	*without conditions*

6 Using لا to express (*neither ... nor...*)

لا ... ولا...	*neither ... nor...*
ما كلمني أحد، لا أبي ولا أمي	*no one has called me, neither my father nor my

Using لم

7 Using لم to negate the past tense

To negate the past tense, لم (*not*) is used before the present tense verb (in the jussive form):

لم أدرس اليوم	*I didn't study today.*
لم أفعل ذلك	*I have not done that.*

8 Using لم to express (*neither ... nor ...*)

لم أقرأ ولم أكتب أي شيء	*I have neither read not written anything.*
لم يدرس الإنجليزية ولم يسافر أبدا إلى إنجلترا	*He didn't study English and has never been to England.*

Using ما

9 In informal colloquial Arabic, to negate verbs in the past tense, ما is used before the verb (in the present tense):

ما تخرجت من هذه الجامعة	*I didn't graduate from this university.*
ما شربت قهوة هذا الصباح	*I didn't drink coffee this morning.*

However, in formal MSA, instead we would say:

لم أتخرج من هذه الجامعة   and   لم أشرب قهوة هذا الصباح

10 To negate the verb (to be (كان in the past tense:

ما كنت في الفصل اليوم	*I wasn't in the class today.*

ليس sing

1 Using ليس to negate nominal sentences

o negate nominal sentences (i.e. non-verbal sentences) with the verb كان
o be) in the present tense, ليس is used and conjugated as follows:

Person	Singular			Dual			Plural		
st person (المُتَكَلِّم)	أَنَا	لَسْتُ	I am not	نَحْنُ	لَسْنا	we are not (dual)	نَحْنُ	لَسْنا	we are not
nd person (المُخَاطَب)	أَنْتَ	لَسْتَ	you (m.) are not	أَنْتُما	لَسْتُما	you (dual) are not	أَنْتُم	لَسْتُم	you (m.) are not
	أَنْتِ	لَسْتِ	you (f.) are not				أَنْتُنَّ	لَسْتُنَّ	you (f.) are not
rd person (الغائب)	هُوَ	لَيْسَ	he is not	هُما	لَيْسا	they (dual) are not	هُمْ	لَيْسُوا	they (m.) are not
	هِيَ	لَيْسَت	she is not				هُنَّ	لَسْنَ	they (f.) are not

or instance:

أنا لست من هنا	I am not from here.
ليس عندي كمبيوتر	I don't have a computer.
ليس عندي وقت	I don't have time!
جامعتنا ليس فيها كلية طب	Our university doesn't have a medical school/faculty.

2 Using لن

o negate the future tense, لن is used before the verb (in the subjunctive):

لن أسافر إلى الأردن الصيف القادم	I won't travel to Jordan next summer.
لن أستطيع السفر خارج البلد بدون جواز سف	I won't be able to travel outside the country without a passport.

3 Using دون

دون	without
دون شروط	without conditions
بدون حليب	without milk

14 Using عدم + noun

عدم التسامح	*intolerance*
عدم الاستقرار	*instability*
عدم الانحياز	*non-alliance*
عدم الوجود	*non-existence*

15 غير + adjective/noun

غير رسمي	*unofficial*
غير كاف	*not sufficient*
غير معقول	*unintelligible*
غير مقبول	*not acceptable*
بغير	*without*
بغير علم	*without knowledge*

16 عديم + noun

عديم اللون	*colourless*
عديم الحركة	*motionless*
عديم الطعم	*tasteless*

ADVERBS (الظرف)

There are many ways to formulate adverbs in Arabic. The most common are:

1 Adverb (noun or adjective + accusative ending)

The most common adverb in Arabic is formed by adding the accusative ending to a noun or adjective. For example:

كثيرا	*many*
قليلا	*little*
جيدا	*well, fully*
جدا	*very*

In context

شكرًا جزيلا	*thank you very much*
حسن جدا	*well done*

16

Adverb (بـ + noun)

Another common adverb used in Arabic is formed by adding the one-letter attached preposition (بـ with) to nouns. For example:

بسهولة	*easily (with ease)*
بصعوبة	*with difficulty*
ببطء	*slowly*
بسرعة	*speedily*

context

مشيت إلى الجامعة بسرعة	*I walked to the university quickly.*
نزلت من الجمل بصعوبة	*I got off the camel with difficulty.*

Adverb (بشكل + adjective)

Another type of adverb is the expression **بشكل** + adjective (i.e. *in a ... way*), as

بشكل بسيط	*easily (in an easy way)*
بشكل عنيف	*violently (in a violent way)*
بشكل منتظم	*regularly (in an organized way)*
بشكل متحضر	*civilly (in a civil way)*

context

درست العربية بشكل منتظم لمدة خمس سنوا	*I studied Arabic regularly for five years.*
ضربت الشرطة المحتجين بشكل عنيف	*The police beat up the protesters violently.*

ADJECTIVES (الصفة)

Adjectives are words that are used to describe nouns. Generally speaking, adjectives are characterized by the following features:

They can be either definite or indefinite

الكتاب جديد	*The book is new.*	الكتاب الجديد	*the new book*

Feminine or masculine

الأستاذ العربي	*the Arab teacher* (m.)
الأستاذة العربية	*the Arab teacher* (f.)

3 Singular

الطالب الجديد   *the new student (m.)*

الطالبة الجديدة   *the new student (f.)*

4 Dual

الطالبان الجديدان   *the (two) new students (nominative case)*

الطالبان الجديدين   *the (two) new students (accusative case)*

5 Plural

Just like nouns, adjectives can have either sound or broken plural.

الطالبات الجديدات   *the new students (f.)*

الطلاب الجدد   *the new students (m.)*

الطلاب الأردنيون   *the Jordanian students (m.)*

الطالبات الأردنيات   *the Jordanian students (f.)*

6 To describe non-human nouns

Note that adjectives that follow non-human nouns in plural are always feminin

مدارس حكومية   *governmental schools*

سيارات قديمة   *old cars*

مساجد إسلامية   *Islamic mosques*

دول عربية   *Arab countries*

علاقات دولية   *international relations*

7 Agreement

Adjectives must agree with the nouns being described in:

a number

أستاذ عربي   *an Arab teacher (sing.)*

أساتذة عرب   *Arab teachers (pl.)*

أستاذان عربيان   *two Arab teachers (dual)*

b gender

رجل مغربي   *a Moroccan man*

امرأة مغربية   *a Moroccan woman*

definiteness

امرأة مغربية   *a Moroccan woman*

المرأة المغربية   *the Moroccan woman*

HE RELATIVE ADJECTIVE (اسم النسبة)

ow to form adjectives from nouns

a rule of thumb, the relative adjective – known as Nisba (**اسم النسبة**) – is
rmed by adding the letter **يّ** (known as Ya' of Nisbah) preceded by the vowel
sra at the end of the noun, as follows:

ة‌اِيّ   +   Kasra vowel   +   noun

ere are some common examples:

ljectives of time

يومي	يوم	*daily*
أسبوع	أسبوع	*weekly*
شهري	شهر	*monthly*
صباح	صباح	*in the morning*
ليلي	ليل	*nightly*

lours

برتقالي	برتقال	*orange*
بني	بن	*brown (from coffee beans)*

tionalities and ethnic origins

عربي	عرب	*Arab, Arabic*
مغربي	المغرب	*Moroccan*
مصري	مصر	*Egyptian*

he noun ends in **ا** we drop it, as in the following examples:

أفريقيّ	أفريقيا	*African*
بريطاني	بريطانيا	*British*
أمريكي	أمريكا	*American*

Religious terms

يهودي	يهود	Jewish, Jew
مسيحي	مسيح	Christian

Miscellaneous

نباتي	نبات	vegetarian
ذهبي	ذهب	golden
مركزي	مركز	central
يساري	يسار	leftist
يميني	يمين	rightist
ملكي	ملك	royal
عالمي	عالم	international
علمي	علم	scientific

Prepositions (converted into Nisba adjectives)

أمامي	أمام	upper, frontal
تحتي	تحت	lower, underneath
فوقي	فوق	upper
خلفي	خلف	rear, backward

If the noun ends in ة (التاء المربوطة) or ا (الألف)

The ending ة (as well as the Fatha vowel) is dropped before adding the Ya' of Nisba.

جامعي	جامعة	academic, university-related
مدرسي	مدرسة	school-related
دولي	دولة	international
ثقافي	ثقافة	cultural
تجاري	تجارة	commercial
سني	سُنّة	Sunni (one of the two main branches of Islam)

r certain words we also add the letter (و) before the (ياء النسبة),
 in:

سنوي	سنة	*annual, yearly*
قروي	قرية	*rural*
بدوي	بادية	*nomadic, Bedouin*

HE DIMINUTIVE (الاسم المصغر)

minutive nouns can be derived from most nouns mainly for the following
asons:

- to express belittling
- to express endearment
- to express contempt and ridicule

ere are two main patterns for the diminutive nouns:

فُعَيْل for trilateral (three consonant) nouns:

كتيب	كتاب	*booklet*
جبيل	جبل	*little mountain*
كليب	كلب	*puppy*
شُجيرة	شجرة	*bush*
بُحَيْرة	بحر	*lake*

فُعَيْل for quadrilateral (four consonant) nouns:

شُمَيْسة	شمس	*sun*
دُوَيْرة	دار	*little house*
شُوَيّة	شيء	*little, slightly* (commonly used in colloquial Arabic)

OMPARATIVES AND SUPERLATIVES (اسم التفضيل)

mparative adjectives

mparative adjectives are normally made by adding **أ** to the beginning of the
ree-letter root of any adjective. This forms the pattern **أفعل**.

Note that comparative adjectives are indefinite and apply to both masculine and feminine. For example:

أَكْبَر	كَبير	big – bigger	أَصْغَر	صَغير	small – smaller
أَجَدّ	جَديد	new – newer	أَقْدَم	قَديم	old (not for people) – olde
أَطْوَل	طَويل	long – longer	أَقْصَر	قَصير	short – shorter
أَبْعَد	بَعيد (عَنْ)	far – further	أَقْرَب	قَريب (مِنْ)	close/near – closer/nearer
أَكْثَر	كَثير	many – most	أَقَلّ	قَليل	few – fewer
أَبْرَد	بارد	cold – colder	أَسْخَن	ساخِن	hot – hotter
أَسْوَأ	سَيِّء	bad – worst	أَحْسَن	حَسَن	good – better
أَغْلى	غالٍ	expensive – more expensive	أَرْخَص	رَخِيص	cheap – cheape
أَسْرَع	سَريع	fast – faster	أَبْطأ	بَطيء	slow – slower
أَثْقَل	ثَقيل	heavy – heavier	أَخَفّ	خَفيف	light – lighter
أَصْعَب	صَعْب	difficult – more difficult	أَسْهَل	سَهْل	easy – easier
أَجْمَل	جَميل	beautiful – more beautiful	أَقْبَح	قَبيح	ugly – uglier
أَوْسَع	واسِع	wide, spacious – more spacious	أَضْيَق	ضَيِّق	narrow – narrower

To express *than* in comparative phrases, you just need to add the preposition مِنْ as in the following examples:

محمد أكبر من أخيه عمر   *Muhammad is older than his brother Omar.*

فاطمة أطول من أختها مريم   *Fatima is taller than her sister Mariar*

Superlative adjectives

Superlative adjectives follow the same pattern as comparatives but they are usually expressed in the definite form, either carrying the definite article ال or not, as in the following examples:

عندي أربعة إخوة وأخوات وأنا الأكبر   *I have four brothers and sisters and I'm the eldest*

عندي أربعة إخوة وأخوات وأنا أكبرهم

I have four brothers and sisters and I'm their eldest

عشت في مدن كثيرة وَادنبرة في رأيي هي أجمل مدينة في أوروبا

I lived in many cities and – in my opinion – Edinburgh is the most beautiful city in Europe.

● **INSIGHT**

Superlative adjectives follow the pattern فُعْلى when they are used as adjectives after a feminine noun. For example:

توجد الصحراء الكبرى في شمال أفريقيا وهي أكبر الصحارى الحارة في العالم

The great desert (Great Sahara) is located in North Africa and it is one of the greatest hot deserts in the world.

ACTIVE AND PASSIVE PARTICIPLES (اسم الفاعل والمفعول)

The Arabic verb has two participles:

- Active participle (اسم الفاعل)
- Passive participle (اسم المفعول)

In general, the active participle describes the property of the subject using the verb from which it is derived, while the passive participle describes the object.

Participles are generally derived using the following patterns:

Participle	Pattern
Active	فاعل
Passive	مفعول

For example, from the verb كتب, we have:

- the active participle كاتب (writer, action of writing)
- the passive participle مكتوب (written)

For triliteral verbs (made up of three letters) we have the following pattern:

Root verb	Active participle		Passive participle	
كتب	كاتب	writer	مكتوب	written
طلب	طالب	student, seeker	مطلوب	wanted, sought after
سكن	ساكن	resident	مسكون	inhabitant, haunted
عمل	عامل	worker	معمول	made

صنع	صانع	worker	مصنوع	manufactured
شرب	شارب	drinker	مشروب	drunk (a drink)
حكم	حاكم	ruler, judge	محكوم	sentenced

Verbs that begin with /أ/ follow the pattern:

أكل	آكل	writer	مأكول	eaten
أخذ	آخذ	taking	مأخوذ	taken

Verbs that end with /أ/ follow the pattern:

قارئ	قرأ	reader, reciter	مقروء	read, readable
مالئ	ملأ	filling	مملوء	overfilled

Verbs that have a long Alif /ا/ in the middle follow the pattern:

كائن	كان	being	مكون	created, formed
نائم	نام	sleeping	منوم	hypnotized

Verbs that begin with the letter /و/ follow the pattern:

والد	ولد	parent	مولود	born
واقف	وقف	standing up	موقوف	suspended

In Arabic, each verb has a unique pattern for deriving both the active and passive participle. The following table lists all the patterns of the verb form from I–X.

Passive participle (اسم المفعول)	Active participle (اسم الفاعل)	Verb form (I–X)	
مَفْعُول	فاعِل	فَعَلَ فَعِلَ	I
مُفَعَّل	مُفَعِّل	فَعَّلَ	II
مُفاعَل	مُفاعِل	فاعَلَ	III
مُفْعَل	مُفْعِل	أفْعَلَ	IV
مُتَفَعَّل	مُتَفَعِّل	تَفَعَّلَ	V
مُتَفاعَل	مُتَفاعِل	تَفاعَلَ	VI
مُنْفَعَل	مُنْفَعِل	انْفَعَلَ	VII

Passive participle (اسم المفعول)	Active participle (اسم الفاعل)	Verb form (I–X)	
مُفْتَعَل	مُفْتَعِل	اِفْتَعَلَ	VIII
-	مُفْعَلّ	اِفْعَلَّ	IX
مُسْتَفْعَل	مُسْتَفْعِل	اِسْتَفْعَلَ	X

REPOSITIONS (حُرُوف الجَرّ)

ne of the greatest challenges students face when learning Arabic – and indeed
nost foreign languages – is the correct use of prepositions, which one to use
nd whether to use them at all.

repositions are used primarily to connect one word to another and, as in
nany other languages, their exact meaning varies sometimes and is primarily
ependent on context.

he following list is a reference guide to the most common prepositions in
rabic listed under different categories:

ttached prepositions

بِ   at, by, with, in

كَ   as, like

لِ   to, for

and-alone prepositions (miscellaneous)

إلى   to, till, until   حَتّى   until, up to, as far as

عَلى   on, on top of, above, against   عَنْ   from, about, on

مِن   from, through   بدون، دون   without

مَعَ   with, together with   ضد   against

عِنْد   at, near, by   في   on (date), in, at (time)

epositions related to place

فَوْقَ   above, on top of   جنب   next to

تَحْتَ   under, below, underneath   بِجانِب   next to

بَيْنَ   between   عبر   across

من بين	among		نحو	approximately, toward
داخل	inside		حول	around, about
خارج	outside		مقابل	opposite
أَمام	in front of		قدام	before, in front of
خَلْفَ	behind			

Prepositions related to time

بَعْدَ	after
قَبْلَ	before
خلال	during
طوال	throughout
منذ	since, for, ago

Prepositions used to express *to have*

مَعَ

عند

لدى

For example:

سافرت مع أصدقائي إلى القاهرة	I have travelled with my friends to Cair
عنده سيارة كبيرة	He has an expensive car.
عندي فكرة	I have an idea.
لديها مال كثير	She has a lot of money.

ARABIC CONNECTORS AND TRANSITIVE WORDS أدوات الربط

Connectors in Arabic are powerful linguistic tools to help you produce cohesive discourse in speaking and writing. The most common connectors are (و) an

(ف). However, there are many types of connector:

▶ Additive connectors: e.g. (و) and, (أو) or, (مثل) such as, (خصوصا):

  ▷ Contrastive connectors: e.g. but (لكن), although (مع أن)

  ▷ Causative connectors: e.g. because (لأن), therefore (لذلك)

26

- Conditional connectors:
  - Sequential connectors: e.g. *second* (أولا، ثانيا), *finally* (أخيرا، ختاما)
  - Summative connectors: e.g. *in general* (بصورة عامة), *in short* (باختصار)

The following list is a reference guide to the most common connectors:

Additive connectors

و	and	إما...أو	either…or
ف	then	من جانبٍ آخر	on the other hand
ف	so that	من جهةٍ أخرى	on the other hand
ثم	then	مثل	such as
أيضا	too	ك	like
أو	or	على سبيل المثال	for example
أم	or	ولا سيما	particularly
كما	also	وبخاصةٍ	especially
بالإضافة إلى	in addition to	خصوصًا	especially
إلى جانب	in addition	بما في ذلك	including
فضلاً عن	let alone	بالإشارة إلى	with regard to
ناهيك	so, too	أي	that is
كذلك	also	بعبارةٍ أخرى	in other words
بل	rather		

Contrastive connectors

لكنْ	but	على عكس	by contrast
إلا أن	however	حتى ولو	even though

أما	but	على الرغم من	in spite of
مقارنة ب	compared to	على أي حال	however (in any case)
مع ذلك	despite	بل	rather
مع أن	although	بل	not only … but also
بينما	whereas	من ناحية أخرى	on the other hand

Causative connectors

إذ	because	لكي	in order to
بما أن	since	لذلك	therefore
لأن	because	بهدف أن	for the purpose of
بسبب	because of	من أجل	for
نظرًا لـ	because	لهذا السبب	for this reason
إذ أن	because	نتيجة لذلك	as a result
بفضل	thanks to		

Conditional connectors

إذ	if	وإلا	otherwise
وإن	even if	على أن	on the condition
في حال	in case	لو	if
مالم	unless	إلا إذا	unless
إن لم	if not	لولا	had it not
بشرط	provided	لو لم	if not
طالما	so long as	ما لم	unless

Sequential connectors

أولاً	first of all	بادئ ذي بدء	first
ثانيًا	second	في النهاية	finally (at the end)
أخيرًا	finally	ختامًا	finally

Summative and other connectors

باختصار	in short	لابد	must
على الأقل	at least	كلما	the more ... the more
بصورة عامة	in general	غني عن البيان	needless to say
في هذه الحال	in this case		

DERIVED VERB FORMS

Most verbs in Arabic follow a set of predefined patterns, which are all derived from the basic trilateral verb form I (فَعَلَ). Western grammarians have assigned Roman numerals I–X to these forms, mainly for ease of memorization and using the root-based dictionaries.

The following table lists the common ten verb forms with their patterns, the general meaning of each pattern and sample verbs in the past tense.

● INSIGHT

Note that many derived verb forms can take several different meanings and as a learner of Arabic you are strongly advised to learn the specific meaning of each verb form individually, based on context, rather than relying on the general meanings in the table that follows.

Examples		Meaning of pattern: usage and application	Pattern الوزن	Verb form
to study	دَرَسَ	This pattern is the basic skeleton of all verb forms, which are all derived from this pattern. It indicates the basic and simple meaning of the verb.	فَعَلَ فَعِلَ فَعُلَ	I
to know	عَلِمَ			
to write	كَتَبَ			

Examples		Meaning of pattern: usage and application	Pattern الوزن	Verb form
عَرَّفَ *to introduce*	عَرَفَ *to know*	1 To express the strengthening or intensifying of the meaning of the basic verb. 2 To express causation.	فَعَّلَ	II
عَلَّمَ *to teach*	عَلِمَ *to know*			
خَرَّجَ *to move out, educate, train*	خَرَجَ *to go out*			
كاتَبَ *to write to each other*	كَتَبَ *to write*	To express a collective action where two or more people are involved in a reciprocal way.	فاعَلَ	III
راسَلَ *to correspond*	رَسَلَ *to send*			
قاتَلَ *to fight, combat (so.)*	قَتَلَ *to kill*			
أَعْلَمَ *to inform*	عَلِمَ *to know*	To convert transitive verbs into intransitive.	أَفْعَلَ	IV
تَعَرَّفَ *to become acquainted*	عَرَّفَ *to introduce*	This is the reflexive of verb form II.	تَفَعَّلَ	V
تَعلَّمَ *to learn*	عَلَّمَ *to teach*			
تَخرَّج *to graduate*	خَرَّجَ *to move out, educate, train*			
تعارَفَ *to become acquainted with one*	عارَفَ *to know one another*	This is the reflexive of verb form III 1 To express a group action. 2 To express pretending to do an action	تَفاعَلَ	VI
تَكاتَبَ *to write to each other*	كاتَبَ *to write to each other*			
تَقاتَل *to fight with one another*	قاتَلَ *to fight, combat (so.)*			

Examples		Meaning of pattern: usage and application	Pattern الوزن	Verb form
اِنْسَحَبَ to withdraw	سَحَبَ to pull, drag	This is the passive of verb form I.	اِنْفَعَلَ	VII
اِنْقَطَعَ to be cut off	قَطَعَ to cut			
اِنْكَسَرَ to get broken	كَسَرَ to break			
اِعْتَرَفَ to confess	عَرَفَ to know	This is the reflexive of verb form I.	اِفْتَعَلَ	VIII
اِجْتَمَعَ to get together, assemble	جَمَعَ to gather			
اِقْتَطَعَ to cut off a part	قَطَعَ to cut			
ـ اِحْمَرَّ to become red		To express the gaining of an attribute (in reference to colours of defects) and translating as to become something.	اِفْعَلَّ	IX
ـ اِخْضَرَّ to become green				
اِسْتَنْصَرَ to seek help	نَصَرَ to help	This is the reflexive of form IV. To express asking for or seeking to obtain something.	اِسْتَفْعَلَ	X
اِسْتَخْرَجَ to extract (take out)	خَرَجَ to go out, exit			
اِسْتَعْلَمَ to enquire (seek information)	عَلِمَ to know			

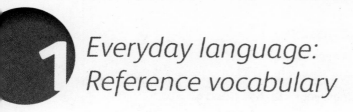

Everyday language: Reference vocabulary

كَما قالَت العَرَب ... As the Arabs say

أَكْبَرُ مِنْكَ بِيَوْم، أَعْلَمُ مِنْكَ بِسَنة

Older than you by a day, more knowledgeable than you by a year.
Arabic proverb

In this unit you will learn essential vocabulary, organized as follows:

الزَّمَن *Time*

▷ *Core vocabulary* مُفْرَدات أساسيّة

▷ *Days of the week* أَيّام الأُسْبوع

▷ *Months of the year* شُهور السَّنة

   ▷ *Arabic, Islamic and Gregorian calendar*

التَّقْويم العَرَبيّ والإسْلاميّ والغَرْبيّ

▷ *Useful expressions of time*

الأَلْوان *Colours*

▷ *Basic colours*

▷ *Secondary colours*

   ▷ *Useful adjectives*

   ▷ *Related verbs*

الأَرْقام *Numbers*

المَقَاسات والأَوْزان والقِياسات *Sizes, weights and measures*

▷ *Core vocabulary* مُفْرَدات أساسيّة

▷ *Weights* الأَوْزان

▷ *Distance* المَسافة

▷ *Area* المِساحة

▷ *Length* الطُّول

▷ *Capacity* السِّعة

▷ *Containers* الأَوْعية

33

Time الزَّمَن

CORE VOCABULARY

أَمْس\البارِحة	yesterday		يَوْم (ج) أَيّام	day
اليَوْم	today		أُسْبوع (ج) أَسابيع	week
غَدًا	tomorrow		شَهْر (ج) شُهور\أَشْهُر	month
الآن	now		سَنة (ج) سَنَوات\سِنين	year
صَباح	morning		الحاضِر	the present
ظُهْر	noon		الماضي	the past
بَعد الظُهْر	afternoon		المُسْتَقْبِل	the future
قَبلَ الظُهْر	before noon		نَهار	daytime
مَساء	evening		وَقْت (ج) أَوْقات	time
لَيْل (ج) لَيال	night		غَسَق	dusk, twilight
مُنْتَصَف اللَيْل	midnight		فَجْر	dawn
ثانية (ج) ثَوان	second		شُروق	sunrise
دَقيقة (ج) دَقائِق	minute		غُروب	sunset
ساعة (ج) ‑ات	hour			

DAYS OF THE WEEK أَيّام الأُسْبوع

يَوْم الأَحَد	Sunday		يَوْم الخَميس	Thursday
يَوْم الاثنَيْن	Monday		يَوْم الجُمُعة	Friday
يَوْم الثُلاثاء	Tuesday		يَوْم السَّبْت	Saturday
يَوْم الأَرْبِعاء	Wednesday			

● INSIGHT

The days of the week can also be written without the word يَوْم

Arabic, Islamic and Gregorian calendar
التَّقْويم العَرَبيّ والإسْلاميّ والغَرْبيّ

The following table is organized as follows:

Gregorian calendar (English)	التَّقْويم الميلادي\الغْريغوريّ
Gregorian calendar (Arabic)	التَّقْويم الغَرْبيّ الميلاديّ
Arabic calendar	التَّقْويم العَرَبيّ
Hijri/Islamic calendar	التَّقْويم الهِجْريّ الإسلاميّ
French calendar (North Africa)	التَّقْويم الفَرنسيّ

January	February	March	April
يَناير	فَبْراير	مارس	أَبْريل
كانونَ الثّاني	شُباط	آذار	نيسان
مُحَرَّم	صَفَر	ربيع الأوَّل	رَبيع الثّاني
جانْفيي	فِيفْري	مارس	أفريل

May	June	July	August
مايو	يونِيو	يوليو	أَغُسْطُس
أيار	حَزيران	تموز	آب
جُمادى الأولى	جُمادى الثانية	رَجَب	شَعْبان
ماي	جْوان	جوييه	أوت

September	October	November	December
سَبْتَمْبَر	أُكْتوبَر	نوفَمْبَر	ديسَمْبَر
أيْلول	تشْرين الأوَّل	تشْرين الثّاني	كانون الأوَّل
رَمَضان	شَوّال	ذو القَعْدة	ذو الحجّة
سِبْتَمْبَر	أكتوبَر	نوفمبر	ديسَمْبَر

This calendar is based on the year 2013.

USEFUL EXPRESSIONS OF TIME

يَوْمِيًّا	daily	فيما بَعْد	subsequently
أُسْبوعِيًّا	weekly	سابِقًا	previously
شَهْرِيًّا	monthly	بُعَيْد	shortly after
سَنَوِيًّا	annually	قُبَيْل	shortly before
في الصَّباح\صَباحًا	in the morning – a.m.	أَبَدًا	never
في المَساء\مَساءً	in the evening – p.m.	نادِرًا	rarely (1)
مُبَكِّرًا\باكِرًا	early	قَلَّما	rarely (2)
ظُهْرًا	noon time	أَحْيانًا	sometimes
حالاً	immediately	عادَةً	usually
الأُسْبوع الماضي	last week	دائِمًا	always
هذا الأُسْبوع\ الأُسْبوع الحالي	this week	فَوْرًا	immediately
		فَجْأَةً	suddenly
الأُسْبوع القادِم	next week	أخيرًا	recently
كُلَّ يَوْم	every day	مُؤَخَّرًا	lately
مَرَّة في الأُسْبوع	once a week	مُتَأَخِّرًا	late
مَرَّتَيْن في الأُسْبوع	twice a week	باستِمْرار	continuously
ثلاث مَرّات في الأُسْبوع	three times a week	حَتْمًا	definitely
بَعْد	after	سَلَفًا	beforehand
قَبْل	before	عاجِلاً أم آجِلاً	sooner or later
بَعْد ذلك	after that	في أَقْرَب فُرْصة مُمْكِنة	as soon as possible
لاحِقًا	afterwards, later on		
ثُمَّ	then		

36

خِلال	during	فِي نَفْس الوَقْت	at the same time
بَيْنَما	while, during	مِن الآن فَصاعِدًا	from now on
حَتَّى	until	على المَدى البَعيد	in the long term
آنَذاك	at that time	على المَدى القَريب	in the short term
حينَما	whenever	في المُسْتَقْبَل القَريب	in the near future
كُلَّما	whenever	في المُسْتَقْبَل البَعيد	in the distant future
مُنْذُ	since	قَريبًا	soon
فُرْصة (ج) فُرَص	opportunity, occasion	كالعادة	as usual
		حَيْث	when
حين\عِنْدَما	when (adv.)	مَرّة (ج) -ات	once
فَتْرَة (ج) -ات	interval of time	مُدّة (ج) مُدَد	period, duration
عَهْد (ج) عُهود	era, age	مُقبِل	forthcoming
قَرْن (ج) قُرون	century	مُؤَقَّتًا	temporarily
عَقْد (ج) عُقود	decade	أثْناء	during

Colours الألْوان

olours may appear as adjectives to describe a noun. So, grammatically, they
nust agree with the noun in gender, case and definition. If they appear with a
nking verb to describe a noun, e.g. *The moon appears yellow*, then they would
nly agree in number.

he numbers are displayed as masculine, feminine and then the plural.

لَوْن (ج) ألْوان   colour

ASIC COLOURS

أَصْفَر - صَفْراء (ج) صُفْر	yellow	أَسْوَد - سَوْداء (ج) سود	black
أَخْضَر - خَضْراء (ج) خُضْر	green	أَبْيَض - بَيْضاء (ج) بيض	white
أَحْمَر - حَمْراء (ج) حُمْر	red	أَزْرَق - زَرْقاء (ج) زُرْق	blue

The well-known tourist attraction, the Alhambra (i.e. *the red one*), originally named 'the Red Fortress' (ٱلْقَلْعَةُ ٱلْحَمْرَاء), is a famous palace built during the 14th century by the Arab/Muslim rulers and located in the city of Granada in Spain. If you visit the Alhambra you will be pleasantly surprised to see calligraphic inscriptions in Arabic all around the palace walls.

SECONDARY COLOURS

بُرْتُقالِيّ	orange	بُرْتُقال	oranges
أُرْجُوانِيّ\ابَنَفْسَجِيّ	purple	أُرْجُوان\ابَنَفْسَج	violet
بُنِّيّ	brown	بُنّ	coffee beans
رَمادِيّ\ارَصاصِيّ	grey	رَماد\ارَصاص	ashes/lead
زَهْرِي\اوَرْدِيّ	pink, rose-coloured	زَهْر\اوَرْد	blossom/roses
ذَهَبِيّ	gold	ذَهَب	gold
فِضِّيّ	silver	فِضّة	silver
كُحْلِيّ	navy blue	كُحْل	kohl (eye cosmetic
زَيْتونِي\ازَيْتِيّ	olive green	زَيْتون	olives
نُحاسِي	copper	نحاس	copper
أَسْمَر\اسَمْراء (ج) سُمْر	brown-skinned	أَشْقَر\اشَقْراء (ج) شُقْر	blond

The basic colours have an irregular feminine form (بَيْضاء، حَمْراء، خَضْراء)،

which follows a consistent pattern. However, any other colours carry the ending (ﺔ) for the feminine form.

Useful adjectives

مُلَوَّن	coloured	بَرّاق	bright
فاتِح	light	لامِع	shiny
غامِق\اداكِن	dark	باهِت	pale

Related verbs

اِحْمَرَّ يَحْمَرُّ اِحْمِرار	to become red
اِخْضَرَّ يَخْضَرُّ اِخْضِرار	to become green
اِصْفَرَّ يَصْفَرُّ اِصْفِرار	to become yellow
اِزْرَقَّ يَزْرَقُّ اِزْرِقاق	to become blue
اِسْوَدَّ يَسْوَدُّ اِسْوِداد	to become black
اِبْيَضَّ يَبْيَضُّ تَبييض	to whiten st.

Numbers الأرْقام

● INSIGHT

The numeral *zero* is originally from medieval Arabic صِفْر. The Arabic numerals (predominantly in use in the East and North Africa), along with algebra, were introduced to the West by Michael Scott in the 13th century. In addition to *zero* the words *to cipher* and *decipher* are also derived from medieval Arabic.

	Cardinal numbers الأَعْداد الأَصْلِيّة (1–10, 11–19, 20–29, 30–100)			Ordinal numbers الأعْداد التَّرْتيبِيّة (1st–100th)	
Standard Arabic numbers	Hindu-Arabic numbers	Arabic name	Ordinal numbers	Arabic	
0	٠	صِفْر	-	-	
1	١	واحِد	1st	الأَوَّل\الأولى	
2	٢	إثْنان	2nd	الثّاني	
3	٣	ثَلاثة	3rd	الثّالِث	
4	٤	أَرْبَعة	4th	الرّابِع	
5	٥	خَمْسة	5th	الخامِس	
6	٦	سِتّة	6th	السّادِس	
7	٧	سَبْعة	7th	السّابِع	
8	٨	ثَمانية	8th	الثّامِن	

9	٩	تِسْعة 9th	التّاسِع
10	١٠	عَشَرة 10th	العاشِر
11	١١	أَحَدَ عَشَر 11th	الحادي\
			الحادِيةعَشَر
12	١٢	إثْنا عَشَر 12th	الثّاني عَشَر
13	١٣	ثَلاثة عَشَر 13th	الثّالث عَشَر
14	١٤	أرْبَعةعَشَر 14th	الرّابع عَشَر
15	١٥	خَمْسة عَشَر 15th	الخامِس عَشَر
16	١٦	سِتّة عَشَر 16th	السّادس عَشَر
17	١٧	سَبْعة عَشَر 17th	السّابع عَشَر
18	١٨	ثَمانية عَشَر 18th	الثّامِن عَشَر
19	١٩	تِسْعة عَشَر 19th	التّاسِع عَشَر
20	٢٠	عِشْرون 20th	العِشْرون
21	٢٠	واحد وعِشْرون 21st	الحادي والعِشْرون
22	٢٢	إثْنان وعِشْرون 22nd	الثّاني وَالعشْرون
30	٣٠	ثَلاثون 30th	الثّلاثون
40	٤٠	أرْبعون 40th	الأَرْبعون
50	٥٠	خَمْسون 50th	الخَمْسون
60	٦٠	سِتّون 60th	السِتّون

40

70	٧٠	سَبْعون	70th	السَّبْعون
80	٨٠	ثَمانون	80th	الثَّمانون
90	٩٠	تِسْعون	90th	التِّسْعون
100	١٠٠	مائة\مئة	100th	المِئَة\المائَة
200	٢٠٠	مائَتان	200th	المِئَتان
1,000	١٠٠٠	ألْف	1,000th	الألْف
1,001	١٠٠١	ألْف وواحِد	1,001th	الألْف وواحِد
2,000	٢٠٠٠	ألْفان	2,000th	الألْفان
10,000	١٠٠٠٠	عَشَرَةُ آلاف	-	-
100,000	١٠٠٠٠٠	مائَةُ ألْف	-	-
1,000,000	١٠٠٠٠٠٠	مَلْيون	-	-
2,000,000	٢٠٠٠٠٠٠	مَلْيونان	-	-
1,000,000,000	١٠٠٠٠٠٠٠٠٠	بَلْيون	-	-
2,000,000,000	٢٠٠٠٠٠٠٠٠٠	بَلْيونان	-	-

STUDY TIP

The standard forms of numbers are widely understood and are the safest to learn initially. However, please note that the spoken form of the numbers varies from one area to another, particularly from 11–19.

11 أرْبَعْتش 14 ثَلَتّعش 13 إثْنَعش 12 حَدَعش
15 ثَمَنْتعش 18 سَبْعَتعش 17 سَتّعش 16 خَمَسْتعش
19 تِسَعْتَعش

● INSIGHT

Arabic numerals are known to have complex grammatical rules that are difficult to learn, even for native speakers, often with varying differences between the written and spoken form. Such rules go beyond the scope of this book and cannot be covered here. To learn more about the grammar of numerals, please refer to one of the suggested grammar references in the *Taking it further* section.

Sizes, weights and measures
المَقاسات والأوْزان والقِياسات

CORE VOCABULARY

مَقاس (ج) -ات	size (e.g. clothing)	قِياس (ج) -ات	measure
وَزْن (ج) أوْزان	weight	مَسافة (ج) -ات	distance
مِساحة (ج) -ات	area	عُمْق	depth
طول	length	سَعة	capacity
عَرْض	width	كَمِّية (ج) -ات	volume
اِرْتِفاع	height	شَكْل (ج) أشْكال	shape

الأوْزان WEIGHTS

غرام\غ	gram (g)	أوقِّية	ounce (oz)
مِلليغرام\مغ	milligram (mg)	رَطْل	pound (lb)
كيلوغرام\كغ	kilogram (kg)	طَنّ	tonne (T)

DISTANCE المَسافة

مِتْر\م	metre (m)
كيلومِتْر\كم	kilometre (km)
ميل\م	mile (mi)
يارْدة	yard (yd)

AREA المساحة

قَدَم	foot (ft)
مِتْر مُرَبَّع	square metre
قَدَم مُرَبَّع	square foot

LENGTH الطول

مِلليمِتْر	millimetre (mm)
سَنْتيمِتْر	centimetre (cm)
بوصة\إنْش	inch (in)
قُطْر (ج) أقطار	diameter

CAPACITY السَّعة

لِتْر\ل	litre
مِلليلِتْر\مل	millilitre (ml)
باينت	pint (pt)
جالون	gallon (gal)
رُبْع جالون	quart (qt)

CONTAINERS الأوْعِية

وِعاء	container	صَفْطة	deck (of cards)
زُجاجة	bottle	قِطْعة	piece
إناء	jar	قَالَب	bar
كَرْتونة	carton	كوب	cup
باكيت	packet	كَأْس من الماء	a glass of water
كيس	bag	قِطْعة جُبْن	a slice or piece of cheese
أنْبوبة	tube	دَزينة\دَسْتة بَيْض	a dozen eggs
عُلْبة	can	عُنْقود عنَب	a bunch of grapes
عُلْبة وَرَقيّة	pack	شَطيرة كَعْكة	a slice of cake
عُلْبة بلاستيكيّة	tub	قالَب شوكولاتة	a bar of chocolate
عُلْبة طَعام	tin	رَغيف خُبْز	a loaf of bread
لَفّة	roll		

SHAPES الأشْكال

مُرَبَّع (ج) -ات	square
دائرة (ج) دَوائِر	circle
مُثلَّث (ج) -ات	triangle
مُسْتَطيل (ج) -ات	rectangle
مُسَطَّح	flat
بَيْضاويّ	oval
كَرَوي	spherical
مُسْتَدير	round
مُكَعَّب	cubic

PERCENTAGES النِّسَب

5%	خَمْسة في المائة
10%	عَشَرة في المائة
20%	عشْرون في المائة
50%	خَمْسون في المائة
100%	مائة في المائة

FRACTIONS الكُسور

With the exception of *half*, fractions in Arabic starting from *a third* onwards are easy to guess and memorize, using mainly the cardinal numbers and the pattern (فُعُل), as shown in the following examples:

Numbers	Fractions	Arabic	Plurals	English
إثْنان	1/2	نِصْف	أَنْصاف	half/halves
ثَلاثة	1/3	ثُلُث	أَثْلاث	third(s)
أَرْبَعة	1/4	رُبُع	أَرْباع	quarter(s)
خَمْسة	1/5	خُمُس	أَخْماس	fifth(s)
سِتّة	1/6	سُدُس	أَسْداس	sixth(s)
سَبْعة	1/7	سُبُع	أَسْباع	seventh(s)
ثَمانِية	1/8	ثُمُن	أَثْمان	eighth(s)
تِسْعة	1/9	تُسُع	أَتْساع	ninth(s)
عَشَرة	1/10	عُشُر	أَعْشار	tenth(s)

> **STUDY TIP**
>
> In order to give compound fractions, you can combine the fractions with cardinal numbers if you wish to say, for instance, *three-quarters*, etc.
>
> 5/2 خَمْسَة أنْصاف   4/5 أَرْبَعَة أخْماس   3/4 ثَلاثَة أَرْباع
>
> Or used in their dual form:
>
> 2/2 two halves نِصْفان   2/3 two thirds ثُلْثان   2/4 two quarters رُبُعان

Describing things وَصْف الأشْياء

كَبير	big	صَغير	small
جَديد	new	قَديم	old (not for people)
طَويل	long	قَصير	short

بَعيد (عَنْ)	far	قَريب (مِنْ)	close/near
كَثير	many	قَليل	few
بارِد	cold	ساخِن	hot
سَيِّء	bad	حَسَن	good
غالٍ	expensive	رَخيص	cheap
سَريع	fast	بَطيء	slow
ثَقيل	heavy	خَفيف	light (in weight)
صَعْب	difficult	سَهْل	easy
مُثيراشَيِّق	exciting	مُمِلّ	boring
سَليم	intact, safe	مَكْسور	broken
جَميل	beautiful	قَبيح	ugly
واسِع	wide, spacious	ضَيِّق	narrow
تافِه	unimportant	مهم	important
غَيْر لَذيذ	tasteless, unsavoury	لَذيذ	delicious
نَظيف	clean	وَسِخ	dirty

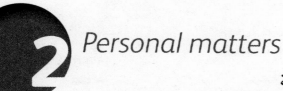

Personal matters

الأُمور الشَّخْصيّة

As the Arabs say ... كَما قالَت العَرَب

لا تَكُن رَطْباً فَتُعْصَر ولا يابساً فَتُكْسَر
Do not be too easy to squeeze or so dry that you break.
Arabic proverb

In this unit you will learn essential vocabulary, organized as follows:

- *Personal details* البَيانات الشَّخْصيّة
  ▷ *Core vocabulary*
- *Forms of address* أشْكال التَّخاطُب
  ▷ *Titles used in letter writing*
- *Human feelings and emotions* المَشاعِر والعَواطِف الإنْسانيّة
  ▷ *Core vocabulary*
  ▷ *Adjectives, opposites and verbal nouns*
  ▷ *Useful verbs*
- *Appearance and clothing* الشَّكْل واللِّباس
  ▷ *Core vocabulary*
  ▷ *Adjectives (related to appearance)*
  ▷ *Accessories* الكَماليّات
  ▷ *Jewellery* المُجَوْهَرات
- *Describing people* وَصْف الأَشْخاص

Personal details البَيانات الشَّخْصيّة

The following information is key personal information, usually found in personal diaries, application forms, CVs, visa entry forms, etc.

CORE VOCABULARY

اسْم (ج) أسْماء	name	تاريخ الميلاد	date of birth
الاِسْم الكامِل	full name	مَكان الميلاد	place of birth

الجِنْسِيّة	nationality	الاسْم الشَّخْصي	personal name
الجِنْس	gender, sex	الاسْم العائلِيّ	surname/family name
ذَكَر	male	الاسْم الأوْسَط	middle name
أُنْثى	female	الاسْم ما قَبْل الزَّواج	maiden name
المِهْنة	profession	العُمْر	age
رَقْم رُخْصة القِيادة	driving licence number	الحالة الاجْتِماعِيّة	social status
تاريخي الدِّراسِيّ	my educational history	مُتَزَوِّج\ة	married
تاريخي العَمَلِيّ	my employment history	أعْزَب\عَزْباء	single (m./f.)
المُؤَهِّلات العلْمِيّة	qualifications	مُطَلَّق\ة	divorced
مَنْشورات	publications	أرْمَل\ة	widowed
اللُّغات	languages	مَهارات واهْتِمامات	skills and interests
مُبْتَدِئ	beginner	الدِّيانة	religion
مُتَوسِّط	intermediate	عُنْوان المَسْكَن	home address
مُتَقَدِّم	advanced	العُنْوان التِّجاري	business/work address
اللُّغة الأمّ	mother tongue	رَقْم الهاتف	telephone number (landline)
كِتابة وَتَحَدُّثاً	written and spoken	رَقْم الهاتف النَقّال	mobile number
التوْقيع	signature	البَريد الإلِكْتْرونيّ	email address
رَقْم هاتِف أحد الأقْرِباء	next of kin phone number	رَقْم البِطاقة الشَّخْصِيّة الوَطَنِيّة	national ID number
رقْم هاتف الطَّبيب	doctor's phone	الرّقْم الوَظيفِيّ	staff number
الفِئة الدَّمَوِيّة	blood type	رَقْم جَواز السَّفَر	passport number
فَصيلة الدَّم	blood group	تاريخ الانْتِهاء	expiry date
		تاريخ الإصْدار	issue date

في حالة الطوارئ (المَرَض أو الحادِث المُفاجِئ) بلِّغ:

in case of emergency (illness or accident), notify:

● **INSIGHT**

In some Arab countries, the Arabic name (usually called الاِسْم الرُّباعيّ *quadrilateral name*) is composed mainly of four items:

الاِسْم   *proper name* (e.g. Muhammad مُحَمَّد)

النَّسَب   *lineage* (lit.): *the first family name: father's first name* (e.g. Abdullah عَبْدُ الله)

النَّسَب   *the second family name: grandfather's first name* (e.g. Khalid خالِد)

النِّسْبة   *surname* (e.g. Al-Misri المِصْريّ)

Full name: مُحَمَّد عَبْدُ الله خالد المصري

Also, Arabs are known to use nicknames and teknonyms:

الكُنْية   *teknonym (a name for a parent derived from their child's name)*

اللَّقَب   *nickname*

It is a common custom among Arabs and Muslims alike to call a man or woman by the name of their firstborn child. The father is nicknamed 'abu (أبو) *father of (child's name)* and the mother 'Umm (أُمّ) *mother of*. So, for instance, the *father and mother of Taha* (طه) are nicknamed:

أُمّ طه   *mother of Taha*   أبو طه   *father of Taha*

So next time you meet an Arab or Muslim, you can easily guess their nickname by finding out the name of their first child.

أشْكال التَّخاطُب orms of address

abs use various forms of address, both in daily informal conversations and in rmal speech and writing. These will depend on the social status of individuals and ey vary between colloquial and standard Arabic. Here are some common titles:

فُلان/ة   *so and so*

يا   *O*   referred to by grammarians as a vocative particle, this is the equivalent of the old-fashioned O, commonly used before the first name or the forms of address below.

سَيِّد	Mr	used formally either spoken or written
سَيِّدة	Mrs	used formally to address married women
مَدام	Mrs (coll.) / Madame (Fr.)	used to address married women from middle/upper class
آنسة	Miss	used to address unmarried women
مادموازيل	Miss (coll.) / Mademoiselle (Fr.)	used to address young unmarried women
دُكْتوراة	Dr	used to address professionals from medical/academic disciplines
أسْتاذاة	teacher, professor (lit.)	a respectful title used to address educated men or women
حاجّة	pilgrim	commonly used to address Muslim men or women who have been on Hajj (pilgrimage to Mecca)
أُخْتي	Madam (coll.)	an informal way to address an acquaintance or stranger
أخي	Sir (coll.)	an informal way to address an acquaintance or stranger
حَضْرَتك \ حَضرتك	(coll.) (m./f.)	a formal and respectful title to address someone of a higher rank or status. This is similar to the French *vous*
شَيْخ (ج) شيوخ	Sheikh, elder (lit.)	commonly used to address a leader or governor

TITLES USED IN LETTER WRITING

In letter writing, there are numerous terms used in Arabic, to name a few:

عَزيزي\عَزيزَتي	my dear (m./f.)		المُحْتَرم	honourable, respected
حَبيبي\حَبيبَتي	my dear, darling, sweetheart (m./f.)		المُخْلِص	sincerely
المُحبّ	lovingly		المُشْتاق	cordially
السَّيِّد	mister			

Human feelings and emotions
المَشاعِر والعَواطِف الإنْسانيّة

شَخْصيّة (ج) -ات	personality	إحْساس (ج) أحاسيس	sense, feeling
سُلوك (ج) سُلوكيّات	behaviour	شُعور (ج) مَشاعِر	feeling
أدَب (ج) آداب	morals	وَعْي	awareness, consciousness
خُلُق (ج) أخْلاق	mannerism	إرادة	determination
سوء الخُلُق	ill manners	أمَل (ج) آمال	hope
عاطِفة (ج) عواطِف	emotion	أُمْنية (ج) أمان	wish
عاطِفيّ	emotional		

STUDY TIP

► Learn vocabulary in thematic groupings or chunks.
► Organize your study of vocabulary and group the new words under:
  ▷ generic categories, e.g. food, furniture, travel, politics
  ▷ sets of everyday words, e.g. numbers, colours, directions, days of the week
  ▷ situations in which they occur, e.g. at the doctor's, job search, at the restaurant
  ▷ functions, e.g. greetings, parting, thanks, apologizing.

ADJECTIVES, OPPOSITES AND VERBAL NOUNS

③ كَما قالَت العَرَب ... As the Arabs say ...

الخَيْرُ بالخَيْرِ والبادي أكْرَم والشَرُّ بالشَّرِّ والبادي أظْلَم

A good act for a good act and the initiator is the more generous;
a bad act for a bad act and the initiator is the more unfair.
Arabic proverb

سَعيد (ج) سُعَدا	happy	مَسْرور	delighted
سَعادة	happiness	سُرور	delight
فَرْحان	glad, joyful	مَرِح	cheerful
فَرْحة	joy	مَرَح	cheerfulness
مُبْتَسِم	cheerful	إسْراف	extravagance

لَطيف (ج) لُطفاء	nice, pleasant, gentle	اِبْتِسام	smiling
لُطْف	niceness	حَزين	sad
ظَريف (ج) ظُرَفاء	pleasant, humorous	حُزْن	sadness
ظَرافة	pleasantness, humour	تَعيس	miserable
حَليم (ج) حُلَماء	forbearing, good-natured	تَعاسة	misery
حُلْم	forbearance	مُطْمَئَن	reassured, at peace
رَقيق (ج) رِقاق	gentle, sensitive	اطْمِئْنان\طُمَأنينة	contentment
رِقّة	gentleness	مُكْتَئَب	depressed
أَنيس	pleasant	اكْتِئاب	depression
أُنْس	amiability	يائِس	despair
حَنون	kind, loving, affectionate	يَأْس	despair
حَنان	affection	قَلِق	worried
طَيّب	kind, good	قَلَق	worry
طيبة	kindness	مَهْموم	worried
وِدّي	friendly	هَمّ	worry
وِدّية	friendliness	خائِف	afraid, scared
وَدود	affectionate	خَوْف	fear
وَدّ	affection	غاضِب	angry
مُحِبّ	loving	غَضَب	anger
حُبّ	love	عَصَبيّ	irritable
مَحْبوب	likeable, popular	عَصَبيّة	nervousness, irritation
حُبّ	love	مُتوتِّر	tense, stressed
مُتَسامِح	forgiving, tolerant	تَوتُّر	tension, stress
تَسامُح	tolerance	مُتَضايِق	annoyed

تَضَايُق	inconvenience, annoyance		مُؤَدَّب	polite
مُسْتَاء	discontent		أَدَب	mannerism
اِسْتِياء	discontent		غير مُؤَدَّب	impolite
كَريم (ج) كُرَماء	generous		قلّة الأدب	lack of manners
كرم	generosity		ثَرْثار	talkative, gossipy
كرامة	self-respect, dignity		ثَرْثَرة	chatter
بَخيل	stingy, miser		نَمَّام	(a) gossip, informer
بُخْل	miserly, avarice		نميمة	gossip
طَمَّاع	greedy		وَقِح	insolent
طَمَع	greed		وَقاحة	insolence
مِضْياف	hospitable		حاد الطَّبْع	hot-tempered
ضِيافة	hospitality		حِدّة الطَّبْع	hot temper
مُسْرِف	extravagant		حَسود/حاسِد	envious
حَسَد	envy		حَيَويّة	vitality
حاقد	spiteful		مُنْتَبِه	alert, awake
حِقْد	hatred		انْتِباه	alertness
مُتَمَلِّق	flattery		مُصَمِّم	determined
تَمَلُّق	flatter		تَصْميم	determination
لا إنْسانيّ	inhuman(e)		حازِم	firm
لاإنْسانيّة	inhumanity		حَزْم	firmness
عَفيف	modest		حاسِم	decisive
عفّة	chastity		حَسْم	decisiveness
مُعْتَدِل	moderate		مُتَيَقِّن	certain
اعْتِدال	moderation		يَقين	certainty
مُتَواضِع	humble		مُتَرَدِّد	reluctant, hesitant
تَواضُع	humbleness		تَرَدُّد	hesitation

مُتَكَبِّر	arrogant	مُرْتاب	doubtful
تَكَبُّر	arrogance	ارْتِياب	suspicion
مُفْتَخِر	proud	مُقْتَنِع	convinced
افْتِخار	pride	اقْتِناع	conviction
مَغْرور	arrogant, egoist	مُهْمِل	careless, negligent
غُرور	arrogance	إهْمال	carelessness
فَخور	proud	كَسول	lazy
فَخْر	pride	كَسَل	laziness
عَفْويّ	spontaneous	شُجاع	brave, courageous
عَفْويّة	spontaneity	شَجاعة	courage
عَنيد	stubborn	جَريء	bold, daring
عِناد	stubbornness	جُرْأة	boldness
غَريب	strange	خَجول\خَجْلان	shy, embarrassed
غَرابة	strangeness	خَجَل	shyness, embarrassment
مُجْتَهِد	hardworking		
اجْتِهاد	diligence	جَبان (ج) جُبَناء	cowardly
مُنْضَبِط	disciplined	جَبانة	cowardice
انْضِباط	discipline	فُضوليّ	curious, inquisitive
مُشْتاق	longing	فُضول	curiosity
شَوْق	longing, yearning	عَنيد	stubborn
جِدّيّ	serious	عِناد	stubbornness
جِدّيّة	seriousness	عاقِل (ج) عُقَلاء	rational
نَشيط (ج) نُشَطاء	active, energetic	عَقْليّة	rationality, sanity
نَشاط	activity	عَقْلانيّ\مَعْقول	reasonable
حَيَويّ	lively, vital	عَقْلانية	rationality

54

مَجْنون (ج) مَجانين	insane, crazy	سَخيف (ج) سُخَفاء	stupid
جُنون	madness	سَخافة	absurdity, silliness
جاهِل (ج) جُهَلاء	ignorant	غَيور	jealous
جَهْل	ignorance	غَيرة	jealousy
عالِم (ج) عُلَماء	knowledgeable, scholar	حَسود	envious
عِلْم	knowledge	حَسَد	envy
مُثَقَّف	knowledgeable	مُشْمَئِزّ	disgusted
ثَقافة	knowledge	اشْمِئْزاز	disgust
عارِف	knowing	مُتَفائِل	optimistic
مَعْرِفة	knowledge	تَفاؤُل	optimism
شَقِيّ (ج) أشْقِياء	naughty, mischievous	مُتَشائِم	pessimistic
شَقاء\شَقاوة	naughtiness	تَشاؤُم	pessimism
مُشاغِب	troublemaker	صادِق	truthful
شَغَب	riot	صِدْق	truthfulness
مُتَهَوِّر	reckless, impatient	نَزيه (ج) نُزَهاء	honest, scrupulous
تَهَوُّر	recklessness	نَزاهة	integrity
مُنْدَهِش	amazed	مُخْلِص	sincere
دَهْشة\انْدِهاش	amazement	إخْلاص	sincerity
مُسْتَغْرِب	astonished, surprised	نَبيل	noble
اسْتِغْراب	astonishment	نُبْل	nobility
مَذْهول	shocked, amazed	مُنافِق	hypocrite
ذُهول	astonishment	نِفاق	hypocrisy
حائِر	confused	شَريف (ج) شُرَفاء	honourable

حَيْرة	confusion	شَرَف	honour
واثِق مِن نَفْسِه	self-confident	أَمين (ج) أُمَناء	honest, loyal
ثِقة بالنَّفْس	self-confidence	أمانة	trustworthiness
مُتْعَب	tired	كَذّاب	liar
تَعَب	fatigue	كَذِب	lying
ذَكيّ (ج) أَذْكِياء	intelligent	صَريح	open, frank
ذَكاء	intelligence	صَراحة	frankness
نَبيه (ج) نُبَهاء	smart	غَدّار	treacherous
نَباهة	smartness	غَدْر	treachery
حَكيم (ج) حُكَماء	wise	خائِن	traitor
حِكْمة	wisdom	خِيانة	betrayal
عَبْقَريّ (ج) عَباقِرة	genius	خادِع	trickster
عَبقرية	genius	خَدْع	deception
غَبيّ (ج) أغْبِياء	stupid	نَصّاب	deceitful
غَباء	stupidity	نَصْب	roguery
مَكّار	sly, cunning	قَسْوة	cruelty
مَكْر	deception	خَشِن	rough, rude
راضي	content, satisfied	خُشونة	roughness
رِضى	satisfaction	مُحْتَرَم	respectful
مِسْكين	miserable, poor	احْتِرام	respect
مُرْتاح	comfortable	مُحْتَقَر	contemptuous
راحة	rest, comfort	احْتِقار	contempt, disdain
مُسْتَريح	relaxed	حَقير	low
اسْتِراحة	rest, comfort	حقْر	despise
مَشْغول	busy	مُهان	humiliated
انْشِغال	busyness	إهانة	humiliation

أَنانيّ	selfish		آسِف	regretful, sorry
أَنانيّة	selfishness, egoism		تَأَسُّف	regret
غَير أَنانيّ	selfless		نادِم	regretful
اِجْتِماعيّ	sociable		نَدامة	regret, remorse
مُنْعَزِل\اِنْعِزاليّ	isolated		مُعَقَّد	complicated
اِنْعِزاليّة	isolation		تَعْقيد	complication
مُتَقَوْقِع	isolated, confined		مُتَناقِض	contradictory
تَقَوْقُع	isolation		تَناقُض	contradiction
مُنْغَلِق	introvert		مُهْتَمّ	interested, concerned
اِنْغِلاق	reclusion		اِهْتِمام	care, concern
مُنْفَتِح	extrovert		مُلِحّ	insistent
اِنْفِتاح	openness		إِلْحاح	insistence
وَحيد	lonely		خارِق\فوق العادة	extraordinary
وِحْدة	loneliness		صَبور	patient
ساذِج	naive, clueless		صَبْر	patience
سَذاجة	naivety		طَموح	ambitious
فَريد	unparalleled		طُموح	ambition
مُتَمَيِّز	unique		مَوْضوعيّ	objective
تَمَيُّز	uniqueness		مَوْضوعيّة	objectivity
مُضْحِك	funny		مَمْنون	grateful
ضَحِك	laughter		الاِعْتِراف بالجَميل	gratefulness
حَسّاس	sensitive		مَحْظوظ	lucky
حَساسيّة	sensitivity		حَظّ	luck
هادِئ	quiet, calm		مَسْؤول	responsible, accountable
هُدوء	calmness		مَسْؤوليّة	responsibility
قاس	cruel			

USEFUL VERBS

شَتَم يَشْتِم شَتْم	to insult
أزْعَج يُزْعِج ازْعاج	to annoy, irritate (so.)
جادَل يُجادِل مُجادلة	to dispute, argue with (so.)
لام يَلوم لَوْم على	to blame (so.)
شَكى يشْكو شَكْوى من	to complain about
بَكى يَبْكي بُكاء	to cry
خان يَخون خِيانة	to betray
خَدَع يَخْدَع خِداع	to deceive (so.)
اعْتَذَر يعتذِر اعْتذار عن	to apologize
سامَح يُسامِح مسامَحة	to forgive
حيَّر يُحَيِّر تحيير	to confuse (so.)
خاف يَخاف خَوْف من	to fear, be afraid of
غار يغير غَيْرة من	to be jealous of

شَعَر يَشْعُر شُعور	to feel
أحسَّ يُحِس إحْساس	to feel
عَطف يَعْطِف عَطْف على	to sympathize with
ابْتَسم يَبْتَسِم ابتِسام	to smile
ضَحَك يَضْحَك ضَحِك	to laugh
تَمَنّى يتمنّى تَمَنّي	to hope, wish
خَجِل يخْجل خَجَل من	to be embarrassed
تَعِب يَتْعَب تعب	to get tired
قَلِق يَقْلَق قَلَق	to be worried
صَبَر يَصْبِر صَبْر على	to be patient with
كَذَب يَكْذِب كَذِب	to lie
غَضِب يَغْضَب غَضَب	to get angry
صَرَخ يَصْرَخ صِراخ	to scream, shout

Appearance and clothing الشَّكل واللِّباس

CORE VOCABULARY

ثَوْب النَّوم	nightgown
بيجامة (ج) -ات	pyjamas
مَلابس داخليّة	underwear
صَدْرة	vest
مَشَدّ صَدْر	bra
رَبْطة عُنُق	tie
جَوْرَب (ج) جَوارب	sock
حِذاء (ج) أحْذية	shoe

لِباس (ج) مَلابِس	clothing
لَبَس يَلْبَس لَبْس	to wear (clothes) (1)
ارْتَدى يَرْتَدي ارْتِداء	to wear (clothes) (2)
خَلَع يَخْلَع خَلْع	to take off
قميص (ج) قِمْصان	shirt
تي شرت	t-shirt
بلوزة (ج) -ات	blouse
مِعْطَف (ج) مَعاطِف	coat

سُتْرة (ج) سِتَر	jacket	خُفّ (ج) أخْفاف	slipper
بَنْطَلون (ج) -ات	trousers/pants	شِبْشِب	flip-flop
بَنْطَلون قَصير	shorts	حَفّاظ (ج) -ات أطْفال	nappy/diaper
تَنّورة (ج) -ات	skirt	خَيّاط (ج) -ون	tailor
فُسْتان (ج) فَساتي	dress	قُطْن	cotton
قَميص نَوْم	nightdress	جِلْد	leather
بَدْلة\بِذْلة (ج) بِذَل	suit (business)	حَرير	silk
ثَوْب السِّباحة	swimsuit	صوف	wool

ADJECTIVES (RELATED TO APPEARANCE)

ضَيِّق	tight	مُحْتَشِم	modest (mainly for clothing,
واسِع	wide, loose	مُتواضِع	is for describing
أنيق	elegant		people)
مُزَيَّن	embroidered, decorated	غير رَسْميّ	casual
مُشَجَّر	patterned	مقْطوع	torn
صِناعِ	synthetic		

الكَماليّات ACCESSORIES		المُجَوْهَرات JEWELLERY	
حَقيبة (ج) حَقائِب	bag	جَوْهَرة (ج) جَواهِر	jewel, jewellery
حَقيبة ظَهْر	backpack	عِقْد (ج) عُقود	necklace
حَقيبة يد	purse	سِوار (ج) أسْوِرة	bracelet
مِحْفَظة (ج) مَحافِ	wallet	خاتِم (ج) خَواتِم	ring
مَظلّة (ج) -ات	umbrella	حَلَق	earrings
قُبَّعة (ج) -ات	hat	سِلْسِلة	chain
قُفّاز (ج) -ات	gloves	ذَهَب	gold
حِزام (ج) أحْزِمة	belt	فِضّة	silver
ساعة يَد	wristwatch	ماس	diamond
نَظّارة (ج) -ات	glasses	لُؤْلُؤ	pearls
نَظّارة شَمْسيّة	sunglasses		

Describing people وَصْف الأشْخاص

أشْقَر	blond	طَويل (ج) طِوال	tall
أسْمَر	tanned	قَصير (ج) قِصار	short
بَرْدان	cold	قَويّ (ج) أقْوِياء	strong
حَرّان	hot	ضَعيف (ج) ضُعَفاء	weak
نائِم	sleeping	تَعْبان	tired
مُسْتَيْقِظ	awake	جَميل	beautiful
مُتَيَقِّظ	alert/attentive	وَسيم	handsome
غافِل	oblivious	قَبيح	ugly
سَليم\صَحيح	fit, sound	بَشِع	offensive, hideous
مَريض (ج) مرْضى	sick	نَحيف	thin
مَشْلول	paralysed	سَمين	overweight
مُعاق	handicapped	فَقير	poor
مُتَخَلِّف عَقْليًّا	mentally disable	غَنيّ	rich
كَفيف	blind	جَوْعان\جائِع	hungry
أعْمى\عَمْياء	blind (m./f.)	عَطْشان	thirsty
أطْرَش\طَرْشاء	deaf (m./f.)	شَبْعان	full, satisfied
أخْرَس\خَرْساء	dumb (m./f.)	مَشْهور	famous
أعْرَج\عَرْجاء	lame (m./f.)	أصْلَع	bald

3 Family and human relations
الأُسْرة والعَلاقات الإنْسانيّة

this unit you will learn essential vocabulary, organized as follows:

Relationships العَلاقات

▷ *My family* عائلَتي

▷ *Extended family* الأُسْرة المُمْتَدّة

▷ *Friendship and human relations* الصَّداقة والعَلاقات الإنْسانيّة

Life events: أحْداثُ الحَياة

▷ *From cradle to grave* مِن المَهْد إلى اللَّحْد

▷ *Birth and childhood* الوِلادة والطُّفولة

▷ *Adolescence and youth* المُراهَقة والشَّباب

▷ *Old age* العُمُر المُتَقَدّم

▷ *Death* المَوْت

▷ *Marriage* الزَّواج

The language of love لُغة الحُبّ

العَلاقات elationships

FAMILY عائلَتي

أُسْرة (ج) أسَ...	*family (1)*	أُمّ (ج) أمَّهات	*mother*
عائلة (ج) -ات	*family (2)*	بِنْت (ج) بَنات	*daughter*
أهْل (ج) أهالي	*family (extended)*	اِبْن (ج) أبْناء	*son*
أفْراد العائلة	*family members*	اِبْنة\بِنْت	*daughter, girl*

61

قَريب (ج) أَقْرِباء	relative	أَخ (ج) إِخْوة	brother
والِد	father	شَقيق (ج) أَشِقّاء	full brother
والِدة	mother	أُخْت (ج) أَخَوات	sister
والِدان	parents (dual)	جَدّ (ج) أَجْداد	grandfather, ancestor
آباء	parents	جَدّة (ج) -ات	grandmother
أَب (ج) آباء	father	الجَدّين	grandparents (dual)
الجَدّ الأَكْبَر	great-grandfather, ancestor	بِنْت خال\خالة	maternal cousin (female)
عَمّ (ج) أَعْمام\ عُمومة	uncle (paternal)	اِبْن أَخ\أُخْت	nephew (brother or sister's son)
عَمّة (ج) -ات	aunt (paternal)	بِنْت أَخ\أُخْت	niece (brother or sister's daughter)
خال (ج) أَخْوال	uncle (maternal)	حَفيد (ج) أَحْفاد	grandchild, grandson
خالة (ج) -ات	aunt (maternal)	حَفيدة (ج) أَحْفاد	granddaughter
اِبْن عَمّ\عَمّة	paternal cousin (male)	تَوْأَم (ج) تَوائم	twin
اِبْن خال\خالة	maternal cousin (male)	تَوْأَمان	twins (dual)
بِنْت عَمّ\عَمّة	paternal cousin (female)		

EXTENDED FAMILY الأُسْرة المُمْتَدّة

نَسيب (ج) أَنْسِباء	in-law	سِلْفة	sister-in-law (husband's sister)
حَمْو (ج) أَحْماء	father-in-law	نَسيب (ج) أَنْساب	brother-in-law
حَماة (ج) حَمَوات	mother-in-law	زَوْج الأُمّ	stepfather
صِهْر (ج) أَصْهار	son-in-law	زَوْجة الأب	stepmother
كُنّة (ج) كَنائن	daughter-in-law	أَخ غير شَقيق	half-brother
سِلْف (ج) أَسْلاف	brother-in-law (husband's brother)	أُخْت غير شَقيقة	half-sister

⑤ كَما قالَتِ العَرَبُ ... As the Arabs say ...

صَديقُكَ مَنْ صَدَقَكَ لا مَنْ صَدَّقَكَ

Your true friend is he who tells you the truth, not he who agrees with everything you say.
Arabic proverb

صَديق (ج) أَصْدِقاء	friend
صاحِب (ج) أَصْحاب	friend, companion, owner
صَداقة	friendship
شَريك (ج) شُرَكاء	partner
تَعارُف	acquaintance
تَعَرَّف يَتَعَرَّف تَعَرُّف على	to be introduced to, to first meet (so.)

أَحْداثُ الحَياة Life events

مِن المَهْد إلى اللَّحْد FROM CRADLE TO GRAVE

عُمْر	age	عَذْراء (ج) عَذارى	virgin (2)
سِنّ	age	بَكارة	virginity
حَياة (ج) حَيَوات	life	أَنْثَويّة\نَسَويّة	feminism
جِنْس (ج) أَجْناس	gender, nationality	أُنوثة	femininity
أُنْثى	female, feminine	رُجولة	masculinity, manhood
ذَكَر	male, masculine	الجِنْس اللَّطيف\	the fair sex
رَجُل (ج) رِجال	man	النّاعِم	
امْرَأة (ج) نِساء	woman	الجِنْس الخَشِن	the strong sex
نِسْوان\نِسْوة	women (pl.)	صَغير السِّنّ (ج)	young
المَرْأة	the woman	صِغار السِّنّ	

بِنْت (ج) بَنات	girl	صَغير (ج) صِغار	young, small
فَتاة (ج) فَتَيات	young girl	كَبُر يَكْبُر كِبَر	to grow up, get older
سَيِّدة (ج) -ات	lady	أمومة	motherhood
بِكْر (ج) أبْكار	virgin (1)	أُبُوّة	fatherhood

الوِلادة والطُّفولة BIRTH AND CHILDHOOD

جَنين	infant	تَرَبّى يَتَرَبّى تَرْبِية	to be brought up
طِفْل (ج) أطْفال	toddler	سَمّى يُسَمّي تَسْمِية	to name (so.)
رَضيع (ج) رُضَّع	baby	خِتان	circumcision
طِفْل (ج) أطْفال	child	مُجالسة الأطْفال	childminding
طُفولة	childhood	مُرَبِّية (ج) -ات	nanny
وَلَد (ج) أوْلاد	boy or son	قابِلة (ج) -ات	midwife
صَبِيّ (ج) صِبيان	boy	طَبيب مُوَلِّد	obstetrician
صَبِيّة (ج) صَبايا	girl	مَوْلود قَبْل الأوان	premature baby
عَيِّل (ج) عِيال	kid	زُجاجة حَليب	baby's bottle
حامِل	pregnant	دُمْية (ج) دُمى	dummy
حَمْل	pregnancy	حَليب أطْفال	baby milk
أنْجَب يُنْجِب إنْجاب	to have children	حَفّاظة (ج) -ات	nappy
وُلِد يولَد وِلادة	to be born	سَرير نَقّال	cot
إجْهاض	miscarriage	عَرَبة أطْفال	pram
وِلادة	birth, delivery	لُعْبة (ج) لُعَب	toy
رَضاعة طَبيعيّة	breastfeeding	طِفْل مُتَبَنّى	adopted child
تَرْبِية	upbringing	تَبَنّى يَتَبَنّى تَبَنّي	to adopt
رَبّى يُرَبّي تَرْبِية	to bring up	يَتيم (ج) يَتامى	orphan

6
كَما قالَتِ العَرَب ... As the Arabs say

قَلْبي عَلى وَلَدي انْفَطَر وَقَلْبُ وَلَدي عَلي حَجَر
My heart bleeds for my child, but my child's heart is made of stone.
Arabic saying

مُراهِق(ج) -ون	teenager, adolescent	بالِغ\راشِد(ج) -ون	adult
فَتى (ج) فِتْيان	young boy/man	قاصِر(ج) -ون	minor
فَتاة (ج) فَتَيات	young girl/woman	شَباب	young people, youth
شابّ (ج) شُبّان	young man	شَبيبة	youth (as an age category)
شابّة (ج) شابات	young woman		

العُمْر المُتَقَدّم OLD AGE

مُتَوَسِّط العُمْر	middle-aged person	شَيْخ (ج) شُيوخ	old man
كُهولة\مُنْتَصَف العُمْر	middle age	شَيْخوخة	old age
أزْمة مُنْتَصَف العُمْر	midlife crisis	عَجوز (ج) عَجائز	old woman
كَبيرالسِّنّ(ج)كِبار السِّنّ	old (age)		

المَوْت DEATH

7
كَما قالَتِ العَرَب ... As the Arabs say

فَإذا لَمْ يَكُنْ مِنَ المَوْتِ بُد فَمِنَ العَجْزِ أَنْ تَموتَ جَباناً
Since death is the one sure destiny we have, why die a coward
when you can be brave?
Arabic poetry

وَفاة\مَوْت	death	دَفْن	burial
مات يَموت مَوْت	to die, pass away (1)	مَقْبَرة (ج) مَقابِر	cemetery

تَوَفّى يَتَوَفّى وَفاة	to die, pass away (2)	قَبْر (ج) قُبور	grave
مُتَوَفّى\راحِل	deceased, departed	شَهادة وَفاة	death certificate
مَرْحوم	deceased (Islamic term)	وَصِيّة (ج) وَصايا	will, testament
جَنازة (ج) -ات	funeral	عَزّى يُعَزّي عَزاء	to offer one's condolences
جُثّة (ج) جُثَث	corpse	شَيَّد يُشَيِّد تَشْييد	to pay tribute to (s‹
نَعْش	coffin	قَتَل نَفْسَه	to kill oneself
دَفَنَ يَدْفُن دَفْن	to be buried	اِنْتَحَر يَنْتَحِر اِنْتِحار	to commit suicide

MARRIAGE الزَّواج

⑧ كَما قالَت العَرَب ... As the Arabs say ...

خِيارُكُمْ خِيارُكُمْ لِنسائِهم

The best among you are those who are best to their wives.
Prophetic saying (Muhammad (PBUH), the Prophet of Islam
(محمد رسول الله

خِطْبة\خُطوبة	engagement	العَروسان	the bride and groo
خاطِب\مَخْطوبة	fiancé/fiancée	شَهْر عَسَل	honeymoon
مَخْطوبة	engaged (female only)	القَفَص الذَّهَبي	the golden cage (of marriage)
خاتَم خِطْبة	engagement ring	لَيْلة الدُّخْلة	wedding night (co
زَوْج (ج) أزْواج	husband	لَيْلة الزِّفاف	wedding night
زَوْجة (ج) -ات	wife	إطار الزَّواج	marriage framewo‹
مُتَزَوِّج\ة	married		

زَوْجان	married couple (dual)	تَزَوَّج يَتَزَوَّج تَزَوُّج	to get married
زَواج\انكاح	marriage	زَواج القاصِرات	child/minor marriage
زَواج مُنَسَّق	arranged marriage	طَلَب يَطْلُب طَلَبَ يَد	to propose (ask for someone's hand in marriage)
زَواج عُرْفي	unofficial marriage		
عَقْد زَواج	marriage contract	زَوَّج يُزَوِّج تَزْويج	to marry off (so.)
شَهادة زَواج	marriage certificate	طلاق	divorce
مَهْر (ج) مُهور	dowry	خُلْع	seeking to be divorced (initiated by the wife)
خاتَم زَواج	wedding ring		
الحَياة الزَّوجيِّ	married life	مُطَلَّق\ة	divorcee
حَفْلة زِفاف	wedding party	طَلَّق يُطَلِّق تَطْليق	to divorce
ثَوْب زِفاف	wedding dress	مُنْفَصِل\ة	separated
عُرْس(ج)أعْراس	wedding	انْفَصَل يَنْفَصِل انْفِصال عَن	to separate
عَروسة (ج) عَرائِس	bridegroom		
عَريس (ج) عِرسان\عُرْس	groom	أرْمَل\ة (ج) أرامِل	widower, widow

أعْزَب (ج) عُزّاب	single, unmarried (male)	عُزوبيّة	bachelorhood, celibacy
عَزْباء (ج) عَزْباوات	single, unmarried (female)	عُنوسة	spinsterhood

The word (عَروس *bride, groom*) can be either gender.

Language of love لُغة الحُبّ

⑩ As the Arabs say ... كَمَا قَالَتِ العَرَب

جُنِنّا بِلَيْلى وهِي جُنَّت بِغَيْرِنا

وأخْرى بِنا مَجْنونة لا نُريدُها

I am madly in love with Laila, but Laila adores someone else; yet quite another girl loves me but she does not quicken my pulse!
Arabic poetry (Majnun Laila, 'Romeo' of the Arab World)

عَلاقة	relationship	شَهْوة	lust
حُبّ	love	غَرام	infatuation
عِشْق	passion	قَبّل يُقَبّل تَقْبيل	to kiss (so.)
كَراهِيّة	hate	قُبْلة (ج) -ات	kiss
أحَبّ يُحِبّ حُبّ	to love (so.)	مارَس الجِنْس	to have sex, ma love (1)
وَقَع يَقَع وُقوع في حُبّ	to fall in love with (so.)	جامَع يُجامِع جِماع	to have sex, ma love (2)
حَبيب (ج) أحْباب\ أحِبّاء\ أحِبّة	beloved, sweetheart, darling	جِنْس(ج) أجْناس	sex, gender
		كَبْت	frustration (sexu
أغْرى يُغْري إغْراء	to seduce, tempt		
خَليل (ج) أخِلّاء	boyfriend		
نَزْوة عابِرة	love affair		

Education and work

التَّعْليم والعَمَل

this unit you will learn essential vocabulary, organized as follows:

التَّعْليم *Education*

> الأَشْخاص *People*

> الأَماكن *Schools and places*

> أَدَوات الدِّراسة *Study tools*

> المَواد الدِّراسيّة *Study subjects*

> *Studying and learning: essential verbs*

الدِّراسة والتَعَلُّم: أَفْعال أَساسيّة

> مُؤَهِّلات *Qualifications*

> أَنْشطة *Activities*

> متنوعات *Miscellaneous*

> لُغَة الصَّف *Classroom language*

> تَعْليمات المُعَلِّم *Teacher instructions*

> تَعْليقات المُعَلِّم *Teacher feedback*

> التَّعْليم الإِلِكْتْرونيّ *E-learning*

العَمَل *Work*

> *Core vocabulary*

> البَحْث عَن وَظيفة *Job search*

Education التَّعْليم

PEOPLE الأَشْخاص

مُتَدَرِّب (ج) -ون	trainee	تِلْميذ (ج) تَلاميذ	pupil
عالِم (ج) عُلَماء	scholar/scien	طالِب (ج) طُلّاب\طَلَبة	student
مُدير (ج) مُدَراء\ناظِر (ج) -ون	principa/head	خِرّيج (ج) -ون	graduate
عَميد (ج) عمداء	dean	مُدَرِّس (ج) -ون	teacher (1)
باحِث (ج) -ون	research	مُعَلِّم (ج) -ون	teacher (2)
خَبير (ج) خبراء	expert	أُسْتاذ (ج) أَساتِذة	teacher (3)
مُتَخَصِّص (ج) -ون	specialis	مُحاضِر (ج) -ون	lecturer
مُفَتِّش (ج) -ون	inspecto	مُدَرِّب (ج) -ون	trainer

● INSIGHT – FEMININE ENDING

For the feminine form of the above professions, simply add the feminine ending (ة\ـة)
e.g. تِلْميذ\تِلْميذة pupil.

● INSIGHT

Note that طالِب is derived from the root verb طلب, which means to seek and to
demand. Hence, طالِب could also signify a seeker, as in طالِب لُجوء asylum seeker

70

الأَماكِن SCHOOLS AND PLACES

حَضانة (ج) -ات	nursery/preschool	دِراسات عُلْيا	higher education
رَوْضة أَطْفال	kindergarten	مَرْكَز (ج) مَراكِز	centre
مَدْرَسة (ج) مَدارِس	school	مَعْهَد (ج) مَعاهِد	institute
مَدْرَسة خاصّة	private school	مُؤَسَّسة (ج) -ات	institution/foundation
مَدْرَسة عامّة\حُكومي	state school	مَكْتَبة (ج) -ات	library
مَدْرَسة دينيّة	religious school	مَكْتَب القُبول	admissions office
كُتّاب	Qu'ranic school	مَكْتَب المُدير	principal's office
مَدْرَسة ابْتِدائيّة	primary school	قاعة مُحاضَرات	lecture hall
مَدْرَسة إعْداديّة	middle/preparatory school	إدارة	administration
مَدْرَسة ثانوية	secondary/high school	أَرْض المَلْعَب	field/playground
كُلِّيّة (ج) -ات	college	غُرْفة الرِّياضة	gym/sports hall
جامِعة (ج) -ات	university	غُرْفة الحاسوب	computer room
حَرَم جامِعيّ	university campus	مَعْمَل\مُخْتَبَر الكيمْياء	chemistry lab
قِسْم (ج) أَقْسام	department	مَعْمَل\مُخْتَبَر العُلوم	science lab

أَدَوات الدِّراسة STUDY TOOLS

كِتاب (ج) كُتُب	book	مِمْحاة	eraser
كِتاب مَدْرَسيّ (ج) كُتُب مَدْرَسيّة	textbook	حُروف الهِجاء	the alphabet
		صَفْحة (ج) -ات	page
دَفْتَر (ج) دَفاتِر	notebook	وَرَقة (ج) أَوْراق	paper
كُرّاس (ج) كَراريس تَمارين	workbook	آلة حاسِبة (ج) آلات حاسِبة	calculator

قاموس (ج) قَواميس	dictionary	سَبّورة (ج) -ات	board
مَوْسوعة (ج) -ات	encyclopedia	طَبْشور (ج) طَباشير	chalk
مَرْجِع (ج) مَراجِع	reference book	جَدْوَل (ج) جَداوِل	timetable
قَلَم حِبْر (ج) أَقْلام حِبْر	pen	كُرْسِيّ (ج) كَراسِيّ	chair
قَلَم رَصاص (ج) أَقْلام رَصاص	pencil	مَقْعَد (ج) مَقاعِد	
مِسْطَرة	ruler	مَكْتَب (ج) مَكاتِب	desk
مِبْراة	sharpener		

المَوادّ الدِّراسيّة STUDY SUBJECTS

مادّة (ج) مَوادّ	subject
مَوْضوع (ج) مَواضيع	topic
مادّة اختيارية (ج) مَوادّ اِخْتِياريّة	optional subject
مادّة إجبارية (ج) مَوادّ إجْباريّة	compulsory subject
لُغة (ج) -ات أَجْنَبيّة	foreign language
التَّاريخ	history
الرِّياضيّات	mathematics
الجَبْر	algebra
الجُغْرافيا	geography
الموسيقى	music
الفَنّ	art

الفُنون الجَميلة	fine arts
الرِّياضة\التَّربيّة البَدَنيّة	sports/physical education (PE)
التَّربية الدِّينيّة	religious education (RE)
التَّربية المَدَنيّة\الوَطنيّة	civics/citizenship
الأدَب	literature
الحُقوق	law
الفَلْسَفة	philosophy
علْم (ج) عُلوم	science
الكيمْياء	chemistry
الفيزْياء	physics
علْم الإجْتِماع	sociology
علْم النَّفْس	psychology
علْم الحاسوب	computer science
تكْنولوجيا المَعْلومات والاتِّصالات	information and communication technology (ICT)
علْم الفَلَك	astronomy
علْم الأحْياء\بيولوجيا	biology
علْم الأرْض\جيولوجيا	geology
علْم البيئة	environmental science
العلوم الإنْسانيّة	humanities/liberal arts
الهَنْدسة	engineering
الهَنْدسة المَدَنيّة	civil engineering
الهَنْدسة المعْماريّة	architecture
هَنْدسة الحاسوب	computer engineering
الإقْتصاد	economics
إدارة الأعْمال	business administration

المُحاسَبة	accounting
الإحْصاء	statistics
الصِّحّة	health
الطِّبّ	medicine
طِبّ الأسْنان	dentistry
التَّمْريض	nursing
الصَّيْدَلة	pharmacy
الطِبّ النَّفْسانيّ	psychiatry

STUDYING AND LEARNING: ESSENTIAL VERBS

الدِّراسة والتَعَلُّم: أَفْعال أساسيّة

كَتَب يِكْتُب كِتابة	to write	دَرَس يَدْرُس دِراسة	to study
قَرَأ يَقْرَأ قِراءة	to read	تَعَلَّم يَتَعَلَّم تَعَلُّم	to learn
ذاكر يُذاكِر مُذاكرة	to review	دَرَّس يُدَرِّس تَدْريس	to teach
راجَع يُراجِع مُراجَعة	to revise	عَلَّم يُعَلِّم تَعْليم	to teach
شَرَح يَشْرَح شَرْح	to explain	حَفَظ يَحْفَظ حِفْظ	to memorize/ to learn by heart
لَخَّص يُلَخِّص تَلْخيص	to summarize		
تَحَسَّن يَتَحَسَّن تَحَسُّن	to improve	سَأَل يَسْأَل سُؤال	to ask
تَقَدَّم يَتَقَدَّم تَقَدُّم	to progress	أجاب يُجيب إجابة	to answer
نَجَح يَنْجَح نَجاح في	to succeed	فَهِم يَفْهَم فَهْم	to understand
فَشَل يَفْشَل فَشَل في	to fail (1)	عَلِم يَعْلَم عِلْم	to know
رَسَب يَرْسَب رُسوب	to fail (2)	عَرَف يَعْرَف مَعْرِفة	to know
تَخَصَّص يَتَخَصَّص تَخَصُّص في	to specialize	شارَك يُشارِك مُشاركة	to participate
صَحَّح يُصَحِّح تَصْحيح	to correct	ساهَم يُساهِم مُساهَمة	to contribute
حَرَّر يُحَرِّر تَحْرير	to edit	حاضَر يُحاضِر مُحاضَرة	to lecture

to notice	لاحَظ يُلاحِظ مُلاحَظة	to think	فَكَّر يُفَكِّر تَفْكير في
to comment	عَلَّق يُعَلِّق تَعْليق	to focus on	رَكَّز يُرَكِّز تَرْكيز على
to analyse	حَلَّل يُحَلِّل تَحْليل	to solve	حَلَّ يَحُلّ حَلّ
to translate	تَرْجَم يُتَرْجِم تَرْجَمة	to attend	حَضَر يَحْضُر حُضور
to apply for	قَدَّم يُقَدِّم تَقْديم طَلَب لـ	to be absent	غاب يَغيب غِياب عن
to graduate	تَخَرَّج يَتَخَرَّج تَخَرُّج	to research	بَحَث يَبْحَث بَحْث في

مُؤَهِّلات QUALIFICATIONS

نَتيجة (ج) نَتائِج	result
دَرَجة (ج) -ات	grade/mark
تَقْرير مَدْرَسيّ	school report
شَهادة (ج) -ات	certificate/degree (academic)
دِبْلوم (ج) -ات	diploma
باكالورْيوس	Bachelor's degree
باكالورْيوس أَدَب	Bachelor of Arts (BA)
باكالورْيوس عُلوم	Bachelor of Science (BSc)
ماجِسْتير	Masters
ماجِسْتير إدارة أَعْمال	MBA (Masters of Business Administration)
دُكْتوراه	PhD/doctorate
بامْتِياز	with distinction
عَنْ جَدارة وإسْتِحْقاق	with merit
مَعَ مَرْتَبة الشَّرَف	with honours
مَهارة (ج) -ات	skill
كَفاءة (ج) -ات	proficiency, ability
مُسْتَوى	level

ACTIVITIES أَنْشِطة

تَمْرين (ج) -ات\تَمارين	exercise/drill
تَدْريب (ج) -ات	training exercise
نَشاط (ج) -ات\أَنْشِطة	activity
واجِب مَنْزِليّ (ج) -ات مَنْزِليّة	homework/essay/assignment
تَقْديم (ج)-ات	presentation
مَشْروع (ج) مَشاريع	project
وَرَقة بَحْثيّة	research paper
أَنْشِطة يَدَويّة\حِرَفيّة	manual activities/craft
تَلْوين	colouring
امْتِحان (ج)-ات	exam
اخْتِبار (ج)-ات	test
امْتِحان كِتابيّ	written assignment
امْتِحان شَفَويّ	oral test
دَرْس (ج) دُروس	lesson
صَفّ (ج) صُفوف	classroom
حِصّة (ج) حِصَص	class/period
فَصْل (ج) فُصول	term/semester
دَوْرة (ج) -ات	course

فَصْل دِراسيّ	term/semester
مُحاضَرة (ج) -ات	lecture
نَدْوة (ج) -ات	seminar
مقابلة شخصية (ج.) مقابلات شخصية	1:1 interview
دُروس خُصوصيّة	private tuition
تَجْرِبة (ج) تَجارِب	experience
خِبْرة عَمَليّة	work experience
تَدْريب مِهَنيّ	apprenticeship/vocational training
تَدْريب	internship
تَمْثيل أَدْوار	role play
مَهارات لُغَويّة	language skills
قراءة	reading
كَتابة	writing
اسْتِماع	listening
كَلام\حِوار	speaking
المَنْطوق	pronunciation
فَهْم المَسْموع	listening comprehension
فَهْم المَقْروء	reading comprehension
إمْلاء	dictation
اسْتِراحة (ج) -ات	break
اسْتِراحة غَداء	lunch break
إجازة (ج) -ات\عُطْلة (ج) عُطَل مَدْرَسيّة	school holiday

متنوعات MISCELLANEOUS

مُسْتَطيل (ج) -ات	rectangle	خَطّ (ج) خُطوط	handwriting
مُثَلَّث (ج) -ات	triangle	سُؤال (ج) أَسْئِلة	question

إجابة (ج) -ات	answer		زاوية (ج) زَوايا	angle
خَطَأ (ج) أَخْطاء	mistake		بَحْث (ج) أَبْحاث	research
فاصِلة (ج) -ات	comma		رسالة (ج) رَسائِل	dissertation
نُقْطة (ج) نُقَط	period, full stop		أُطْروحة (ج) -ات	
هامِش (ج) هَوامِش	margin		مَنْهَج (ج) مَناهِج	curriculum/ syllabus
رَقْم (ج) أَرْقام	number		مِنْحة (ج) مِنَح	scholarship/ grant
مُعادَلة (ج) -ات	equation		رسُوم التَّعْليم	tuition
مَسْأَلة رياضيّة (ج) مَسائِل رياضيّة	mathematical problem		مَصاريف الدِّراسة	
			تَمْويل	finance
شَكْل (ج) أَشْكال	shape		مُساعَدات ماليّة	financial aid
دائِرة (ج) دَوائِر	circle		قَرْض دِراسيّ (ج) قُروض دِراسيّة	student loan
مُرَبَّع (ج) -ات	square			

● INSIGHT – AL-QAEDA

In addition to its meaning as *grammar/rule*, the Arabic word **قاعدة** can mean *base/ foundation*. It is from this meaning that the international organization **القاعدة** (Al-Qaeda) derives its name. In Arabic, Al-Qaeda can be referred to by **تَنْظيم القاعدة** (*The Al-Qaeda Organization*) or just **القاعدة** (*The Base*).

There is also a well-known book widely studied by non-Arab speaking Muslims who wish to learn to read the Qur'anic Arabic script called (**القاعدة النورانيّة**), i.e. *The Luminous Rule*. This book was published well before the emergence of the group Al-Qaeda and students might simply refer to it as Al-Qaeda!

CLASSROOM LANGUAGE لُغَة الصَّف

عِنْدي سُؤال	I have a question.
ما مَعْنى ... ؟	What does ... mean?
كَيْف نَكْتُب/نقول ... بالعَرَبيّة؟	How do we write/say ... in Arabic?

78

مَرَّة أُخْرى\ثانية لَوْ سَمَحْت؟   *One more time, please?*

لا أَعْرِف   *I don't know.*

لا أَفْهَم   *I don't understand.*

تَعْليمات المُعَلِّم   TEACHER INSTRUCTIONS

إقْرَأ\إقْرَئي   *read*

أعِد\أعيدي   *repeat*

أُكْتُب\أُكْتُبي   *write*

قُلْ\قولي   *say*

تَرْجِم\تَرْجِمي   *translate*

صِفْ\صِفي   *describe*

اذْكُر\اذْكُري   *mention*

اسْتَعْمِل\اسْتَعْمِلي   *use*

اسْتَمِع وأعِد   *Listen and repeat.*

هل فَهِمْتُم؟   *Do you (pl.) understand?*

تفضّل\تفضّلي   *Please/go ahead.*

إقْرَأ\إقْرَئي النَّص التالي   *Read the following text.*

أُكْتُب\أُكْتُبي الكَلِمات المُناسِبة في الفَراغات   *Write the appropriate words in the spaces.*

اسْتَمِع\اسْتَمِعي إلى الحِوار التالي   *Listen to the following dialogue.*

أجِبْ\أجيبي عَن السُّؤال   *Answer the question.*

أكْمِل\أكْمِلي الجُمَل   *Complete the sentences.*

افْتَح\افْتَحي كِتابك   *Open your book.*

المُعَلِّم تَعْليقات TEACHER FEEDBACK

مُمْتاز!	Excellent!	جَيِّد	Good.
إجابة صَحيحة!	Correct answer!	جَيِّد جِدًّا!	Very good!
صَحيح	That's correct!	أَحْسَنْتَ!	Well done!

التَّعْليم الإلِكْترونيّ E-LEARNING

التَّعْليم الإلِكْتروني	e-learning
تَعْليم عَبْرَ الإنْتِرْنِت	online learning
تَعْليم افْتِراضيّ	virtual learning
تَعْليم مُدْمَج\مَزيج	blended learning (BL)/mixed-mode learning
تَعْليم جَوّال\نَقّال	mobile learning
بيئة التَّعْليم الافْتِراضيّ	virtual learning environment (VLE)
تَقْييم تَرْبَويّ إلِكْترونيّ\عَلى الإنْتِرْنِت	e-assessment/online assessment
اِخْتِبار إلِكْترونيّ (ج) -ات إلِكْترونيّة	e-test/e-quiz
نَشاط إلِكْترونيّ (ج) أَنْشِطة إلِكْترونيّة	e-activity
رِحْلة مَعْرِفيّة باسْتِخْدام الإنْتِرْنِت	webquest
مَكْتَبة رَقْميّة (ج) مَكاتِب رَقْميّة	digital library
مَكْتَبة إلِكْترونيّة (ج) مَكاتِب إلِكْترونيّة	e-library
كِتاب إلِكْترونيّ (ج) كُتُب إلِكْترونيّة	e-book
كِتاب رَقْميّ (ج) كُتُب رَقْميّة	digital book
قاموس إلِكْترونيّ (ج) قَواميس إلِكْترونيّة	e-dictionary
قاموس عَلى الإنْتِرْنِت	online dictionary
سَبّورة تَفاعُليّة	interactive whiteboard (IWB)
بَثّ الدُّروس الإلِكْترونيّة عَلى الإنْتِرْنِت	course-casting

مَدْرَسة إلِكْتْرونيّة	online school
جامِعة إلِكْتْرونيّة	online university
جامِعة افْتِراضيّة	virtual university
فَصْل افْتِراضيّ (ج) فُصول افْتِراضيّة	virtual classroom
نَدْوة عَلى الإنْتِرْنت	webinar/web-based seminar
دَرْس عَلى الإنْتِرْنت (ج) دُروس عَلى الإنْتِرْنت	online lesson
فيديو تَعْليميّ	video tutorial
مُتَعَلِّم إلِكْتْرونيّ	e-learner/online learner
مُدَرِّس إلِكْتْرونيّ	e-tutor/online tutor
مُحْتَوى تَعْليميّ عَلى الإنْتِرْنت	online educational content
تَطْبيقات تَعْليميّة لِلْجَوّال	mobile educational apps

العَمَل Work

كَما قالَتِ العَرَب ... As the Arabs say ...

إنَّ اللهَ يُحِبُّ إذا عَمِلَ أَحَدُكم عَمَلاً أَنْ يُتْقِنَهُ

*Certainly, Allah loves for one of you when performing
a deed to perform it with perfection.*
Prophetic saying (Muhammad (PBUH))

ORE VOCABULARY

وَظيفة (ج) وَظائف	job
مِهْنَة (ج) مِهَن	profession, trade
عَمَل (ج) أَعْمال	work
شُغْل (ج) أَشْغال	work, profession

حِرْفة (ج) حِرَف	craft, profession
تَوْظيف	employment
بِطالة	unemployment
العَمَل لِلْحِساب الخاصّ	self-employment
سيرة مِهَنِيّة\مَسار عَمَلِيّ	career
مهنة	occupation

البَحْث عَنْ وَظيفة JOB SEARCH

مُقابَلة شَخْصِيّة	job interview	وَظيفة شاغِرة	job vacancy
مُؤَهِّل (ج) -ات	qualification	طَلَب عَمَل	application
خِبْرة (ج) -ات	experience	اسْتِمارة طَلَب	application form
عَقْد (ج) عُقود	contract	سيرة ذاتِيّة (ج) سِيَر ذاتِيّة	curriculum vitae, CV

في المَكْتَب AT THE OFFICE

إجازة (ج) -ات	leave, holidays	وَظيفة بِدَوام كامِل	full-time job
إجازة غَيْر مَدْفوعة الأجْر	unpaid leave	وَظيفة بِدَوام جُزْئِيّ	part-time job
إجازة مَدْفوعة الأجْر	paid holidays	أوْقات\مَواقيت العَمَل	office hours
إجازة مَرَضِيّة	sick leave	مُرَتَّب (ج) -ات	salary (1)
شَهادة مَرَضِيّة	sick note	راتِب (ج) رَواتِب	salary (2)
إجازة سَنَوِيّة	annual holiday	دَخْل (ج) دُخول	income
عُطَل رَسْمِيّة	national holidays	رِزْق (ج) أرْزاق	living, provision
إقالة (ج) ات	dismissal	تَرْقِية (ج) -ات	promotion

82

مَعاش (ج) -ات	pension (1)	نِقابة (ج) -ات	union
راتِب التَّقاعُد	pension (2)	إِضْراب (ج) -ات	strike
مُهِمّة عَمَل	business trip	مُضْرِب عَن العَمَل	striker (work)
غَداء عَمَل	business lunch	ضَريبة (ج) ضَرائِب	tax, taxation
اجْتِماع (ج) -ات	meeting	مَطْلَب (ج) مَطالِب	demands
غُرْفة اجْتِماعات	meeting room	ظُروف العَمَل	working conditions
جَدْوَل أَعْمال\أَجِّنْدة	agenda	مُسْتَوى المَعيشة	standard of living
تَرَأَّس يَتَرَأَّس تَرَأُّس	to chair (a meeting)	عِلاوة (ج) -ات	pay raise
تَقْديم (ج) -ات	presentation	مُعَدَّل البِطالة	unemployment rate
عَرْض (ج) عُروض	proposal	الدَّخْل القانونيّ الأَدْنى	legal minimum wage
مُتَحَدِّث (ج) -ون	speaker		

ROFESSIONS المِهَن

ommon professions مِهَن شائِعة

صاحِب العَمَل	employer	مُبْتَدِئ (ج) -ون	apprentice
مُوَظَّف (ج) -ون	employee, worker (1)	خَبير (ج) خُبَراء	expert
عامِل (ج) عُمّال	employee, worker (2)	مُدَقِّق حِسابات	auditor
العامِلون	staff	وَكيل (ج) وُكَلاء	agent

التَّعْليم والعَمَل 4 *Education and work* 83

سِكْرتيراة	secretary	زَميل (ج) زُمَلاء	colleague
مُوَظَّف استقبال	receptionist	رَئيس تَنْفيذيّ	chief executive
مُسْتَشار (ج) -ون	consultant	مُوَظَّف تَنْفيذيّ	executive
مُساعِد (ج) -ون	assistant	مُدير (ج) مُدَراء	director, manager
مُساعِد شَخْصيّ	personal assistant	مُدير عامّ	managing director
مُوَظَّف حُكوميّ	civil servant	مُتَدَرِّب (ج) -ون	trainee

Specialist professions مِهَن مُتَخَصِّصة

Note that the majority of vocabulary related to specialist professions and occupations is in fact grouped together by theme and listed under the relevant unit. For instance, professions such as *teacher, lecturer, trainer,* etc. are within the first part of this unit, while Unit 8 (Travel, tourism and trade) has professions like *driver, pilot, sailor,* etc.

Industries الصِّناعات

(14) كَما قالَت العَرَب ... As the Arabs say
سَبْع صْنايع وبَخْتُه ضايع
Master of seven (i.e. many) trades, but has no luck!
Jack of all trades, master of none!
Colloquial Arabic saying

For industries, you could use the term قِطاع (ج) -ات, i.e. *sector* before the following industries, e.g. (قطاع التَّعْليم).

التَّوْزيع	distribution	أَعْمَل في	I work in ...
التَّعْليم	education	المُحاسَبة	accounts
التَّصْدير	export	الإعْلان	advertising
الموضة\الأَزْياء	fashion	الزِّراعة	agriculture
القِطاع الماليّ	finance	البُنوك	banking

84

خِدْمة المَطاعِم	catering	الخَدَمات الصِّحِّيّة	health services
الخِدْمة العامّة	civil service	الاسْتيراد	import
البِناء والتَّشْييد	construction	التَّأْمين	insurance
التِّجارة	commerce	تكْنولوجيا المَعْلومات والاتِّصالات	ICT
الخَدَمات التَّرْفيهيّة	leisure services	العَقار	property
الخَدَمات اللوجِستِ	logistics	الشِّراء	purchasing
الصِّناعة	manufacturing	صِناعة الغَزْل والنَّسيج	textile industry
التَّسْويق	marketing	السِياحة	tourism
الطِّبّ	medicine	النَّقْل والمُواصَلات	transport
الإعْلام	media	البَيْع بالجُمْلة	wholesale
الإنْتاج	production		

الأَقْسام DEPARTMENTS

قِسْم (ج) أَقْسام	department	الشُّؤون القانونيّة	legal
مرْكَز رَئيسيّ	head office	خِدْمة العُمَلاء	customer service
فَرْع (ج) فُروع	branch	مَبيعات	sales
شُؤون الأَفْراد	personnel department	الإدارة	administration
إدارة المَوارِد البَشَريّ	human resources	قِسْم الحِسابات	accounts department

USEFUL VERBS

عَمِل يَعْمَل عَمَل	to work	أقال يُقيل إقالة	to fire (so.)
مارَس يُمارِس مُمارَس	to practise	طَرَد يَطْرُد طَرْد مِنَ العَمَل	to fire, expel (so.)

أَدار يُدير إدارة   to manage   اسْتَقال يَسْتَقيل   to resign (from)
اسْتقالة من

وَظَّف يُوَظِّف تَوْظيف   to hire   تَقاعَد يَتَقاعَد تَقاعُد   to retire

---

STUDY TIP

Look out for derivatives. Split up words in order to extract the derivatives which share a common root or stem; e.g. some of derivatives of the root (عِلْم – *to know*) that you might come across are:

عِلْم (ج) عُلوم	*knowledge*	تَعَلُّم	*learning*
مَعْلوم	*known*	مُعَلِّم (ج) -ون	*teacher*
عالِم (ج) عُلَماء	*knowledgeable, scientist*	تَعْليم	*teaching*
مُتَعَلِّم (ج) -ون	*student, learner*	مَكْتَب اسْتِعْلامات	*information desk*

5 Food and drink

الطَّعام والشَّراب

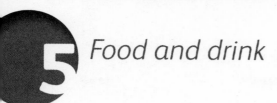
In this unit you will learn essential vocabulary, organized as follows:

▸ Food and drink الطَّعام والشَّراب

▷ Core vocabulary

▷ Meals and mealtimes الوَجَبات

▷ Meals الوَجْبات

▷ Drinks المَشْروبات

▷ Dairy produce مُنْتَجات الأَلْبان

▷ Bread الخُبْز

▷ Fruits الفَواكِه

  ▷ Citrus fruits الحِمْضِيّات

  ▷ Berries التّوت

  ▷ Tropical fruits فَواكِه اسْتِوائِيّة

  ▷ Dried fruit and nuts الفَواكِه الجافّة والمُكَسَّرات

▷ Vegetables الخُضْرَوات

▷ Herbs and spices الأَعْشاب والتَّوابِل

▷ Fish and meat السَّمَك واللَّحْم

  ▷ Fish سَمَك ▷ Poultry طُيور

  ▷ Seafood فَواكِه البَحْر ▷ Game طُيور الصَّيْد

87

Food and drink الطَّعام والشَّراب

CORE VOCABULARY

طَعام	food	مَذاق\نَكْهة	taste, flavour (2)
مَأْكولات	foods	أَكَل يَأْكُل أَكْل	to eat
وَجْبة (ج) -ات	meal	تَناوَل يَتَناوَل تَناوُل	to eat (a meal)
شَهيّة	appetite	شَرِب يَشْرَب شُرْب	to drink
طَعْم (ج) طُعوم	taste, flavour (1)	ذاق يَذوق ذَوْق	to taste

MEALS AND MEALTIMES الوَجْبات

فُطور	breakfast	أَفْطَر يُفْطِر	to have breakfast
غَداء	lunch	تَغَدّى يَتَغَدّى	to have lunch
عَشاء	dinner	تَعَشّى يَتَعَشّى	to have dinner

● INSIGHT

إفْطار may also refer to a *sundown meal*, breaking the fast during fasting days whether in Ramadan or any other day of the year.

سُحور Suhoor (lit. *a pre-dawn meal*) is an Islamic term referring to the first meal Muslims consume just before dawn before fasting, during the Islamic month of Ramadan or any other day of the year.

الوَجْبات MEALS

بطاطا مَقْليّة	chips	حساء\شوربة	soup
مَعْكَرونة	pasta, macaroni	مَرَق	stock, broth
بيتْزا	pizza	سَلَطة	salad
كاري	curry	سَنْدويتْش	sandwich
		بَرْغَر	burger

المَشْروبات DRINKS

قَهْوة	coffee	مَشْروب (ج) -ات	drink (1)
شوكولاتة ساخِنة	hot chocolate	شَراب (ج) أَشْرِبة	drink (2)
كولا	cola	مَشْروبات غازيّة	soft drinks
مَشْروبات كُحوليّة	alcoholic drinks	عَصير (ج) عَصائِر	juice
خَمْر\نَبيذ	wine	ليمونادة\مَشْروب لَيْمون	lemonade
بيرة\جعّة	beer		
شامْبانيا	champagne	ماء (ج) مِياه	water
عِرْق سوس	liquorice drink	مِياه مَعْدِنيّة	mineral water
		شاي	tea

● INSIGHT – YOU ALREADY SPEAK ARABIC!

The English words *syrup*, *sherbet* and *sorbet* are loanwords derived from the Arabic word

(شَراب), lit. *beverage* or *drink*.

مُنْتَجات الألْبان DAIRY PRODUCE

لَبَن زَبادي	yogurt	حَليب	milk
كريم\قِشْدة	cream	لَبَن	milk, yogurt (coll.)
بَيْض	eggs	زُبْدة	butter
		جُبْن	cheese

الخُبْز BREAD

خُبْز	bread		عَجين	dough
عيش	bread (coll.)		خَميرة	yeast
رَغيف (ج) أَرْغِفة	loaf of bread			

الفَواكه FRUIT

فاكِهة (ج) فَواكِه	fruit (1)		إجّاص\كُمَّثْرى	pear
ثَمَرة (ج) ثِمار	fruit (2)		دُرّاق\خَوْخ	peach
مَوْز	banana		بَرْقوق	plum
تُفّاح	apple		كَرَز	cherry
عِنَب	grape		بِطّيخ أَخْضَر	watermelon
رُمّان	pomegranate		بِطّيخ أَصْفَر\شَمّام	melon
مِشْمِش	apricot			

الحِمْضيّات Citrus fruits

بُرْتُقال	orange		لَيْمون حامِض	lime
لَيْمون	lemon		جريب فروت\الَيْمون هِنْديّ	grapefruit

● INSIGHT – YOU ALREADY SPEAK ARABIC!

Citrus fruits such as lemons, lime and oranges were first introduced to the Mediterranean region by the Arabs during the Middle Ages. *Lemon* was taken from لَيْمون, *lime* from لَيْمة and *orange* from نَرَنْج. The latter is originally from the Old French 'orenge', from the Modern Latin 'pomum de orenge', and from the Italian 'narancia', which is a form of the Arabic Naranj "نَرَنْج" originally taken from Persian 'narang'.

التّوت Berries

فَراوْلة	strawberry	توت مُعَلّق	raspberry
توت	berry	توت أَسْوَد مُعَلّق	blackberry
توت أَزْرَق	blueberry		

فَواكِه اِسْتِوائِيّة Tropical fruit

أَناناس	pineapple	أفوكادو	avocado
جَوْز الهِنْد	coconut	فاكهة كيوي	kiwi fruit
مَنْجة	mango	كَرَز	cherry

الفَواكِه الجافّة والمُكَسَّرات Dried fruit and nuts

زَبيب	raisin	جَوْز "عَيْن الجَمَل"	walnut
تَمْر	dates (dried)	بُنْدُق	hazelnut
بَلَح	dates (fresh)	جَوْز البرازيل	Brazil nut
تين	figs (fresh and dried)	جَوْز الهِنْد	coconut
بَرْقوق ناشِف	prune	كاجو	cashew
لَوْز	almond	فُسْتُق	pistachio
فول سودانيّ	peanut		

الخُضْرَوات VEGETABLES

خُضْرَوات\خُضار	vegetables (green)	سَبانِخ	spinach
بَطاطِس\بَطاطا	potato	ذُرة	sweetcorn
طَماطِم\بَنْدورة	tomato	لَفْت	turnip
بَصَل	onion	فَطْر	mushroom
جَزَر	carrot	قَرْع	pumpkin

خَسّ	lettuce		زَهْرة\قَرْنَبيط	cauliflower
خِيار	cucumber		بازِلّاء	peas
فُلْفُل	pepper		فول	broad beans
كوسا	courgette		حمَّص	chickpeas
كرنب\مَلْفوف	cabbage		عَدَس	lentils
فِجْل	radish		أرُزّ	rice
بامية	okra		دَقيق\طَحين	flour
باذِنْجان	aubergine		قَمْح	wheat
خُرْشوف	artichoke			

الأَعْشاب والتَّوابِل
HERBS AND SPICES

عُشْب (ج) أَعْشاب	herb, plant		كُزْبَرة	coriander
كَرْفَس	celery		بَقْدونِس	parsley
نَعْناع	mint		ثوم	garlic
زَعْتَر	thyme		زَنْجَبيل	ginger
بَهارات\تَوابِل	spices		كَمون	cumin
مِلْح	salt		قَرَنْفُل	cloves
فُلْفُل أَسْوَد	black pepper		مَريميّة	sage
فُلْفُل	pepper		خَلّ	vinegar
فُلْفُل أَحْمَر	paprika		زَيْت	oil
قَرْفة	cinnamon		زَيْتون	olive
زَعْفَران	saffron		زَيْت زَيْتون	olive oil

السَّمَك واللَّحْم
FISH AND MEAT

| لَحْم (ج) لُحوم | meat | | لَحْم خِنْزير | pork |
| لَحْم خَروف | lamb | | نَقانِق | sausages |

92

لَحْم بَقَر	beef	لَحْم أَرْنَب	rabbit
لَحْم عِجْل	veal		

طُيور Poultry

دَجاج	chicken	ديك رومِيّ	turkey

طُيور الصَّيْد Game

لَحْم إوَزّ	goose	لَحْم حَمام	pigeon
ديك بَرِّيّ	pheasant	لَحْم بَطّ	duck

سَمَك Fish

تونة\طونة	tuna	سَلَمون	salmon
سَرْدين	sardine	سَلَمون مُرَقَّط	trout
قُدّ	cod	حَبّار	squid
حدوق\قَديد	haddock	أُخْطُبوط	octopus

فَواكِه البَحْر Seafood

جَمْبري\رُبْيان	prawn	سَلْطَعون\سَرَطان البَحْر	lobster
سَرَطان	crab	مَحّار	oyster

● INSIGHT

All the above items (fruit, vegetables and meat) are listed in the group plural form (e.g. **تُفَّاحات, لَيْمونات**) rather than in sound plural (e.g. **تُفَّاح, لَيْمون**). However, most of the vocabulary above can be expressed in the singular form using the feminine ending **(ة\ـة)**, for instance: **تُفَّاحة, لَيْمونة, رُمّانة, تَمْرة.**

حَلَوِيّات DESSERTS

حَلَوِيّات	desserts, sweets	فَطيرة (ج)	pie, pancake
حَلْوى (ج) حَلَوِيّات	sweets	سُكَّر	sugar

بَسْكَويت	biscuit	مُرَبّى	jam
آيْس كريم\بوظة	ice cream	مُرَبّى بُرْتُقال	marmalade
كَعْك\كيك	cake	عَسَل	honey

● **INSIGHT – YOU ALREADY SPEAK ARABIC!**

The term *candy* is originally taken from the Arabic القَنْد or القَنْدي, i.e. *liquid of sugar cane* which was originally borrowed from Persian *qand*.

FOOD-RELATED WORDS

مُغَذّي	nutritious	ساخِن	hot (temperature)
تَغْذِية	nutrition	مُرّ	bitter
لَذيذ\طَيِّب\شَهيّ	delicious	حامِض	sour
جائِع (ج) جِياع	hungry	فاسِد	spoiled
جوع	hunger	مُتَعَفِّن	rotten
عَطْشان	thirsty	مَحْروق	burned
عَطَش	thirst	مُدَخَّن	smoked (fish)
شَبْعان	full (eating)	مَسْلوق	boiled
نَباتيّ	vegetarian	مَقْليّ	fried
نَيِّء\انَيْء	raw	مَشْويّ	grilled
طازِج	fresh	مُحَمَّر	roasted
طَبيعيّ	natural	في الفُرْن	baked
عُضْويّ	organic	مَحْشيّ	stuffed
لَيِّن	tender	مَفْروم	minced
ناشِف	dry	مُقَرْمَش	crunchy
حُلْو	sweet	مُقَطَّع إلى شَرائِح	sliced
حارّ	hot (spicy)		

EATING AND COOKING الأَكْل والطَّبْخ

وَصْفة (ج) -ات	recipe	غلّى يَغْلّي غَليا غَليان	to boil (water)
مِقْدار (ج) مَقادير	ingredient	سَلَق يَسْلُق سَلْق	to boil (vegetables)
طَبَخ يَطْبُخ طَبْخ	to cook (1)	قَشَّر يُقَشِّر تَقْشير	to peel (e.g. a vegetable)
طَهَى يَطْهى طَهْيا طَهْو	to cook (2)	قَطَّع يُقَطِّع تَقْطيع	to cut
سَخَّن يُسَخِّن تَسْخين	to heat up (st.)	شَريحة (ج) شَرائح	slice piece
خَلَط يَخْلُط خَلْط	to mix	قِطْعة (ج) قِطَع	to bake
مَزَج يَمْزِج مَزْج بـ	to mix with	خَبَز يَخْبِز خَبْز	to eat
صَبّ يَصُبّ صَبّ	to pour (1)	أَكَل يَأْكُل أَكْل	
سَكَب يَسْكُب سَكْب	to pour (2)		
حَرَّك يُحَرِّك تَحْريك	to stir		

At a restaurant في المَطْعَم

CORE VOCABULARY

مَطْعَم (ج) مَطاعِم	restaurant	قائمة المَشْروبات	the drinks menu
نادِل (ج) نَوادِل	waiter	مُقَبِّلات	starters
كارسون	waiter (coll.)	الوَجْبة الرَّئيسيّة	main course
طَبَق (ج) أَطْباق	dish, course	حَلَويّات	desserts
قائمة الطَّعام	the menu	فاتورة	bill

USEFUL PHRASES

لَدَيَّ نِظام غِذائيّ خاصّ	I have a special diet.	هل تُريدُ شايًا أم قَهْوة؟	Can I offer you a cup of coffee?

أَتْبِعُ نِظام غِذائيّ	I am on a diet.	إنَّه لَذيذٌ جِدًّا	It is really delicious!
أنا عِنْدي حَساسيّة مِن ...	I am allergic to ...	إنَّه لا يُعْجِبُني	I don't like it.
أنا لا آكُل...	I don't eat ...	أُريد...	I'd like ...
أنا نَباتيّ	I am vegetarian.	طاوِلة لـ...	a table for ...

SPOKEN EXPRESSIONS

All these expressions mean 'Bon appetit!/Enjoy your meal' in different dialects.

بالهَناء والشِّفاء	(MSA and most Arabic dialects)
هَنيئًا	(MSA)
الله يهَنّيك	(standard response)
بِصِحّة وَعافية	(MSA and most Levant dialects)
صَحْتين	(Lebanese and Levant dialects)
بالصِّحة	(North African dialects)

POPULAR ARAB DISHES وَجَبات عَرَبيّة مَشْهورة

To give you a taste of the Arabic dishes which vary from the East to the West of the Arab world, here is a short list of the most popular dishes:

Northwest African dishes

كُسْكُس	couscous (a North African traditional Berber dish of semolina cooked by steaming and served with meat and vegetables)
طاجين	tajine (a Berber dish made with meat, poultry or fish together with vegetables or fruit)
حَريرة	harira (the traditional Berber soup of the Maghreb)
بَسْطيلة	pastilla (a traditional Moroccan pie stuffed with meat, sugar, almonds and crêpe-like werqa ورقة dough)
شاي أَخْضَر بالنَّعْناع	green Moroccan tea (with mint)

Middle Eastern dishes

الخُبْز العَرَبيّ	pitta bread
فَلافِل\طَعْميّة	falafel (a deep-fried ball of chickpeas and fava beans)

حُمُّص   *hummus (a chickpea dip with sesame seed paste)*

كُبّة   *kibbeh (fried meat stuffed with pine nuts and cracked wheat)*

مَقْلوبة   *makloubeh (dish of meat, rice and cauliflower)*

تَبّولة   *tabbouleh (finely chopped salad made with fresh parsley)*

مَحْشي وَرَق العِنَب   *waraq enab (stuffed vine leaves)*

كَباب شاميّ/كُفْتة   *kebab shami (kebab made from minced lamb and chickpeas)*

مُلوخيّة   *mulukhiyya (leafy vegetable cooked in chicken stock)*

كُشَري   *kushari (rice, macaroni and lentils with tomato sauce)*

مَنْسَف   *mansaf is a Bedouin spit-roasted lamb served with rice and pine nuts*

فول مُدَمَّس   *ful medames (spicy broad bean stew)*

طَحينة   *tahina*

بابا غَنّوج   *baba ghannoush (aubergine dip)*

عُرْسيّة   *urceiya (an Omani rice dish similar to harissa rice)*

هَريسة   *harissa*

Desserts

كُنافة   *kenafeh (Levantine cheese pastry soaked in sweet syrup)*

بَقْلاوة   *baklava*

مُهَلَّبيّة   *muhalbia (dessert made with milk or cream and sugar)*

بَسْبوسة   *basbousa (cake made of semolina soaked in syrup)*

أُمّ عَليّ   *umm ali (an Egyptian dessert made of puff pastry, milk and nuts)*

قَطائف   *kataif (a fine vermicelli-like pastry)*

رُزّ بِحَليب   *rice pudding*

At home

في المَنْزِل

In this unit you will learn essential vocabulary, organized as follows:

- **At home في المَنْزِل**
  - ▷ *Core vocabulary*
  - ▷ *People* الأَشْخاص
  - ▷ *House rooms and furniture* الغُرَف والأَثاث
    - ▷ *Rooms* الغُرَف
    - ▷ *Living room* غُرْفة الجُلوس\الصّالون
    - ▷ *Dining room* غُرْفة الطَّعام
    - ▷ *Kitchen* في المَطْبَخ
    - ▷ *Bathroom* الحَمّام
    - ▷ *Bedroom* غُرْفة النَوْم
- **Outdoors خارج البَيْت**
  - ▷ *In the garden* في الحَديقة
  - ▷ *Tools* أَدَوات
  - ▷ *Useful phrases*
- **Housework الأَعْمال المَنْزِلِيّة**
  - ▷ *Useful verbs*

99

At home في المَنْزِل

CORE VOCABULARY

بَيْت (ج) بُيوت	house		مَحَلَّة (ج) -ات	area
منزِل (ج) مَنازِل	residence		شِقّة (ج) شِقق	apartment
سَكَن مَسْكَن (ج) مَساكِن	home, residence, where one lives		مَبْنًى (ج) مَبان	building
			بِناية (ج) -ات\ا	apartment building
حَيّ (ج) أَحْياء	quarter		عِمارة (ج) -ات	
فيلا (ج) فِلَل	villa		جِدار (ج) جُدْران	wall
مَزْرَعة (ج) مَزارِع	farm		حائِط (ج) حَوائِط	wall (room)
غُرْفة (ج) غُرَف	room (1)		سَقْف (ج) سقُوف	ceiling
حُجْرة (ج) حُجرات	room (2)		سَطْح (ج) سُطوح	roof
طابَق (ج) طَوابِق	floor (1)		مَمَرّ (ج) -ات\صالة	
دَوْر (ج) أَدْوار	floor (2)		(ج) ات	hall (way), corridor
باب (ج) أَبْواب	door		مِصْعَد (ج) مَصاعِد	lift
مَدْخَل	entrance		سُلَّم (ج) سَلالِم	stairs, ladder
بَوّابة (ج) -ات	gate		شُرْفة (ج) شُرُفات	balcony
مِفْتَاح (ج) مَفاتيح	key		إيجار	rent
قُفْل (ج) أَقْفال	lock		مَفْروش	furnished
جَرَس (ج) أَجْراس	bell		بَهْو\فِناء داخِليّ	foyer/internal courtyard
حارة (ج) -ات	neighbourhood		دُرْج مُتَحرّك	escalator

الأَشْخاص PEOPLE

جار (ج) جيران	neighbour		صاحِب البَيْت\رَبّ البَيْت	landlord
مُسْتَأْجِر (ج) -ون	tenant		رَبّة بَيْت	housewife

100

HOUSE ROOMS AND FURNITURE الغُرَف والأثاث

Rooms الغُرَف

غُرْفة الجُلوس\المَعيشة	living/sitting room
غُرْفة الأكْل\الطَّعام\السُّفْرة	dining room
غُرْفة الاسْتِقْبال\الضُّيوف	reception room
المَطْبَخ	kitchen
غُرْفة النَّوْم	bedroom
الحَمّام	bathroom
غُرْفة الخادِمة	maid's room
مَخْزَن	store
غُرْفة الحارِس\الأَمْن	safe room

غُرفَة الجُلوس\الصالون Living room

أثاث	furniture	لوحَة فنية (ج) -ات فنية	painting
طَاوِلة (ج) -ات	table	صورة (ج) صُوَر	picture
كُرْسيّ (ج) كَراسي	chair	تِلْفاز\تلفزيون	television
أَريكة (ج) أَرَائك\كَنبة\صوفة	sofa	مُتَحَكِّم عن بُعْد	remote control
سَجّادة (ج) سَجّاد	carpet	مِصْباح (ج) مَصابيح	lamp
أَرْضيّة (ج) -ات	floor	نور (ج) أنوار	light

شَمْعة (ج) -ات	candle	رُفوف كُتب\مَكْتَبة (ج) مكتبات	bookcase
مِرْوحة (ج) مَراوح	fan	مَكْتَب (ج) مَكاتِب	desk
مُكيِّف هَواء	air conditioner	شُبّاك (ج) شَبابيك	window (1)
سَخّان (ج) -ات\مِدْفَأَة	heater	نافذة (ج) نَوافِذ	window (2)
		سِتارة (ج) سَتائِر	curtain

غُرْفة الطَّعام Dining room

سِكّين (ج) سَكاكين	knife	مائدة الطَّعام\السُّفْرة	dinner table
فِنْجان (ج) فَناجين	coffee cup	غطاء الطّاولة	tablecloth
زُجاجة (ج) -ات	bottle	مِنْديل (ج) مَناديل	napkin
عُلْبة (ج) عُلَب	can	طَبَق (ج) أطْباق	dish
عُود أسْنان (ج) أعْواد أسْنان	toothpick	صَحْن (ج) صُحون	plate
صينيّة (ج) -ات\صوان	tray	كوب (ج) أكْواب\قَدَح (ج) أقْداح	cup
منْضَدة	table	كأْس (ج) كُؤوس	glass
مَسّاكة الأشْياء السّاخِنة	oven glove	صَحْن فِنْجان	saucer
مُحَرِّكة	stirrer	زُبْديّة (ج) زبادي\ سُلْطانيّة (ج) -ات	bowl
مِصْفاة	sifter	إبْريق (ج) أبَاريق	jug
غِرْبال	sieve	شَوْكة (ج) -ات	fork
ماصّة\مَصّاصة\ شفّاطة	drinking straw	ملْعَقة (ج) مَلاعِق	spoon (1)
		مِعْلَقة (ج) مَعالِق	spoon (2)

في المَطْبَخ Kitchen

غَلّاية	kettle	ثَلّاجة (ج) -ات	fridge
خَلّاط (ج) -ات	mixer/blender	فُرْن (ج) أفران	oven
غَسّالة صُحون	dishwasher	مَوْقِد (ج) مَواقِد	stove, hob
غَسّالة (ج) -ات	washing machine	كَهْرَباء	electricity
مُهْمَلات	rubbish	غاز	gas
سَلّة مُهْمَلات	dustbin	قِدْرة (ج) قُدور	pot
		قَلّاية	frying pan

الحَمّام Bathroom

حَمّام (ج) -ات	bathroom/bath
دَوْرة مياه\مِرْحاض (ج) مَراحيض	toilet (1)
تواليت	toilet (2) (coll.)
حَوْض (ج) أَحْواض الاِسْتِحْمام	bathtub
دوش (ج) -أدشاش	shower
وَرَق تواليت	toilet paper
مِغْسَلة (ج) مَغاسِل	sink, basin
صُنْبور (ج) صَنابير	tap
فوطة (ج) فُوَط	towel (1)
مِنْشَفة (ج) مَناشِف	towel (2) (coll.)
صابونة (ج) -ات	soap
شامْبو	shampoo
مُنَعِّم الشَّعْر	conditioner
عِطْر (ج) عُطور	perfume

مِشْط (ج) أَمْشاط	comb
لُوفة\لِيفة	sponge
فُرْشاة أَسْنان	toothbrush
مَعْجون أَسْنان	toothpaste
شَفْرة (ج) -ات حِلاقة	razor
صابون حِلاقة	shaving cream
مُجَفِّف الشَّعْر	hairdryer

غُرْفة النَّوْم Bedroom

فِراش (ج) أَفْرِشة\سَرير (ج) أَسِرّة	bed
مَرْتَبة (ج) مَراتِب	mattress
لِحاف (ج) لُحُف	quilt
وِسادة (ج) وَسائد\مِخَدّة (ج) مَخادّ	pillow
مِنْضَدة	bedside table
سَاعَة مُنَبِّه	alarm clock
مُنَبِّه الحَريق	fire alarm
دُرْج (ج) أَدْراج	drawer
رَفّ (ج) رُفوف	shelf
خِزانة (ج) خَزائِن	cupboard
خِزانة مَلابِس (ج) خَزائِن مَلابِس	wardrobe
عَلّاقة ثِياب (ج) عَلّاقات ثِياب	clothes hanger
تَسْريحَة (ج) -ات	dresser
مِرْآة (ج) مَرايا	mirror

خارِج البَيْت Outdoors

باحَة	courtyard	مِياه المَجاري	sewage	
كَراج	garage	عَزْل	insulation	
سور (ج) أسْوار	fence			

في الحَديقة IN THE GARDEN

حَديقة (ج) حَدائق\		شَجَرة (ج) أشْجار	tree
بُسْتان (ج) بَساتين	garden	أعْشاب ضارّة	weeds
عُشْب (ج) أعْشاب	lawn, grass	بِرْكة (ج) -ات	pond
نَبات (ج) -ات	plant	نافورة (ج) -ات	fountain
زَهْرة (ج) زُهور	flower		

أدَوات TOOLS

أداة (ج) أدَوات	tool	بُرْغي (ج) بَراغي	screw
مِكْنَسة (ج) مَكانِس	broom	مَفَكّ (ج) -ات	screwdriver
مِمْسَحة (ج) مَماسِح	mop	مِفْتاح براغ	spanner, wrench
مِكْواة (ج) مَكاوي	iron	مِنْشار (ج) مَناشير	saw
مَقَصّ (ج) -ات	scissors	دَهّان (ج) -ات	paint
مِطْرَقة (ج) مَطارق	hammer	صَمْغ	glue
مِسْمار (ج) مَسامير	nail	شَريط لاصِق	tape

USEFUL PHRASES

لِلْبَيْع	for sale
لِلإيجار	for rent
في مَنْطقة سَكَنيّة	in a residential area

في الضَّواحي	*in the suburbs*
في الطَّابَق الأوَّل	*on the first floor*
في الطَّابَق الأرْضيّ\السُّفْليّ	*in the basement*
في العُلِّيّة	*in the attic*
طابَق عُلْويّ	*upstairs*
طابَق سُفْليّ	*downstairs*
على الطاولة	*on the table*
تحت الطاولة	*under the table*
فوق الطاولة	*above the table*
بجانب النَّافذة	*beside the window*
مَنْزليّ	*domestic*
شُؤون مَنْزليّة\داخليّة	*domestic affairs*
اسْتِخْدام مَنْزليّ	*domestic use*

الأعمال المنزلية Housework

قام يَقوم قِيام بالأعْمال المَنْزِليّة	*to do housework*
نَظَّف يُنَظِّف تَنْظيف	*to clean*
رَتَّب يُرَتِّب تَرْتيب	*to tidy up*
غَسَل يَغْسِل غَسْل	*to wash*
مَسَح يَمْسَح مَسْح	*to wipe*
كَنَس يَكْنِس كَنْس	*to sweep*

USEFUL VERBS

سَكَن يَسْكُن سَكَن	*to live/to reside*
أجَّر يُؤَجِّر تَأْجير	*to let*

اِسْتَأَجَر يَسْتَأْجِر اِسْتِئْجار	to rent
اِنْتَقَل يَنْتَقِل اِنْتِقال من	to move (off)
فَتَح يَفْتَح فَتْح	to turn/switch on
أَغْلَق يُغْلِق إغْلاق	to turn/switch off (1)
قَفَل يَقْفِل قَفْل	to turn/switch off (2)

● INSIGHT – YOU ALREADY SPEAK ARABIC!

In this unit, there are two Arabic loanwords that have entered the English language:

▶ *Sofa*: originally from صُفَّة, i.e. *a couch or bench*. This term was adopted into Turkish and entered Western Europe from Turkish in the 16th century.

▶ *Mattress*: from مَطْرَح, which was originally borrowed in Sicily from Arabic and derived from the root word طرح, i.e. *to throw down*. The literal meaning of mattress is *the thing thrown down*.

---

19   As the Arabs say ... كَما قالَتِ العَرَب

صاحِبُ البَيْتِ أَدْرى بالّذي فيه

The landlord is most aware of what his house contains.
Arabic proverb

STUDY TIP

Write words for objects around your house and stick them to the objects using sticky labels r notes. Use a visual dictionary to help you find items quickly. As a revision exercise, look round you and see how many objects you can name in Arabic.

7 In town

في المَدينة

this unit you will learn essential vocabulary, organized as follows:

التَّجَوُّل في المَدينة *Getting around town*
▷ Core vocabulary

المَحَلات التِّجاريّة والتَّسَوُّق *Shops and shopping*

في السّوبِرْماركِت *At the supermarket* ▷

▷ Useful verbs

▷ Useful adjectives

لافتات المَحَلّات *Shop signs and signboards* ▷

الخِدْمات والتَّرْفيه *Services and entertainment* ▷

في مَكْتَب البَريد *At the post office* ▷

في الفُنْدُق *At the hotel* >

خِدْمات الطَّوارِئ *Emergency services* >

البِنايات *Buildings*
> Core vocabulary

الأشْخاص والمِهَن *People and professions*

> Core vocabulary

> Useful phrases

etting around town التَّجَوّل في المَدينة

RE VOCABULARY

street	شارِع (ج) شَوارِع	city	مَدينة (ج) مُدُن
avenue	شارِع واسِع\جادّة	village	قَرْية (ج) قُرى

شارِع جانِبيّ	side street	ضاحِية (ج) ضَواحي	suburb
طَريق (ج) طُرُق	road	مَنْطِقة\مِنْطِقة (ج) مَناطِق	region, area
طَريق سَريع	highway	مَنْطِقة صِناعيّة	industrial complex
موقِف سَيّارات	car park	جِسْر (ج) جُسور	bridge
موقِف حافِلات	bus stop	مَيْدان (ج) مَيادين	square (1)
يافِطة (ج) -ات	sign (1)	ساحة (ج) -ات	square (2)
لافِتة(ج) -ات	sign (2)	وَسَط المَدينة\البَلَد	city centre (1)
رَصيف (ج) أرْصِفة	pavement, sidewalk	مركز المدينة	city centre (2)
مَصْرَف (ج) مَصارِف	drain, sewag	ناصِية (ج) نَواص	corner (at a junction)
		تَقاطُع طُرُق	intersection

المَحَلّات التِّجاريّة والتَّسَوُّق   SHOPS AND SHOPPING

مَتْجَر هَدايا	gift shop	مَحَلّ (ج) -ات	shop (1)
مَتْجَر مُجَوْهَرات	jeweller	دُكّان (ج) دَكاكين	shop (2)
مَتْجَر حَيَوانات أليفة	pet shop	مَتْجَر (ج) متاجِر	shop (3)
مَتْجَر أثاث	furniture sho	مَرْكَز تَسَوُّق	shopping centre, shopping mall
مَتْجَر سِلَع مُسْتَعْمَلة	second-han shop		
صالون حِلاقة	hair salon	سوق (ج) أسْواق	market
بوتيك	boutique	مُمْتاز سوق\سوبِّرْمارْكِت	supermarket
مَكْتَب عَقارات	estate agen	بَزار (ج) -ات	bazaar (Persian for souk)
وِكالة\مَكْتَب سَفَر	travel agen		
عَرْض (ج) عُروض	offer	مَقْهى (ج) مَقاه	café, coffee shop
تَخْفيض (ج) -ات	discount, reduction	مَخْبَز(ة) (ج) مَخابِز	bakery, pastry
		مَلْبَنة\مَحْلَبة (ج) -ات	dairy shop

110

مَغْسَلة (ج) -ات	laundrette	هَديّة (ج) هَدايا	gift, present
مَحَلّ خُضْرَوات\خُضْري	grocery	إيصال (ج) -ات	receipt
بَقّالة (ج) -ات	small grocery shop	سِعْر (ج) أَسْعار	price (1)
بائع سَمَك	fishmonger	ثَمَن (ج) أَثْمان	price (2)
بائع زُهور	florist	كِلْفة\كُلْفة (ج) كُلَف	cost
بائع جَرائد	news-stand	مِحْفَظة (ج) مَحافظ	wallet
عَطّار	perfume/ spice shop	كيس (ج) أَكْياس	bag, sack
جَزّار\اللَحّام	butcher	بَقْشيش\إكْراميّة	tip (coll.)
خَيّاط	tailor's		
مَتْجَر أَحْذية	shoe shop		

في السوبِرْماركِت AT THE SUPERMARKET

مُنْتَجات الخُبْز	bakery (products)	لُحوم وَدَواجِن	meat and poultry
مُنْتَجات الأَلْبان	dairy (products)	مَشْروبات	drinks
فَواكه	fruits	حَلَويات	confectionery
خُضَرَوات	vegetables	أَدَوات الحَمّام	toiletries
سَمَك	fish	مُنْتَجات مَنْزِليّة	household products
أَغْذية مُسْتَحْضَرة	deli	مُنْتَجات الرُّضَّع	baby products
وَجَبات سَريعة	convenience food	مَجَلات	magazines
أَغْذية مُجَمَّدة	frozen food	أَدَوات كَهْرَبائيّة	electrical goods

USEFUL VERBS

اشْتَرى يَشْتَري شِراء	to buy
باع يَبيع بَيْع	to sell
تَسَوَّق يَتَسَوَّق تَسَوُّق	to shop

كَلَّفَ يُكَلِّفُ تَكْليف — to cost

اسْتَبْدَلَ يَسْتَبْدِل — to exchange (an item)
اسْتِبْدال بِ

اتَّفَقَ يَتَّفِق اتِّفاق على — to agree (on a deal)

فاصَلَ يُفاصِل — to haggle, bargain (1)
مُفاصَلة على

ساوَمَ يُساوِم — to haggle, bargain (2)
مُساوَمة على

تاجَرَ يُتاجِر مُتاجَرة في — to trade in

USEFUL ADJECTIVES

رَخيص	cheap	مُزَيَّف	fake
غال	expensive	مُصْطَنَع	artificial
مَجّاني	free	طبيعيّ	natural

SHOP SIGNS AND SIGNBOARDS لافِتات المَحَلّات

لِلْبَيْع	for sale	اسْحَب	pull
مَفْتوح	open	دَوْرَة المِياه	toilet, WC
مُغْلَق	closed	خاصّ	private
مُغْلَق لِلصَّلاة	closed for prayer	رِجال	men
ادْفَع	push	سَيِّدات	ladies

SERVICES AND ENTERTAINMENT الخِدْمات والتَّرْفيه

حانة (ج) -ات	bar	مَسْرَح (ج) مَسارِح	theatre
مَعْرِض (ج) مَعارِض	gallery, exhibition	حَديقة حَيَوان	zoo
سينَما (ج) -ات	cinema, movie theatre	حَديقة (ج) حَدائق	park, gard

112

في مَكْتَب البَريد THE POST OFFICE

مَكْتَب بَريد	post office	خَتْمُ البَريد	postmark
ساعي البَريد	postman	صُنْدوقُ بَريد	postbox
طابع (ج) طَوابِع	stamp	طَرْد (ج) طُرود	package
مَظْروف \ظَرْف \مُغَلَّف	envelope	بالبَريد الجَوّي	by airmail
رِسالة (ج) رَسائل	letter, message (1)	بَريد مُسَجِّل	registered mail
خِطاب (ج) -ات	letter, message (2)	بَريد مُسْتَعْجَل	recorded mail (UK)

في الفُنْدُق THE HOTEL

خِدْمة الغُرَف	room service	غُرْفة مُزْدَوَجة	double room
سَرير وَإفْطار (B & B)	bed and breakfast	غُرْفة لِفَرْد واحِد	single room
حَجْز	reservation	غُرْفة لِفَرْدَيْن	twin room
اسْتِقْبال (ج) -ات	reception	تَنْظيف جافّ	dry cleaner

خِدْمات الطَّوارِئ EMERGENCY SERVICES

سَيّارة إسْعاف	ambulance	فِرْقة الإطْفاء	fire brigade
حَريق	fire (lit. burning)	عَرَبة إطْفاء الحَريق	fire engine
مَرْكَز إطْفاء الحَريق	fire station	طَفّاية حَريق	fire extinguisher

البِنايات Buildings

CORE VOCABULARY

بِناية (ج) -ات	building	ناطِحة سَحاب	skyscraper
بَيْت (ج) بُيوت	house, home	مَصْنَع (ج) مَصانِع	factory
مَنْزِل (ج) مَنازِل	house, residence		

مَكْتَبة (ج) -ات	library or bookshop bookstore
مَحَطّة (ج) -ات	station
مَطار (ج) -ات	airport
مُتْحَف (ج) مَتاحِف	museum
قَصْر (ج) قُصور	palace
قَلْعة (ج) قِلاع	castle
بُرْج (ج) أَبْراج	tower
مُدَرَّج (ج) -ات	auditorium, amphitheatre
جامِع (ج) جَوامِع	mosque
مَسْجِد (ج) مَساجِد	mosque (lit. place of prostration)
كَنيسة (ج) كَنائِس	church
مَصْرِف (ج) مَصارِف	bureau de change, bank
صَرّاف آلي	cashpoint, ATM
دَفْعُ الحِساب	checkout
دَرَج مُتَحَرِّك	escalator
مِصْعَد (ج) مَصاعِد	lift, elevator
طابِق (ج) طَوابِق	floor (1)
دور (ج) أَدْوار	floor (2)
الطّابِق الأَرْضي	ground floor
الطّابِق الأَوَّل	first floor
الطّابِق الثّاني	second floor

مَسْكَن (ج) مَساكِن	home
شَقّة (ج) شُقَق	flat, apartment
عِمارة (ج) -ات	building, block of flats/apartments
فيلّا (ج) فِلَل	villa
وِحْدة سَكَنِيّة	housing unit
مُجَمَّع سَكَني	housing compound
شَرِكة (ج) -ات	company
مَرْكَز (ج) مَراكِز	centre
مَبْنى مَكاتِب	office building
مَبْنى البَلَدِيّة	town hall
كَنيس (ج) كُنُس	synagogue
مَعْبَد (ج) مَعابِد	temple
كاراج\مَرْأَب	garage
مُسْتَشْفى (ج) مُسْتَشْفَيات	hospital
البورْصة	stock exchange
قِسْمُ الشُّرْطة	police station
صيدَلِيّة (ج) -ات	pharmacy
مَطْعَم (ج) مَطاعِم	restaurant
فُنْدُق (ج) فَنادِق	hotel
مَكْتَبُ تَأْمين	insurance agency

114

صِرافة	(currency) exchange	الطّابِق العُلْوي	upper floor
بَنْك (ج) بُنوك	bank	الطّابِق السُّفْلي	basement

الأشْخاص والمِهَن eople and professions

عَميل (ج) عُمَلاء	customer	خَبّاز	baker
حَدّاد	blacksmith	جَزّار	butcher, slaughterer
كَهْرَبائي	electrician	حَلّاق	hairdresser
خَيّاط	tailor	سائِق	driver, chauffeur
رَجُل مَطافئ	firefighter	مُهَندِس مِعْماري	architect
بَنّاء (ج) بَنّاؤون	builder	نَجّار	carpenter, joiner
ميكانيكي	mechanic	حارِس (ج) حُرّاس	guard
مُصَوِّر	photographer	حَمّال	porter, carrier
سَبّاك	plumber	بَوّاب	doorkeeper, doorman
خَدّام	servant	بائِع (ج) باعة	salesman, dealer
خَدّامة	maid	تاجِر (ج) تُجّار	merchant
ساعي البَريد	postman, mailman	اسْكافيّ	shoemaker
خُضَري	greengrocer (coll.)	شُرْطيّ	police officer
بَقّال (ج) -ون بَقّالة	grocer		

أيّ خِدْمة؟	May I help you?
بِكَمْ هَذا؟	How much is this?
هَلْ هَذا آخِر سِعْ	Is this the final price?

رِياض
Riad (a traditional Moroccan house or palace with an interior garden or courtyard)

مَجْلِس (ج)مَجالِس
Majlis (lit. *a place of sitting*, which is used to describe various types of special gatherings, be they social, administrative or religious. The word is derived from

جَلَسَ, *to sit*. The English equivalent is *council* or *sitting room*.)

STUDY TIP

Make the vocabulary you acquire your own. In other words, personalize the new words by using contexts that you are personally familiar with, e.g. your family, childhood memories or travel experience. If you are writing a story or dialogue, write about experiences that are directly related to your life.

8 Travel, tourism and trade
السِّياحة والسَّفَر والتِّجارة

كَما قالَت العَرَب ... As the Arabs say ...

كُنْ في الدُّنْيا كَأنَّك غَريبٌ أو عابِرُ سَبيل

Be in this world as if you were a stranger or a traveller.
Prophetic saying (Muhammad (PBUH), the Prophet of Islam
(محمد رسول الله

In this unit you will learn essential vocabulary, organized as follows:

السَّفَر *Travel*
▷ Core vocabulary
▷ Means of transport وَسائِل النَّقْل والمُواصَلات
▷ Facilities and infrastructure تَسْهيلات ومَرافِق البِنْية التَّحْتِيّة
▷ Travel essentials أساسِيّات السَّفَر
▷ People الأشْخاص
▷ Useful verbs and nouns
▷ Road and instruction signs عَلامات الطَّريق
السِّياحة *Tourism*
▷ Core vocabulary
▷ Places to visit أماكِن للزِّيارة
▷ Famous tourist sites in the Arab world مَعالِم سِياحيّة مَشْهورة
في العالَم العَرَبيّ
▷ Useful verbs
▷ Adjectives
الإقْتِصاد والتِّجارة *Economy and trade*
▷ Core vocabulary
▷ People الأشْخاص
▷ Trade and commerce التِّجارة
▷ Useful verbs
▷ Finance المَوارِد الماليّة
▷ Islamic finance التَّمْويل الإسْلامَيّ
▷ Natural resources المَوارِد الطَّبيعيّة

117

السَّفَر Travel

CORE VOCABULARY

سَفَر (ج) أسْفار	travel	مَشْيًا على الأقْدام	on foot
رِحْلة (ج) -ات	journey	قيادة\سياقة	driving
جَوْلة (ج) -ات	trip/tour	طَيَران	flight
بَرًّا	over land	دَرَجة أولى	first class
جَوًّا	by air	دَرَجة سياحيّة	tourist class
بَحْرًا	by sea	دَرَجة اقْتصاديّة	economy class
بالقطار	by train	دَرَجة رِجال أعْمال	business class

MEANS OF TRANSPORT وَسائل النَّقْل والمُواصَلات

دَرّاجة (ج) -ات	bicycle	مِتْرو أنْفاق	underground, subway, metr
درّاجة ناريّة	motorcycle	عَبّارة (ج) -ات\ا	ferry
سَيّارة (ج) -ات	car	مَرْكب (ج) مَراكِب	
تاكسي\سَيّارة أُجْرة	taxi	سَفينة سياحيّة	cruise ship
باص (ج) -ات	bus (1)	ناقِلة (ج) -ات	tanker
أوتوبيس (ج) -ات	bus (2)	سَفينة حاويات	container ship
حافِلة (ج) -ات	coach	عابِرة (ج) -ات	passenger ship
شاحِنة (ج) -ات	truck/lorry	قارِب (ج) قوارِب\ا	
طائِرة (ج) -ات	aeroplane (1)	زَوْرَق (ج) زَوارِق	boat (smaller)
طَيّارة (ج) -ات	aeroplane (2)(coll.)	مِرْوَحيّة\طَوّافة\	
قطار (ج) -ات	train	هليكوبتر (ج) -ات	helicopter

118

FACILITIES AND INFRASTRUCTURE

تَسْهيلات ومَرافِق البِنْيَة التَّحْتيّة

مُواصَلات عامة	public transport	ميناء (ج) مَوانيء	seaport
مُرور	(road) traffic	شارِع (ج) شَوارِع	street/road
علامات مُرور	traffic signs	طَريق (ج) طُرُق	main road
إشارات مُرور	traffic lights/signals	طَريق سَريع	motorway/highway
مَحَطّة (ج) -ات	station	طَريق ريفي	country road
مَحَطّة قطار\حافلات	train/bus station	طَريق ثانَويّ	secondary road
مَحَطّة بَنْزين	petrol station	تَقاطُع طُرُق	junction
مَوقِف (ج) مَواقِف	stop (train, bus)	مُفْتَرَق طُرُق	crossroads
مَطار (ج) -ات	airport	غُرْفة انْتِظار	waiting room
مَوْقِف سَيّارات (ج) مَواقِف سَيّارات	car park	مِنصّة (ج) -ات	platform
رَصيف (ج) أَرْصِفة	pavement/sidewalk	ازْدِحام	overcrowding, traffic congestion
نَفَق (ج) أَنْفاق	tunnel		
جِسْر (ج) جُسور	bridge		
بَوّابة (ج) -ات	gate (e.g. at an airport)		

أساسيات السَّفَر TRAVEL ESSENTIALS

جَدْوَل (ج) جَداوِل	timetable/schedule	سَفير (ج) سُفَراء	ambassador
تذْكَرة (ج) تَذاكِر	ticket	قُنْصُليّة	consulate
حَجْز	reservation/booking	قُنْصُل (ج) قَناصِل	consul
تذْكَرة ذَهاب	single/one-way ticket	كاميرا\آلة تَصْوير	camera
ذَهاب وإيّاب\ذَهاب وعَوْدة	return journey	حَقيبة (ج) حَقائِب	bag, suitcase (1)
مَكْتَب تَذاكِر	ticket office	شَنْطة (ج) شُنَط	bag, suitcase (2) (coll.)
		خَريطة (ج) خَرائِط	map

مَقْعَد (ج) مَقاعِد	seat (e.g. on plane)
إِجْراءات	procedures
جَواز سَفَر (ج) جَوازات سَفَر	passport
تَأْشيرة (ج) -ات	visa (1)
فيزا (ج) -ات	visa (2) (coll.)
سِفارة	embassy

بِطاقة بَريديّة (ج) -ات بَريديّة	postcard
رُخْصة قِيادة (ج) رُخَص قِيادة	driving licence
عَدّاد (ج) -ات	meter (in a taxi)
جُمرك (ج) جَمارِك	customs
شُرْطة الحُدود	border police
تَأْمين	insurance

الأَشْخاص PEOPLE

مُسافِر (ج) -ون	traveller
رَحّالة (ج) -ون	explorer
راكِب (ج) رُكّاب	passenger
سائِق (ج) -ون	driver
سَوّاق (ج) -ين	driver (coll.)
قاطِع تَذاكِر	conductor, inspector

طَيّار (ج) -ون	pilot (1)
قائِد طائِرة	pilot (2)
مُضيف (ج) -ون	steward, cabin crew
قائِد سَفينة	ferry captain
بَحّار (ج) بَحّارة	sailor

● INSIGHT – YOU ALREADY SPEAK ARABIC!

The Arabic word أَميرُ البِحار means commander of the seas, a title in use in

Arabic Sicily and continued by the Normans in Sicily in a Latinized form, and adopted successively by the Genoese and the French. In modern French the word is Amiral.

An English form under King Edward III (14th century) was Amyrel of the Se. Insertion of the d was influenced by allusion to the common Latin admire.

SEFUL VERBS AND NOUNS

ذَهَب يَذْهَب ذَهاب	to go	نَزَل يَنْزِل نُزول من	to disembark, to get off (e.g. a vehicle)
سافَر يُسافِر سَفَ	to travel	ساق يَسوق سِياقة	to drive (1)
وَصَل يَصِل وُصو	to arrive	قاد يَقود قِيادة	to drive (2)
رَجَع يَرْجِع رُجو	to return	لَفَّ يَلِفَّ لَفَّ	to turn (coll.)
حَجَز يَحْجُز حَجْ	to book, to make a reservation	أَسْرَع يُسْرِع إِسْراع	to speed
غَيَّر يُغَيِّر تَغْيير	to change, to amend (e.g. a reservation) (1)	أَبْطَأ يُبْطِأ إِبْطاء	to slow down
عَدَّل يُعَدِّل تَعْديل	to change, to amend (2)	وَقَف يَقِف وُقوف	to stop, to park, to brake
أَلْغى يُلْغي إِلْغاء	to cancel (e.g. a reservation)	زَمَّر يُزَمِّر تَزْمير	to sound (honk) the horn
مشى يَمشي مَشْ	to walk		
رَكِب يَرْكَب رُكوب	to ride, to board	طار يَطير طَيَران	to fly
صَعَد يَصْعَد صُعود عَلى	to board	أَقْلَع يُقْلِع إِقْلاع	to take off (aeroplane)/ to set out (ship)
رَكِب يَرْكَب رُكو عَلى\مَتْن	to embark	هَبَط يَهْبِط هُبوط	to land
طَلَع يَطْلَع طُلوع	to get on, to get in (e.g. a vehicle) (coll.)	تَأَخَّر يَتَأَخَّر تَأَخُّر	to be delayed
		تَعَطَّل يَتَعَطَّل تَعَطُّل	to be cancelled (e.g. trip)

عَلامات الطَّريق AD AND INSTRUCTION SIGNS

خُروج	Exit	مُغْلَق	Closed
دُخول	Entry	ادْفَع	Push
وُصول	Arrivals	اسْحَب	Pull
ذَهاب	Departures	خاصّ	Private
مَفْتوح	Open	قِفْ	Stop

مَمْنوع الوُقوف	No stopping / parking	تاكْسيات\سَيّارات أُجْرة	Taxis
مَمْنوع التّصْوير	No photography	خَطَر	Danger
الرّجاء عَدَم	Please do not …	خَفِّف السُّرْعة\هَدِّئ السُّرْعة\تَمَهَّل	Slow down!
عُمّال يَشْتَغِلون	Roadworks / Men at work	انْتَبِه\احْذَر	Caution! / Take care!
تَحْويلة	Diversion	افْسَح\افْسَح الطَّريق	Give way
تَفْتيش	Inspection	مَمْنوع التَّدْخين	No smoking
		مَمْنوع المُرور\مَمْنوع الدُّخول	No entry

As the Arabs say … كَما قالَت العَرَب

السَّفَر يُسْفِر عن أَخْلاق الرِّجال

Travel reveals a person's character.
Arabic proverb

السِّياحة Tourism

CORE VOCABULARY

غُرْفة مُنْفَرِدة	single room	سِياحة	tourism, sightseeing
غُرْفة مُزْدَوَجة	double room	سِياحيّ	touristic
خِدْمة الغُرَف	room service	سائِح (ج) سُيّاح	tourist
اسْتِقْبال	reception	دَليل سِياحيّ	tour guide / tourist guidebook
إقامة كامِلة	full board	فُنْدُق (ج) فَنادِق	hotel
إقامة نِصْف كامِلة	half board	بَيْت شَباب\نُزُل شَباب	youth hostel
جَناح (ج) أَجْنِحة	suite	دار ضِيافة\بَيْت ضِيافة	guest house
تَكْييف هَواء	air-conditioning	غُرْفة (ج) غُرَف	room

122

PLACES TO VISIT أماكِن للزِّيارة

مَعالِم سِياحيّة	tourist sites	كَنيسة (ج) كَنائِس	church
مَتْحَف (ج) مَتاحِف	museum, gallery	كَنيس (ج) كُنُس	synagogue
مَعْرَض (ج) مَعارِض	exhibition	مَعْبَد (ج) مَعابِد	temple
آثار	ruins	مَسْجِد (ج) مَساجِد	mosque
قَصْر (ج) قُصور	palace	مَسْرَح (ج) مَسارِح	theatre
قَلْعة (ج) قِلاع	castle/citadel	ضَريح (ج) أَضْرِحة	shrine
سور (ج) أَسْوار	wall (city wall)	بُرْج (ج) أَبْراج	tower
حَديقة حَيوانات	zoo	ساعات الدَّوام الرَّسْميّ	business hours
مَيْدان (ج) مَيادين\ ساحة (ج) ساحات	square, plaza		

FAMOUS TOURIST SITES IN THE ARAB WORLD
مَعالِم سِياحيّة مَشْهورة في العالَم العَرَبيّ

هَرَم (ج) أَهْرام	pyramid
أَهْرامات الجيزة	the pyramids of Giza, Egypt
وادي المُلوك	Valley of the Kings, Egypt
مَكْتَبة الإسْكَنْدَريّة	the Royal Library of Alexandria, Egypt
سيناء	Sinai, Egypt
البَحْر الأَحْمَر	the Red Sea, Egypt
البَحْر المَيّت	the Dead Sea
البَتْراء	Petra, Jordan
وادي رَم	Wadi Rum, Jordan
مَسْجِد قُبّة الصَّخْرة	The Dome of the Rock, Jerusalem
المَسْجِد الأَقْصى	al-Aqsa Mosque, Jerusalem

بَعْلَبَك	Baalbek, Lebanon
قلعة الحصن	Krak des Chevaliers, Syria
تَدْمُر	Palmyra, Syria
قَرْطاج	Carthage, Tunisia
مَسْجِدالحَسَنالثّاني	Hassan II Mosque, Morocco
فاس البالي	Fes al-Bali (old Fes), Morocco
الصَّحْراءالمَغْرِبيّة	the Sahara Desert, Morocco

USEFUL VERBS

تَجَوَّل يتَجَوَّل تَجَوُّل	to tour, to travel around	دَفَع يَدْفَع دَفْع	to pay
زار يَزور زيارة	to visit	قَضى يَقْضي قَضاء	to spend (money or time)
رَحَّب يُرَحِّب تَرْحيب	to welcome (so.)	اشْتَرى يَشْتَري شِراء	to buy
إسْتقْبال يَسْتَقْبِل إسْتَقْبَل	to receive	كَلَّف يُكَلِّف كُلْفة	to cost
نَزَل يَنْزِل نُزول	to stay (hotel)		

ADJECTIVES

قريب	near	مَجّانيّ	free of charge
بَعيد	far, distant	مُزدَحِم	crowded
مشغول	busy	تاريخيّ	historical
فاضي	vacant (room) (coll.)	مُعاصِراحَديث	contemporary modern

Economy and trade الإقْتِصاد والتّجارة

CORE VOCABULARY

إقْتِصاد	economics	اليَد\القُوّة العامِلة	labour
اقْتِصاديّ	economical	مَوارِد بَشَريّة	human resources

نُمُوّ اقْتِصاديّ	economic growth	اخْتِراع	invention
تَطَوُّر\تَنْمِيّة	development	إعانة	subsidy
قِطاع خاص	the private sector	إنْتاج	production
قِطاع عام	the public sector	تَوْزيع	distribution
خَصْخَصة	privatization	تَوْسيع	expansion
عَوْلَمة	globalization	خِدْمة (ج) -ات	service
صادِرات	exports	دُوَل مُتَقَدِّمة	developed countries
وارِدات	imports	دُوَل مُتَخَلِّفة	underdeveloped countries
صِناعة	industry, manufacturing	دُوَل نامِيّة	developing countries
صِناعيّ	industrial		
مَصْنوع	manufactured (product)	السّوق السّوداء	black market
الاقْتِصاد العالَميّ	the global economy	السّوق المُشْتَرَكة	the Common Market
الاقْتِصاد الجَديد	the new economy	السّوق الحُرّة	duty-free market
اقْتِصاد المَعْلومات الشَّبَكيّة	networked information economy	شَراكة	partnership
إصْلاح اقْتِصاديّ	economic reform	مُبادَرة (ج) -ات	initiative
سِياسة التَّقَشُّف	austerity	صَفْقة (ج) -ات	deal, bargain
مُكافحة التَّقَشُّف	anti-austerity	عَقْد (ج) عُقود	contract, agreement
اقْتِصاد الحَجْم	economy of scale	عَقْد إيجار	lease contract
بِنْية تَحْتِيّة	infrastructure	عَقْد بَيْع	sales contract
بَطالة	unemployment	مُخاطَرة	risk
احْتِكار (ج) -ات	monopoly, cartel	انْدِماج	amalgamation, merger, integration
تَنافُس	competition	إنْفاق	spending
مُسْتَوى المَعيشة\العَيْش	living standard		

مُخاطرة	risk
اِنْتِعاش	recovery
إيراد (ج) -ات	revenue
اِحْتِياطي	reserve
تَحْويل	transfer
اِنْخِفاض (ج) -ات	reduction
تَقْليد\مُحاكاة	imitation
اِصْطِناعي	artificial
تَكْلِفة	cost, expense
تَفاوُض	negotiation
قابِل للتَّفْويض	negotiable
حَظْر اِقْتِصاديّ	economic boycott
حَظْر تِجاريّ	trade embargo
مُعَدَّل النَّمُو	growth rate

النّاتِج المَحَلِّيّ الإجْماليّ	GDP (gross domestic product)
رَفاهة	luxury
رَخاء	prosperity
اِزْدِياد (ج) -ات	increase
صُعود	rise
تَذَبْذُب	fluctuation
تَرْخيص (ج) تَراخيص	authorization
تَصْفِية	settlement
تَعْويض	compensation
تَفْتيش	inspection
اِنْهِيار	crash
ركود	recession, stagnation

الأَشْخاص PEOPLE

مُساهِم (ج) -ون	shareholder
مُسْتَثْمِر (ج) -ون	investor
مُعير (ج) -ون	lender (1)
مُسْتَعير (ج) -ون	borrower (1)
دائِن (ج) -ون	lender (2)
مَدين (ج) -ون	borrower (2)
شَريك (ج) شُرَكاء	partner
كَفيل (ج) كُفلاء	sponsor
أمين الصُّنْدوق\المال	treasurer

اِقْتِصاديّ (ج) -ون	economist
مُسْتَهْلِك (ج) -ون	consumer
مَزُوِّد\مُمَوِّن	supplier, provider
عامِل (ج) عُمال	worker
زَبون (ج) زَبائِن	customer
مُمَوِّل (ج) -ون	financier
تاجِر (ج) تُجّار	trader, merchant, dealer
بائِع (ج) -ون	seller
سِمْسار (ج) سَماسِرة	broker
مُضارِب (ج) -ون	speculator

TRADE AND COMMERCE التّجارة

تِجارة	commerce, trade	بِضاعة (ج) بَضائع	merchandise
تِجاريّ	commercial	مَوارِد	resources
تاجَرَ يُتاجِر مُتاجَرة في	to trade in	مُنْتَج (ج) -ات	products
اِشْتَرى يَشْتَري شِراء	to buy	سِلْعة (ج) سِلَع	commodity
		مَوادّ اِسْتِهْلاكيّة	consumer goods
باعَ يَبيع بَيْع	to sell	مَوادّ تِجاريّة	commercial articles
بالجُمْلة	wholesale	مارْكة مُسَجَّلة	registered trade mark
بالتَّقْسيط	in instalments	تَصْفِية	clearance, liquidation
مَصْروف (ج) مَصاريف	expenditure	تَخْفيضات\تَنْزيلات	sales, reductions
تَعامُل	dealing, trading	خَصْم (ج) خُصومات	discount
تَبادُل تِجاريّ	trade exchange	مُساوَمة\مُفاصَلة	haggling
تَسْويق	marketing	مَزاد عَلَنيّ	auction
قُوّة الشِّراء	purchasing power	مَزاد على الإنْتَرْنِت\ إِلِكْترونيّ	online auction
اِسْتِهلاك	consumption		
ضَمانة (ج) -ات	guarantee, warranty	مَوْقِع تَرْويج العَلامة التِّجاريّة	brand-building site
تَوْصيل\تَسْليم	delivery	مَوْقِع للتِّجارة الإلِكْترونيّة	e-commerce site
تَبَرُّع	donation		

USEFUL VERBS

اِزْداد يَزْداد اِزْدياد	to increase (v.i.) (1)	اِسْتَثْمَر يستثمر اَسْتِثْمار	to invest
زادَ يَزيد زِيادة	to increase (v.t.) (2)	صَدَّر يصدّر تصدير	to export

اِنْخَفَض يَنْخَفِض	to decrease	أَنْتَج يُنْتِج إنتاج	to produce
اِنْخِفاض		اِسْتورد يستورد	to import
خفَّض يخفِّض	to reduce	اِسْتيراد	
تخفيض		أَثر يؤثر تأثير	to influence
طوَّر يطوِّر تطوير	to develop	أَنْفَق ينفق إنفاق	to spend
نفذ ينفذ تنفيذ	to implement	كَلَّف يكلف تكليف	to cost

المَوارِد الماليّة FINANCE

كَما قالتِ العَرَب ... As the Arabs say ...
(23)
المالُ الحَرام لا يَدوم
Illegal unlawful money will never last.
Arabic proverb

مال	wealth, assets, money	إفْلاس	bankruptcy
نَقْد (ج) نُقود	money	أزْمة الدُّيون	debt crisis
رَأس مال (ج) رُؤوس أَمْوال	capital	أزْمة ماليّة	financial crisis
		اِنْهيار ماليّ	financial meltdown
ثَرْوة (ج) -ات	wealth	رُكود\كَساد	recession
تَكْلُفة (ج) تَكاليف	cost	تَدَهْوُر	decline, slump
نَفَقة (ج) -ات	expenses	تَضَخُّم	inflation
سوق العُمْلة الأجْنَبيّة	foreign currency market	مُضارَبة	speculation
		سَهْم (ج) أَسْهُم	share
سوق الأوْراق الماليّة	stock market	أرْصدة وأسْهُم	equity
بورْصة	stock exchange	رَهْن (ج) رُهون	mortgage (1)
اِسْتِثْمار (ج) -ات	investment	رَهان (ج) -ات	mortgage (2)
رِبْح (ج) أَرْباح	profit	تَخْفيضات	cutbacks
مُرْبِح	profitable	عَجْز	deficit

128

خَسارة\خُسران	loss	عُقوبات اِقْتصاديّة	economic sanctions
مُفْلِس	bankrupt	رَسْم (ج) رُسوم	charge, customs, tax
مُقَاطَعة	boycott	ضَريبة (ج) ضَرائب	tax
تَجْميد الأمْوال	freezing of assets	ضَريبة الدَخْل	income tax
غَسيل الأمْوال	money laundering	ضَريبة القيمة المُضافة	VAT (value added tax)
مُعَدَّل التَّضَخُّم	rate of inflation	ضَريبة الأرْباح الرّأسْماليّة	CGT (capital gains tax)
تَخْفيض القيمة	devaluation	الاِحْتياطيّ الاِتّحاديّ	the Federal Reserve
العام الماليّ\السَّنة الماليّة	the financial year	البَنْك الدُّوَليّ	the World Bank
بَيْت المال	treasury	البَنْك المَرْكَزيّ الأوروبيّ	ECB (European Central Bank)
عُمْلة صَعْبة	hard currency	صُنْدوق النّقْد الدُّوَليّ	IMF (International Monetary Fund)
عُمْلة سَهْلة	soft currency	مِنْطقة اليورو	the eurozone
دَخْل	income		
ميزانيّة	budget		
أمَّن يُؤَمِّن تَأمين على	to insure		
تَأمين	insurance		
تَأمين على الحَياة	life insurance		
تَأمين على الحوادث	accident insurance		

التَّمْويل الإسْلاميّ ISLAMIC FINANCE

المَصْرَفيّة الإسْلاميّة	Islamic banking
رَهْن عَقاريّ حَلال	halal mortgage, Sharia compliant finance
رِبا	usury

NATURAL RESOURCES المَوارِد الطَّبيعيّة

نَفْط	oil	مَنْجَم (ج) مَناجِم	mine
بِترول	petroleum	النَّفْط الخامّ	crude oil
الذَّهَب الأسْوَد	black gold (oil or coal)	وَقود أُحْفوري	fossil fuel
غاز طَبيعي	natural gas	نَقَّب يُنَقِّب تَنْقيب	to drill (natural resource)
حَقْل نَفْط	oilfield	حَفَرَ يَحْفَر حَفْر	to dig
برميل (ج) بَراميل	barrel	رَيّ	irrigation
الفَحْم الحَجَريّ	coal	زِراعة	agriculture, farming

Money مال

AT THE BANK في البَنْك

بَنْك (ج) بُنوك	bank	عُمْلة وَرَقيّة	note
مَصْرَف (ج) مَصارِف	bank, bureau de change	عُمْلة أجْنَبيّة	foreign currency
حِساب (ج) -ات	account	عُمْلة صَعْبة	hard currency
رَصيد (ج) أرْصِدة	balance	سِعْر (ج) أسْعار	price, rate
رَقْم حِساب	account number	قيمة (ج) قِيَم	value
حِساب مَصْرَفيّ	bank account	مَبْلَغ (ج) مَبالِغ	amount
حِساب جار	current account	دين (ج) دُيون	debt
حِساب تَوْفير	savings account	مَدْيون	borrower, indebted, someone in debt
صَرّاف آليّ	cashpoint/ATM	دائِن	creditor
تَحْويل مَصْرَفيّ	bank transfer	تَحْويل	transfer

130

خَصْم مُباشِر	direct debit	قَرْض (ج) قُروض	loan
سِعْر الصَّرْف	exchange rate	مُدَّخَرات\تَوْفير	savings
عُمولة (ج) -ات	commission	فائِدة (ج) فَوائِد	interest (bank)
مال (ج) أَمْوال	money	بِطاقة ائْتِمان	credit card
نَقْد (ج) نُقود	cash	بِطاقة الخَصْم المُباشِر	debit card
عُمْلة (ج) -ات	currency	وَديعة (ج) وَدائِع	deposit
عُمْلة نَقْدِيّة	coin	شيك (ج) -ات	cheque

5

كَما قالَتِ العَرَب ... As the Arabs say ...

المَدْيون حِمارُ الدّائِن

A man in debt is his creditor's donkey.
Arabic saying

INSIGHT – YOU ALREADY SPEAK ARABIC!

uring the 3rd century CE, banks in Persia issued letters of credit known as *chak* (In New
ersian script: **چک**). In post-Islamic Arabic documents this word appears as **صَكّ**.
uslim traders are known to have used the cheque or *şakk* system since the time of
arun al-Rashid (9th century) of the Abbasid Caliphate.

EFUL VERBS

كَسَب يَكْسَب كَسْب	to earn
صَرَف يَصْرِف صَرْف	to spend
وَفَّر يُوَفِّر تَوْفير	to save
سَحَب يَسْحَب سَحْب	to withdraw
أَوْدَع يودِع إيداع	to deposit

اِسْتَلَف يَسْتَلِف
اِسْتِلاف
to borrow (money)

اِسْتَعَار يَسْتَعير
اِسْتِعارة
to borrow (items)

سَلَّف يُسَلِّف
تَسْليف
to lend (money)

أعار يُعير إعارة
to lend (items)

اِسْتَثْمَر يَسْتَثْمِر
اِسْتِثْمار
to invest

العُمْلات العَرَبِيّة ARAB CURRENCIES

الدِّرْهَم	Dirham (Dh) (Morocco, UAE)
الرِّيال	Riyal (Qatar, Saudi Arabia, Oman, Yemen)
الدّينار	Dinar (Kuwait, Jordan, Libya, Tunisia, Iraq, Bahrain, Algeria)
اللّيرة	Pound (Syria, Lebanon)
الجنيه المِصْريّ	Egyptian pound

العُمْلات الدوليّة INTERNATIONAL CURRENCIES

الجنيه	Pound (£)	اليورو	Euro (€)
الدّولار	Dollar ($)	الينّ	Yen (¥)

132

9 Health and the body
الجَسَد والصِّحة

In this unit you will learn essential vocabulary, organized as follows:

The human body الجَسَد البَشَريّ
▷ Core vocabulary

▷ *The head and face* الرَّأس والوَجْه
▷ *The mouth* الفَم
▷ *The hand* اليَد
▷ *Internal organs* الأعْضاء الدّاخِليّة
▷ *Body systems* أجْهِزة الجِسْم
▷ *The five senses* الحَواسّ الخَمسّ

Health الصِّحة
▷ Core vocabulary
▷ Useful expressions

Illnesses and injuries الأمْراض والإصابات
▷ *Illnesses* الأمْراض
▷ *Injuries* الإصابات

At the hospital في المُسْتَشْفى
▷ Core vocabulary
▷ *Hospital departments* أقْسام المُسْتَشْفى
▷ *In the operating theatre* في غُرْفة العَمَليات
▷ *Emergencies* حَالات الطّوارئ

133

- *At the doctor's* عِنْد الطَّبيب
  - ▷ Core vocabulary
- *At the pharmacist* عِنْد الصَّيْدَلِيّ
- *At the dentist* عِند طبيب الأَسْنان
- *Personal hygiene* النَّظافة الشَّخْصيّة

The human body الجِسْم البَشَريّ

CORE VOCABULARY

جِسْم (ج) أجْسام	body (1)	مِرْفِق (ج) مَرافِق	elbow
جَسَد (ج) أجْساد	body (2)	ظَهْر (ج) ظُهور	back
عُضْو (ج) أعْضاء	organ, member (organization)	مُؤَخِّرة	bottom
جِلْد (ج) جُلود	skin	رِجْل (ج) أرْجُل	leg
صَدْر (ج) صُدور	chest	فَخِذ (ج) أفْخاذ	thigh
ثَدْي (ج) أثْداء	bust, breast	رُكْبة (ج) رُكَب	knee
كَتِف (ج) أكْتاف	shoulder	كاحِل (ج) كواحِل	ankle
ذِراع (ج) أذْرُع	arm	قَدَم (ج) أقْدام	foot
ساعِد (ج) سَواعِد	forearm		

> ● INSIGHT
>
> The two terms (رِجْل, *leg*) and (رَجُل, *man*) are obviously both derived from the same root words (R-J-L) ل ج ر. In fact, the etymological meaning of this root word signifies *to go on foot* or *someone who stands on one's feet*, which is not necessarily gender-specific and رِجال, pl. of رجل, could include men and women. However, the term رجل has predominately taken the meaning of masculinity and manhood in Modern Standard Arabic.

THE HEAD AND FACE الرَّأس والوَجْه

رَأْس (ج) رُؤُوس	head	لِحْية (ج) لِحَى	beard
جُمْجُمة (ج) جَماجِم	skull	جَبين (ج) جُبُن	forehead (1)

دِماغ (ج) أَدْمِغة	brain	جَبْهة (ج) -ات	forehead (2)
وَجْه (ج) وُجوه	face	خَدّ (ج) خُدود	cheek
عَيْن (ج) عُيون	eye	رَقْبة (ج) رِقاب	neck
أُذُن (ج) آذان	ear	حُنْجُرة (ج) حَناجِر	throat (1)
أَنْف (ج) أُنُوف	nose	حَلْق (ج) حُلوق	throat (2)
شَعْر	hair	ذِقْن (ج) ذُقون	chin
شارِب (ج) شَوارِب	moustache	فَكّ (ج) فُكوك	jaw

● INSIGHT

The term جَبْهة is also used in politics in reference to organizations such as:

الجَبْهة الإسْلاميّة   *The Islamic Front*

الجَبْهة الشَّعْبيّة لِتَحْرير فِلَسْطين   *The Popular Front for the Liberation of Palestine (PFLP)*

See Unit 16 (Politics and the military) for a detailed list of popular political and nonpolitical organizations in the Arab world.

As the Arabs say ... كَما قالَتِ العَرَب
اللّي مَكْتوب عالْجَبين لازِم تُشوفُه العين

What is written on the forehead will inevitably be seen by the eye.
Everyone will certainly meet their destiny. (English equivalent)
Colloquial Arabic saying

THE MOUTH الفَمّ

فَمّ (ج) أفْواه	mouth	سِنّ (ج) أسْنان	tooth
شَفة (ج) شِفاه	lip	لُعاب	saliva
لِسان (ج) ألْسِنة	tongue		

● INSIGHT

Grammatically speaking, most parts of the body which occur in pairs are feminine:

يَد	hand	عَيْن	eye
فَخِذ	thigh	ساق	leg
		أُذُن	ear

On the other hand, parts of the body which are not in pairs are usually masculine:

وَجْه	face	رَأْس	head
صَدْر	chest	قَلْب	heart
حَنْجَرة	throat	ظَهْر	back

THE HAND اليَد

وُسْطى	middle finger	يَد (ج) أَياد	hand
بُنْصُر	ring finger	رِسْغ (ج) أَرْساغ	wrist
خُنْصُر	little finger	أُصْبُع (ج) أَصابِع	finger/toe
قَبْضة (ج) -ات اليَد	fist	ظُفْر (ج) أَظافِر	fingernail/toenail
راحة (ج) -ات اليَد	palm	إِبْهام (ج) أَباهيم	thumb/big toe
		سَبّابة (ج) -ات	index finger

⟨28⟩ كَما قالَتِ العَرَب ... As the Arabs say

ما حَكَّ جِلْدُكَ مِثْلَ ظُفْرِك

Nothing can scratch your body better than your own nail.
Arabic proverb

INTERNAL ORGANS الأَعْضاء الدّاخِليّة

رِئة (ج) -ات	lung	عِرْق (ج) عُروق	vein
مَعِدة (ج) مَعِد	stomach	دَمّ (ج) دِماء	blood
بَطْن (ج) بُطون	abdomen	عَضَلة (ج) -ات	muscle

136

ضِلْع (ج) ضُلوع	rib	كَبِد (ج) أكْباد\كُبود	liver
مِفْصَل (ج) مَفاصِل	joint	كِلْية (ج) كُلى	kidney
عَظْم (ج) عِظام	bone	أمْعاء	intestine
العَمود الفِقَريّ	backbone	شَرْيان (ج) شَرايين	artery

● INSIGHT

The Arabic term for *heart* is قَلْب (ج) قُلوب, derived from the root word Q-L-B (ق ل ب) which means *to turn around, turn over, turn upside down* and *overthrow*.

This meaning is evident in the following Islamic prayer, one of the most frequent supplications used by Muslims:

يا مُقَلِّب القُلوب ثَبِّت قَلْبي عَلى دينِكَ

O Turner of the hearts, keep my heart firm in your religion.

Here are some more related words derived from the same root:

قَلْب   *reversal, overturn, conversion*

انْقِلاب   *overthrow, coup d'état*

مَقْلوبة   *Makloubeh* (which translates as *upside down*) is a traditional dish from the Arab Levant which is flipped upside down when served, hence the name.

BODY SYSTEMS أجْهِزة الجِسْم

الجِهاز التَنَفُّسيّ	respiratory system	الجِهاز الدَّوْريّ	circulatory system
الجِهاز الهَضْميّ	digestive system	الجِهاز التَّكاثُريّ\التَّناسليّ	reproductive system
الجِهاز العَصَبيّ	nervous system	جِهاز المَناعة	immune system

THE FIVE SENSES الحَواسّ الخَمْس

حاسّة (ج) حَواس	sense	نَظَر يَنْظُر نَظَر إلى	to look at
البَصَر	sight	شاهَد يُشاهِد مُشاهدة	to watch
السَّمْع	hearing	سَمِع يَسْمَع سَمْع	to hear
الشَّمّ	smell	اسْتَمَع يَسْتَمِع اسْتِماع إلى	to listen to
اللَّمْس	touch	شَمّ يَشُمّ شَمّ	to smell

9 Health and the body جَسَد والصّحة

التَذَوُّق	taste		لَمَس يَلْمَس لَمْس	to touch
رَأى يَرى رُؤية	to see		ذاق يَذوق ذَوْق	to taste

Health الصِّحة

CORE VOCABULARY

صِحّة	health		وِقاية	prevention
الطِبّ	medicine (field)		عِلاج	treatment

USEFUL EXPRESSIONS

بالسَّلامة\سَلامتك   *Wishing you a safe recovery.*

الله يِشْفيك\شَفاك الله   *May God cure you.*

أَتَمَنّى لك شِفاءً سَريعًا   *Wishing you a speedy recovery.*

Illnesses and injuries الأمْراض والإصابات

مَرَض (ج) أمْراض	disease		وَجَع (ج) أوْجاع	pain
مُزْمِن	chronic		أَلَم (ج) آلام	pain
مُعد	contagious, infectious		أَذى	pain
عَدْوى	infection		صُداع	headache
وَباء	epidemic			

> ● INSIGHT – YOU ALREADY SPEAK ARABIC!
>
> The words *soda* and *sodium* are originally based on the Arab word صُداع, meaning *headache*.

الأمْراض ILLNESSES

سُعال	cough		عُسْر هَضْم	indigestion
سعل يَسْعُل سُعال	to cough		تَقلُّصات	cramps
عَطْسة	sneeze		أَلَم البَطْن\المَعِدة	stomach-ache
عَطَس يَعْطِس عَطْس	to sneeze		الِتهاب	infection

دَوْخة، دُوار	dizziness	رَشْح، زُكام، بَرْد	cold
غَثَيان	nausea	حُمّى	fever
تَقَيُّؤ	vomiting	قَشْعَريرة	chill
ضَغْط الدَّم	blood pressure	إنْفلونزا	flu
نَزيف الأنْف	nosebleed	رَبْو	asthma
نَزيف	haemorrhage	أَرَق	insomnia
نَزَف يَنْزِف نَزيف	to bleed	حُموضة	heartburn
تَسَمُّم	poisoning	إسْهال	diarrhoea
ارْتِجاج	concussion	إمْساك	constipation
الإيدز (نَقْص المَناعة المُكْتَسَبة)	AIDS	بَثْرة	blister
السّيدا	SIDA (Syndrome de l'Immunodéficience Acquise) French for AIDS, commonly used in Arab countries across North Africa	مَرض السُّكَّر	diabetes
		مَرض السَّرَطان	cancer
		التهاب المفْصَل	arthritis
		جَلْطة (ج) -ات	clot
		جَلْطة دِماغيّة	stroke

الإصابات INJURIES

إصابة	injury	كَسْر (ج) كُسور	fracture
مُصاب (ج) -ون	injured	كَدْمة (ج) -ات	bruise
إصابة بالرَّأس	head injury	لَدْغة (ج) -ات	sting
وَرَم (ج) أوْرام	swelling	عَضّة (ج) -ات	bite
صَدْمة (ج) -ات	shock	حَرْق (ج) حُروق	burn
صَدْمة كَهْرَبائيّة	electric shock	جُرْح (ج) جُروح	wound, cut
		جَريح (ج) جَرْحَ	wounded, injured

● INSIGHT

There is an important distinction to note in Arabic between *injured* مُصاب and *wounded* جَريح. The latter is much more serious than the former, but both are regularly used in the media.

At the hospital في المُسْتَشْفى

CORE VOCABULARY

مُسْتَشْفى (ج) مُسْتَشْفَيات	hospital	وحْدة العناية المُرَكَّزة	intensive care unit
عِيادة (ج) -ات	clinic	إحالة	referral
عَنْبَر (ج) عنابر	ward	مُسْتَشار	consultant
أوْقات الزِّيارة	visiting hours		

HOSPITAL DEPARTMENTS أقْسام المُسْتَشْفى

الجِّراحة	surgery	النِّساء والولادة	gynaecology
الأطْفال	paediatrics	الأمْراض الجِلْدِيّة	dermatology
الأمْراض النَّفْسِيّة	psychiatry	الأشِعّة	radiology
الولادة	maternity	القلْب والأوْعِية الدَّمَويّة	cardiology
العِظام	orthopaedic		

IN THE OPERATING THEATRE في غُرْفة العَمَليّات

جَرّاح (ج) -ون	surgeon	بَتْر	amputation
عَمَليّة (ج) -ات	operation	تَشْريح	autopsy/post-mortem
غُرْفة عَمَليّات	operating theatre	زَرْع القلْب	heart transplant
جراحة	surgery	عَمَليّة تَجْميل	plastic surgery
تَخْدير	anaesthesia		

حالات الطُّوارِئ EMERGENCIES

مُسَكِّنات الألَم	painkillers	حالة طارِئة (ج) -ات طارِئة	emergency
إنْعاش	resuscitation	سَيّارة إسْعاف	ambulance
غَيْبوبة	coma	إسْعافات أوَّليّة	first aid
أزْمة قَلْبِيّة	heart attack	خِزانة أدْوِية	medical cabinet

At the doctor's عِند الطَّبيب

CORE VOCABULARY

عَرَض (ج) أعْراض	symptom	طَبيب (ج) أطِبّاء	doctor (medical)
عالَجَ يُعالِج مُعالَجة	to treat (medical)	مَريض (ج) مَرْضى	patient
		مُمَرِّض (ج) -ون	nurse
شَفى يَشْفي شِفاء	to cure (a disease)	تَمْريض	nursing
ميعاد (ج) مَواعيد	appointment	وَصْفة طِبّية (ج) -ات طِبّية	prescription
غُرْفة انْتِظار	waiting room	فَحَصَ يَفْحَص فَحْص	to examine medically
سَمّاعة (ج) -ات	stethoscope	فَحْص طِبِّيّ (ج) فُحوص طِبّية	medical examination
مِقْياس (ج) مَقاييس الحَرارة	thermometer	تَنَفَّسَ يَتَنَفَّس تَنَفُّس	to breathe
أشِعّة إكْس	X-ray	شَعَرَ يَشْعُر شُعور بـ	to feel (pain, emotion)
حَقَنَ يَحْقِن حَقْن	to inject	وَجَعَ يوجع وَجَع	to hurt (head, stomach, etc.)
لِقاح	vaccine	تَحَسَّنَ يَتَحَسَّن تَحَسُّن	to get better
		اِخْتِبار (ج) -ات	test

At the pharmacist عند الصَّيْدَلِيّ

جُرْعة (ج) -ات	dose (e.g. of medicine)	صَيْدَلِيّة (ج) -ات	pharmacy
مَرْهَم (ج) مَراهِم	cream, ointment	صَيْدَلِيّ	pharmacist
مُطَهِّر (ج) -ات	disinfectant	دَواء (ج) أَدْوِية	medicine
ضَمّاد	bandage, dressing	قُرْص (ج) أَقْراص	pill, tablet
شَراب	syrup, drink	مُضادّ حَيَوِيّ	antibiotic

At the dentist عند طبيب الأَسْنان

خَلْع	extraction	طَبيب أَسْنان	dentist
تاج	crown	سِنّ (ج) أَسْنان	tooth
طَقْم أَسْنان	dentures	أَلَم أَسْنان	toothache
نَظافة الأَسْنان	dental hygiene	فَحْص الأَسْنان	check-up
مَعْجون أَسْنان	toothpaste	تَسَوُّس	decay
فُرْشاة أَسْنان	toothbrush	حَشْو	filling
فَرَش يَفْرُش فَرْش	to brush (teeth)	مِثْقَب	drill

Personal hygiene النَّظافة الشَّخْصِيّة

مُزيل العَرَق	deodorant	نَظافة شَخْصِيّة	grooming
عِطْر (ج) عُطور	perfume	دُشّ	shower
جيل الاِسْتِحْمام	shower gel	أخد دُشّ	take a shower
صابون	soap	اِغْتَسَل يَغْتَسِل اِغْتِسال	wash oneself
		اِسْتَحَمّ يَسْتَحِمّ اِسْتِحْمام	take a bath

مُوس حِلاقة كَهْرَبائِيّ	electric razor	حِلاقة	shaving
رَغْوة حِلاقة	shaving foam	حَلَق يَحْلُق حَلْق	to shave (hair)
مُوس حِلاقة	shaving razor		

STUDY TIP

Learn words in pairs. Make it a habit to learn vocabulary in singular and plural forms at the same time. Don't memorize a noun without its plural! For example:

كِتاب (ج) كُتُب\أُسْبوع (ج) أسابيع\طالِب (ج) طُلّاب

Try applying the same advice for when learning opposites (e.g. بَعيد\قَريب or

.(مُدَرِّس\مُعَلِّم\أُسْتاذ) and synonyms (بَرْدَحَرّ).

10 The wider world

العالَم

30

كَما قالَتِ العَرَب ... As the Arabs say ...

يا أَيُّها النَّاس إنَّا خَلَقْناكُمْ مِنْ ذَكَرٍ وَأُنْثَىٰ

وَجَعَلْناكُمْ شُعوبًا وَقَبائِلَ لِتَعارَفوا إِنَّ أَكْرَمَكُمْ عِنْدَ اللهِ أَتْقاكُمْ

O mankind! We created you from a single (pair) of a male and a female,
and made you into nations and tribes, that ye may know each other.
Indeed, the most honoured of you in the sight of God is (he who is) the
most righteous.

Qur'anic verse (Al-Hujurat 49:13 الحُجُرات)

this unit you will learn essential vocabulary, organized as follows:

The world العالَم
 ▷ Core vocabulary
 ▷ Continents and major regions القارَّات والأَقاليم الرَّئيسيَّة
 ▷ Directions الاتِّجاهات

The Arab world العالَم العَرَبيّ
Arab League member states الدُّوَل الأَعْضاء في جامَعة الدُّوَل العَرَبيَّة
 ▷ The Middle East الشَّرْق الأَوْسَط
 ▷ Maghreb (Northwest Africa) شَمال إفْريقْيا والمَغْرِب العَرَبيّ
 ▷ Other African Arab-speaking countries دُوَل إفْريقيَّة أُخْرى
Arab cities مُدُن عَرَبيَّة
 ▷ The Middle East الشَّرْق الأَوْسَط
 ▷ Maghreb (Northwest Africa) شَمال إفْريقيا والمَغْرِب العَرَبيّ

Arab-speaking regions المَناطِق النَّاطِقة باللُّغَة العَرَبيَّة
Continents and major regions القارَّات والمَناطِق الرَّئيسيَّة
 ▷ Europe أوروبا
 ▷ Africa إفْريقْيا

145

The world العالَم

CORE VOCABULARY

مَكان (ج) أَماكن	place/location	عالَم (ج) عَوالِم	world	
مَوْقِع (ج) مَواقِع	location/site	أَرْض (ج) أَراض	earth	
مَنْطَقة (ج) مَناطِق	region/area	الكُرة الأَرْضيّة	globe	
ضاحية (ج) ضَواح	suburb	قارّة	continent	
حَيّ (ج) أَحْياء	district	بَلَد (ج) بُلْدان\دَوْلة	country	
قَرْية (ج) قُرى	village	(ج) دُوَل		
الرّيف	the countryside	وَطَن (ج) أَوْطان	homeland	
أَطْلَس	atlas	عاصمة (ج) عَواصم	capital	
مَسافة (ج) -ات	distance	إقْليم (ج) أقاليم	region	
مَساحة (ج) -ات	area	خَريطة (ج) خَرائط	map	

CONTINENTS AND MAJOR REGIONS قارّات والأقاليم الرّئيسيّة

أَمْريكا الجَنوبيّة	South America	افْريقْيا	Africa
أَمْريكا الوُسْطى	Central America	أوروبا	Europe
قارة أُسْتْراليا	Australia	آسْيا	Asia
القارة القُطْبيّة الجَنوبيّة	Antarctica	الشَّرْق الأقْصى	Far East
القُطْب الشَّماليّ	Arctic	الشَّرْق الأدْنى	Near East
		أَمْريكا الشَّماليّة	North America

الاتِّجاهات DIRECTIONS

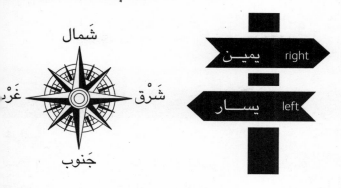

شَمال

غَرب شَرق

جَنوب

يمين right

يسار left

العالَم العَرَبيّ The Arab world

● **INSIGHT – THE LEAGUE OF ARAB STATES**

The *League of Arab States* (**جامعة الدُّوَل العَرَبيّة**), commonly known as the *Arab League* (**الجامِعة العَرَبيّة**), is a regional organization of Arab countries located in and around North Africa and Southwest Asia. It was formed in 1945 and currently has 22 members. All the countries listed are members of the League.

Can you decipher the calligraphic writing in the League's logo?

STUDY TIP

Note that the word **جامعة** is also widely used to mean *university*, as in:

جامِعة القَرَويّين، فاس، المَغْرِب *University of al-Qarawiyyin, Fes, Morocco*

Arab League member states

الدُّوَل الأَعْضاء في جامَعة الدُّوَل العَرَبِيّة

THE MIDDLE EAST الشَّرْق الأَوْسَط

الدُّوَل Countries		العاصِمة Capital		Nationality الجِنْسِيّة
العِراق	Iraq	بَغْداد	Baghdad	عِراقيّ
السُّعوديّة	Saudi Arabia	الرِّياض	Riyadh	سُعوديّ
اليَمَن	Yemen	صَنْعاء	Sana'a	يَمَنيّ
سوريا	Syria	دِمَشْق	Damascus	سوريّ
فِلَسْطين	Palestine	القُدْس	Jerusalem	فِلَسْطينيّ
الأُرْدُن	Jordan	عَمّان	Amman	أُرْدُنيّ
الإمارات العَرَبيّة المُتَّحِدة	United Arab Emirates (UAE)	أبو ظَبي	Abu Dhabi	إماراتي
لُبْنان	Lebanon	بَيْروت	Beirut	لُبْنانيّ
عُمان	Oman	مَسْقَط	Muscat	عُمانيّ
الكُوَيْت	Kuwait	الكُوَيْت	Kuwait city	كُوَيْتيّ
قَطَر	Qatar	الدَّوْحة	Doha city	قَطَريّ
البَحْرَيْن	Bahrain	المَنامة	Manama	بَحْرينيّ

● INSIGHT

While it is common in English for all nouns and adjectives of countries, languages and people always to begin with a capital letter, in Arabic there are no capital letters and some countries are definite while others are indefinite.

شَمال إفْريقْيا والمَغْرِب العَرَبيّ (MAGHREB (NORTHWEST AFRICA

الدُّوَل	Countries	العاصِمة	Capital	الجِنْسيّة Nationality
المَغْرِب	Morocco	الرِّباط	Rabat	مَغْرِبيّ (ج) مَغارِبة
الجَزائِر	Algeria	الجَزائِر	Algiers	جَزائِريّ
تونِس	Tunisia	تونِس	Tunis	تونِسيّ
ليبْيا	Libya	طَرابُلُس	Tripoli	ليبيّ
موريتانْيا	Mauritania	نواكْشوط	Nouakchott	موريتانيّ

دُوَل إفْريقيّة أُخْرى OTHER AFRICAN ARAB-SPEAKING COUNTRIES

الدُّوَل	Countries	العاصِمة	Capital	الجِنْسيّة Nationality
مِصْر	Egypt	القاهِرة	Cairo	مِصْريّ
السّودان	Sudan	الخُرْطوم	Khartoum	سودانيّ
الصّومال	Somalia	مَقْديشْيو	Mogadishu	صوماليّ
جُزُر القَمَر	Comoros	موروني	Moroni	قَمَريّ

● **INSIGHT – RECOGNIZING THE NAMES OF ARAB COUNTRIES**

The names of some Arab countries are more easily recognizable than others due to their similar pronunciation in Arabic and English.

Here are some examples:

Libya, Oman, Qatar, Mauritania, Syria

سورْيا، موريتانْيا، قَطَر، عُمان، ليبْيا

However, although others are familiar to the English ear, they usually carry the definite article (الـ) /al-/ i.e. *the*, such as:

Bahrain, Kuwait, Yemen, Iraq

العِراق، اليَمَن، الكُوَيْت، البَحْرَيْن

The official name of most Arab countries is often quite lengthy and mostly only used in official documents rather than in daily conversations.

While the majority are *republics* (جُمْهوريّة، (ج) - ات) such as:

جُمْهوريّة مِصر العَرَبيّة   *Arab Republic of Egypt*

الجُمْهوريّة اللبنانيّة   *Lebanese Republic*

الجُمْهوريّة الجَزائريّة الدّيمُقْراطيّة الشّعْبيّة   *People's Democratic Republic of Algeria*

others are *kingdoms* (مَمْلَكة، (ج) مَمالك) such as:

المَمْلَكة العَرَبيّة السُّعوديّة   *Kingdom of Saudi Arabia*

مَمْلَكة البَحْرَيْن   *Kingdom of Al-Bahrain*

المَمْلَكة المَغْرِبيّة   *Kingdom of Morocco*

or *sultanates* (سَلْطَنة) such as:

سَلْطَنة عُمان   *Sultanate of Oman*

and others are simply known as *state of …* such as:

دَوْلة قَطَر   *State of Qatar*

دَوْلة ليبْيا   *State of Libya*

(which was known under the leadership of Ghaddafi until 2011 as الجَماهيريّة العَرَبيّة اللّيبيّة الشّعْبيّة الاشْتِراكيّة العُظْمى i.e. *Great Socialist People's Libyan Arab Republic*)

What Arab countries do these coats of arms represent?

مُدُن عَرَبيّة rab cities

addition to the capital cities, the following is a list of some of the major cities
some Arab countries.

الشَّرْق الأَوْسَط E MIDDLE EAST

مُدُن عَرَبيّة	Arab cities	دُوَل عَرَبيّة	مُدُن عَرَبيّة	Arab cities	دُوَل عَرَبيّة
الزَّرقاء	Zarqa	الأُرْدُن	الإِسْكَنْدَريّة	Alexandria	مِصْر
ارْبِد	Irbid		الجيزة	Giza	
دُبَي	Dubai	الإمارات العَرَبيّة المُتَّحِدة	أَمّ دَرْمان	Omdurmàn	السّودان
الشّارقة	Sharjah		بور سودان	Port Sudan	
طَرابُلُس	Tripoli	لُبْنان	المَوْصِل	Mosul	العِراق
صَيْدا	Sidon		البَصْرة	Basra	
صَلالة	Salala	عُمان	المَدينة المُنَوَّرة	Medina	السُّعوديّة
نِزْوى	Nizwa		مَكّة	Mecca	
الأَحْمَد	Ahmadi	الكُوَيْت	الحَديدة	Al-Hudaydah	اليَمَن

حَوَلي — Hawally			عَدَن — Aden	
المَحْرَق — Muharraq	البَحْرَيْن	حُمْص — Homs		سورْيا
الرِّفاع — Riffa		حَلَب — Aleppo		
الوَكير — Al-Wakair	قَطَر	بَيْت لَحْم — Bethlehem		لَسْطين
الرَّيّان — Al-Rayyan		غَزّة — Gaza		

MAGHREB (NORTHWEST AFRICA) مال إفْريقْيا والمَغْرِب العَرَبيّ

بِنْغازي — Benghazi	ليبْيا	الدّار البَيْضاء — Casablanca		المَغْرِب
مِصْراتة — Misrata		مُرّاكُش — Marrakech		
صْفاقِس — Sfax	تونِس	وَهْران — Oran		الجَزائر
سوسة — Sousse		قُسَنْطينة — Constantine		
انْواديبو — Nouadhibou	موريتانْيا			
النِّعْمة — Néma				

152

1 **Morocco** (المَغْرب) literally means *The West*. Historically, medieval Arab historians and geographers referred to Morocco as (المَغْرب الأَقصى) *The Farthest West*. The name Morocco originates from the Spanish *Marruecos*, from the medieval Latin *Morroch*, which referred to the name of the former Almoravid and Almohad capital, Marrakech (مُرّاكُش). In Turkish, however, Morocco is referred to as *Fas* in reference to the ancient capital, *Fes/Fez* (فاس).

2 **Casablanca** (الدّار البَيْضاء) in Morocco is famous as the name of the 1942 American romantic drama film filmed in the same city. The name (الدّار البَيْضاء) means literally *White House* and the city is nicknamed Casa/kaza/ (البيت الأبيض) by the locals. Do not confuse (الدّار البَيْضاء) with (البيت الأبيض), which both share the same translation: *the White House*!

3 **Yemen** (اليَمَن) is thought to derive from (يَمين), meaning *on the right side*, as the south is on the right when facing the sunrise. Another suggestion is that it derives from (يُمْن) meaning *felicity*, as the region is fertile. The Romans called it *Arabia Felix* (Happy Arabia).

4 **Jerusalem** is commonly known in Arabic as (القُدس), meaning *The Holy* or *The Holy Sanctuary*. In Hebrew it is referred to as أورُشليم (ירושלים).

5 **Cairo** (القاهِرة), the capital of Egypt, means literally *The Vanquisher* or *The Conqueror*. It is also called (أمّ الدُّنْيا), meaning *the mother of the world*.

6 **Medina** (المَدينة), one of the primary cities of Saudi Arabia, is officially known as (المَدينة المُنَوَّرة), i.e. *the radiant city*, but is commonly referred to as (المَدينة), i.e. *the city*. In pre-Islamic times, the city was known as Yathrib (يَثْرِب) but then renamed by Muhammad, the prophet of Islam (PBUH), as (مَدينَة النَّبيّ), i.e. *The City of the Prophet*.

Arab-speaking regions
المَناطِق النّاطِقة باللُّغَة العَرَبيّة

العالَم العَرَبيّ	the Arab world
الشَّرْق الأَوْسَط	the Middle East
الشَّرْق الأَوْسَط الكَبير	the Greater Middle East

دُوَل الخَليج	the Gulf states
شَمال إفْريقْيا	North Africa
المَغْرِب العَرَبيّ	the Maghreb
المَشْرِق العَرَبيّ	the Mashriq
شبْه الجَزيرة العَرَبيّة	the Arabian Peninsula
هَضَبة\مرتفعات الجولان	the Golan Heights
الشّام\بِلاد الشّام\سوريّة الكُبْرى	the Levant/Greater Syria
سَيْناء	Sinai
السُّوَيْس	the Suez
الأراضي المُحْتَلّة	the Occupied Territories
الضِّفّة الغَرْبيّة	the West Bank
قِطاع غَزّة	the Gaza Strip

Continents and major regions
القارات والمَناطِق الرَّئيسيّة
أوروبا EUROPE

النِّمْسا	Austria	إيرْلَنْدا	Ireland
بَلْجيكا	Belgium	إيطاليا	Italy
بريطانْيا	Britain	لوكْسَمْبورغ	Luxembourg
بُلْغاريا	Bulgaria	مالْطا	Malta
الجُمْهوريّة التْشيكيّة	Czech Republic	هولَنْدا	the Netherland
قُبْرُص	Cyprus	النَّرْويج	Norway
الدّانمارْك	Denmark	بولَنْدا	Poland
انْجِلْتَرا	England	البُرْتُغال	Portugal
فِنْلَنْدا	Finland	رومانِيا	Romania

154

فَرَنْسا	France	روسيا	Russia
أَلْمانيا	Germany	إِسْكُتْلَنْدا	Scotland
الْيونان	Greece	إِسْبانيا	Spain
هُنْغاريا\المَجَر	Hungary	السُّوَيْد	Sweden
آيْسْلَنْدا	Iceland	سُويسْرا	Switzerland
أوكْرانْيا	Ukraine	دَوْلة مَدينة الفاتيكان	Vatican City
المَمْلَكة المُتَّحِدة	United Kingdom	ويلْز	Wales

افْريقْيا FRICA

تشاد	Chad	مالي	Mali
إريتْريا	Eritrea	موزَمْبيق	Mozambique
إِثْيوبيا	Ethiopia	نَيْجيريا	Nigeria
غامْبيا	Gambia	السِّنِغال	Senegal
كينيا	Kenya	جنوب إفريقيا	South Africa
مَدَغَشْقَر	Madagascar	زِمْبابْوي	Zimbabwe

آسِيا SIA

أَفْغانِسْتان	Afghanistan	كوريا الشمالية	North Korea
بَنْغْلاديش	Bangladesh	باكستان	Pakistan
الصّين	China	الفلبين	the Philippines
الهِنْد	India	كوريا الجنوبية	South Korea
إنْدَونيسْيا	Indonesia	سريلانكا	Sri Lanka
إيران	Iran	تايلندا	Thailand
اليابان	Japan	أوزباكستان	Uzbekistan
كازاخِسْتان	Kazakhstan	فيتنام	Vietnam
ماليزيا	Malaysia		

الأمريكتين AMERICAS

جَمايْكا	Jamaica	الأرْجَنْتين	Argentina
الْمَكْسيك	Mexico	الْبْرازيل	Brazil
بيرو	Peru	كَنَدا	Canada
أَمْريكا/الوِلايَات الْمُتَّحِدة الأمْريكيَّة	United States of America	شيلي	Chile
		كولومْبيا	Colombia
فِنَزْويلا	Venezuela	كوبا	Cuba

أُسْتْراليا AUSTRALASIA

أُسْتْراليا	Australia	نيوزيلَنْدا	New Zealand	غينيا الجَديدة	New Guine

> **STUDY TIP**
> Try to learn the names of countries in a real context by consulting a colourful map of the worl●
> either in print or online.

الجِنْسيّات Nationalities

> ● **INSIGHT – NATIONALITY ADJECTIVES**
>
> In Arabic, all country nationality adjectives end with the suffix (يّ \ة). This suffix is
> known in Arabic grammar as (ياء النِّسْبة), i.e. the Ya' of the relative adjective. This
> Ya', when added to a noun, changes it to an adjective, such as in:
>
> فِلَسْطين (country) + ي = فِلَسْطينيّ \ة (nationality m./f.)
>
> لُبْنان + ي = لُبْنانيّ (ج) ون
>
> مِصْر + ي = مِصْريّ (ج) ون
>
> Also, notice that once the country name is suffixed with Ya' of Nisbah, the definite
> article of the country name must be omitted; for example:
>
> المَغْرِب - مَغْرِبيّ (ج) مَغاربة
>
> الأردن - أردني (ج) ون

156

COMMON NATIONALITIES جِنْسِيّات شائعة

عَرَبيّ (ج) العَرَب	*Arabs*
إنجليزي (ج) الإنْجْليزا الإنْكْليز	*English*
فَرَنْسِيّ (ج) -ون	*French*
أوروبيّ (ج) -ون	*Europeans*
إسْبانيّ (ج) الإسْبان	*Spaniards*
ألْمانيّ (ج) الألْمان	*Germans*
الرّوس	*Russians*

أَمْريكيّ (ج) -ون ا	*Americans*
الأَمْريكان	
افْريقيّ (ج) الأفارقة	*Africans*
أَسْيَويّ (ج) -ون	*Asians*
هِنْديّ (ج) الهُنود	*Indians*
صينيّ (ج) -ون	*Chinese*
يابانيّ (ج) -ون	*Japanese*

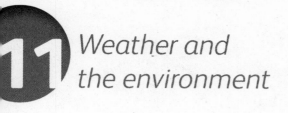

11 Weather and the environment

الطّقس والبيئة

this unit, you will learn essential vocabulary, organized as follows:

Weather الطّقس
▷ Seasons of the year فُصول السّنة
▷ Core vocabulary
▷ The weather forecast تَوَقُّعات الطّقس
  ▷ Useful phrases
  ▷ Describing the weather وَصْف الطّقس
  ▷ More phrases
Oceans and seas المُحيطات والبِحار
▷ The oceans المُحيطات
▷ The water environment بيئات مائيّة
Nature and the environment الطّبيعة والبيئة
▷ Core vocabulary
▷ Geological hazards المَخاطِر الجيولوجيّة
▷ Environmental issues القَضايا البيئيّة
▷ Useful verbs
▷ Plants النّباتات
▷ Animals الحَيوانات
▷ Farm animals حيوانات المَزْرَعة
▷ Birds الطّيور
▷ Mammals and wild animals الثَّدْييّات والحَيوانات البَرّيّة

159

▷ Reptiles الزَّواحِف
▷ Fish السَّمك
▷ Insects الحَشَرات

Weather الطَّقس

SEASONS OF THE YEAR فُصول السَّنة

فَصْل (ج) فُصول	season	الرَّبيع	spring
الصَّيْف	summer	الخَريف	autumn/fa
الشِّتاء	winter		

CORE VOCABULARY

طَقْس (ج) طُقوس	weather (1)	بَرْق (ج) بُروق	lightning
جَوّ (ج) أَجْواء	weather (2)	رَعْد (ج) رُعود	thunder
مُناخ	climate	إعْصار (ج) أعاصير	hurricane
غِلاف جَوّي	atmosphere	زَوْبَعة (ج) زَوابِع	tornado
شَمْس (ج) شُموس	sun	غَيْمة (ج) غيوم	cloud (1)
أشِعّة الشَّمْس	sunshine	سَحابة (ج) سُحب	cloud (2)
قَمَر (ج) أقْمار	moon	قَوْس قُزَح	rainbow
مَطَر (ج) أمْطار	rain	نَجْم (ج) نُجوم	star
ثَلْج (ج) ثُلوج	snow, ice	حَرّ/حَرارة	heat
ريح (ج) رِياح	wind	دَرَجة الحَرارة	temperature
عاصِفة (ج) عَواصِف	storm, gales	بَرْد/بُرودة	cold (n.)
ضَباب	fog	دِفْء	warmth
صَقيع	frost	رُطوبة	humidity

STUDY TIP

To consolidate your learning of weather-related vocabulary, make it a habit to check Arabic weather forecasts regularly online, by watching live Arabic TV and/or by reading summarize weather updates of major Arab cities.

Among the most popular Arabic news websites, which also provide live TV coverage, are:

BBC Arabic (بي‌بي‌سي‌عربي), Al-Jazeera (الجزيرة) and Al-Arabiya (العَرَبيّة)

تَوَقُّعات الطَّقْس THE WEATHER FORECAST

Useful phrases

نَشْرة جَوِّية	weather forecast (TV)
كَيْفَ حال الجَوّ\الطَّقْس؟	How's the weather?
كَمْدَرَجة الحَرارة	What's the temperature?
أَمْس	yesterday
اليَوْم	today
غَداً	tomorrow
خلال الأيّام القَليلة المُقْبِلة	over the next few days

وَصْف الطَّقْس Describing the weather

الجَوّ...	it is ...	مُثْلِج	snowy/icy
مُشْمِس	sunny	صاف\صَحْو	clear
حارّ\ساخِن	hot	مُعْتَدِل	moderate, mild, temperate
دافِئ	warm	غائِم	cloudy
بارِد	cold	عاصِف	stormy
بارِد جِدّاً\مُتَجَمِّد	freezing	رَطْب	wet, damp, humid
مُمْطِر\ماطِر	raining, rainy	جافّ	dry
الثَّلْج يَتَساقَط	snowing		

More phrases

الطَّقْس جَيِّد	the weather is good	بُقَع ضَباب	fog patches
الطَّقْس سَيِّء	the weather is bad	ظُروف القِيادة خَطيرة	dangerous driving conditions
حَالة الطَّقْس تَزْداد سُوءًا	the weather is getting worse	خَطَر الفَيَضان	risk of flooding

حَالة الطَّقْس تَتَحَسَّن	the weather is improving	دَرَجة الحَرَارَة سَتَكون	the temperature will be ... degrees
يُمْكِنُك أن .... تَتَوَقَّع	you can expect ...	دَرَجة مِئَوِيّة\ سِنْتيغْرَاد	celsius/centigrade
رياح خَفيفة\قَويّة	light/strong winds	فَهْرِنْهايْت	fahrenheit
غُيوم\سَحاب	clouds	دَرَجة الحَرَارة تَرْتَفِع\تَنْخَفِض	the temperature is rising/falling
هُبوب الرِّياح	gusts of wind		
رَخّات مَطَر غَزيرة	heavy showers	دَرَجة الحَرَارة عالية	the temperature is high
فَتَرات مُشْمِسة	sunny intervals	دَرَجة الْحَرَارة مُنْخَفِضة	the temperature is low
فَتَرات مُشْرِقة \ زاهية	bright periods	دَرَجة الحَرَارة الكُبْرى	maximum temperature
نَوْبات مَطَر طَويلة	prolonged spells of rain	دَرَجة الحَرَارة الصُّغْرى	minimum temperature
ضَباب الصَّباح	morning mist		

المُحيطات والبِحار Oceans and seas

THE OCEANS المُحيطات

مُحيط (ج) -ات	ocean	المُحيط الهادِئ	Pacific Ocean
المُحيط الأطْلسيّ	Atlantic Ocean	المُحيط المُتَجَمِّد الشَّماليّ	Arctic Ocean
المُحيط الهِنْديّ	Indian Ocean	المُحيط المُتَجَمِّد الجَنوبيّ	Antarctic Ocean

بَحْر (ج) بِحار	sea	البَحْر الأَحْمَر	the Red Sea
بُحَيْرة (ج) -ات	lake (diminutive n.)	البَحْر الأَسْوَد	the Black Sea
بِرْكة (ج) بِرك	pond	البَحْر المَيِّت	the Dead Sea
بَحْر العَرَب	Arabian Sea	نَهْر (ج) أَنْهار	river
الخَليج العَرَبيّ	Arab Gulf	نَهْر النّيل	the Nile river
البَحْر الأَبْيَض المُتَوَسِّ	the Mediterranean	وادي (ج) وديان	valley
بَحْر الشَّمال	the North Sea	ساحِل (ج) سَواحِل	coast
بَحْر البَلْطيق	the Baltic		

● INSIGHT – YOU ALREADY SPEAK ARABIC!

The word *Swahili* or *Kiswahili* originally comes from the Arabic (سَواحِل), i.e. *coasts* (pl. of ساحِل).

شاطِئ (ج) شَواطِئ	beach	خَطَر/مُجازَفة	hazard
مَوْج (ج) أَمْواج	wave	جَبَل جَليديّ	iceberg
المَدّ والجَزْر	tides	نَقْل بَحْريّ	shipping
مَضْيَق (ج) مَضايِق	strait (derived from ضَيِّق, i.e. narrow)	تَوَقُّعات النَّقْل البَحْريّ	shipping forecast
تَيّار (ج) -ات	current, tide	بَحْر هائِج	rough sea
مَرْجان	coral	بَحْر هادِئ	calm sea

Nature and the environment الطَّبيعة والبيئة

كَما قالَتِ العَرَب ... As the Arabs say

وجَعَلْنا مِنَ الماءِ كُلَّ شَيْءٍ حَيّ أَفَلا يُؤْمِنون

And we made every living thing from water.

Qur'anic verse (The Prophets 21:30 الأَنْبِياء)

CORE VOCABULARY

الطَّبيعة — nature

سَماء (ج) سَماوات — sky, heaven

أرْض (ج) أراضٍ — earth, land

عالَم (ج) عَوالِم — world

كَوْكَب (ج) كَواكِب — planet

مَناظِر طبيعيّة — landscape

جَبَل (ج) جِبال — mountain

جَبَليّ — mountainous

(مُناخ جَبَليّ e.g. mountainous climate)

صَحْراويّ — desert-like (e.g. desert dress لِباس صَحْراويّ)

● **INSIGHT – YOU ALREADY SPEAK ARABIC!**

Gibraltar is an Arabic loanword taken from (جَبَل طارق, lit. *the Mountain of Tariq*).
A British overseas territory since 1704, it was conquered in 710 CE by a Muslim leader
named Tariq Ibn Ziyad (طارق ابن زياد), after whom the mountain was named.
In fact, there are many places in Spain that start with *Gibral* (جَبَل), such as *Gibralfaro*
(جَبَل فاروق), i.e. *Mountain of Lighthouse*.

واحة (ج) -ات — oasis

غابة (ج) -ات — jungle, forest

دَغْل (ج) أدغال — bush, rainforest

شلال (ج) -ات — waterfall

حَقْل (ج) حُقول — field

سَهْل (ج) سُهول — plain

غار (ج) أغْوار — cave (1)

مَغارة (ج) -ات — cave (2)

جُرْف — cliff

صَخْرة (ج) صُخور — rock

حَجَر(ة) (ج) حِجارة — stone

تَلّ (ج) تِلال — hill

قِمّة (ج) قِمَم — peak

صَحْراء (ج) صَحارى — desert

كَثيب (ج) كُثْبان — sandhill, dune

رَمْل (ج) رِمال — sand

This is a popular greeting expression Arabs use when welcoming someone to their home.
The greeting was originally as follows, which was shortened later on:

حَلَلْتَ أَهْلاً وَنَزَلْتَ سَهْلاً
(سَهْل). *You have stopped among your people and you have descended upon a plain*

● INSIGHT – FEMININE WORDS WITHOUT THE FEMININE
ENDING ة\ا

There are many feminine nouns that do not carry the feminine ending, such as:

صَحْراء	desert	دُنْيا	world
أَرْض	earth	رِيح	wind
شَمْس	sun	بِئْر	well
نار	fire		

المَخاطِر الجِيولوجِيّة EOLOGICAL HAZARDS

زِلْزال (ج) زَلازِل	earthquake	مُسْتَنْقِع (ج) -ات	swamp
بُرْكان (ج) بَراكين	volcano	نار (ج) نيران	fire
فَيَضان (ج) -ات	flood	حريق الغابات	forest fire
تُسونامي	tsunami		

القَضايا البِيئِيّة NVIRONMENTAL ISSUES

بيئَة (ج) -ات	environment	ضَوْضاء،ضَجّة	noise
حماية البيئة	environmental protection	تَلَوُّث ضَوْضائِيّ	noise pollution
عِلْم البيئة	ecology	تَجارِب نَوَوِيّة	nuclear testing
النُّظُم البيئية	ecosystem	إشْعاع	radiation

نُفايات مُشِعّة	radioactive was[te]	أمْطار حِمْضِيّة	acid rain
طاقة	power, energy	ظاهرة الاِحْتِرار العالَميّ	global warming
طاقة نَوَوِيّة	nuclear power		
طاقة شمْسِيّة	solar power	ظاهرة الاِحْتِباس الحَراريّ	greenhouse effect
طاقة الرِّياح	wind power		
طاقة قابلة للتَّجْديد	renewable energ[y]	اِرْتفاع مُسْتَوى سَطْح البَحْر	sea level rise
طاقة غير متجددة	non-renewable energy	تَغَيُّر المُناخ	climate change
مَحَطّةتَوْليد الطاقة الكَهْرُبائيّة	power station	طَبقة الأوزون	ozone layer
		مُعَدَّلة وراثيًّا	GM (genetically modified)
إعادة تَدْوير	recycling	سُمّ (ج) سُموم	poison
مَوارد طبيعيّة	natural resourc[es]	تَلَوُّث	pollution
مُسْتدامة	sustainable	تَلَوُّث الهَواء	air pollution
تَنْمية مُسْتدامة	sustainable development	تَلَوُّث المياه	water pollution

USEFUL VERBS

حَمى يَحْمي حماية	to protect	دَمَّر يُدَمِّر تَدْمير	to destroy
حافَظ يُحافِظ حِفاظ على	to conserve	لَوَّث يُلَوِّث تَلْويث	to pollute

النّباتات PLANTS

نَبات (ج) -ات	plant	شَجَرة (ج) أشْجار	tree
عُشْب (ج) أعْشاب	grass	خَشَب (ج) أخْشاب	wood
زَهْرة (ج) زُهور	flower	وَرَق (ج) أوْراق	leaf
وَرْدة (ج) ورود	rose	فَرْع (ج) فُروع	branch
شَوْك (ج) أشْواك	thorn	جَذْر (ج) جُذور	root
غُبار	dust, dust cloud	تُرْبة	soil
تُراب (ج) أتْرِبة	soil, dust	طين	mud

166

الحيوانات ANIMALS

حَيَوان (ج) -ات   animal

حَيَوانات المزرعة FARM ANIMALS

حِمار (ج) حَمير	donkey	قِطّة (ج) قَطَط	cat
جَمَل (ج) جِمال	camel	كَلْب (ج) كِلاب	dog
ثَوْر (ج) ثيران	bull, ox	بَقَرة (ج) -ات	cow
عِجْل (ج) عُجول	calf	غَنَم (ج) أغْنام	sheep
بَهيمة (ج) بَهائم	cattle, livestock	خَروف (ج) خِراف	lamb
أرْنَب (ج) أرانِب	rabbit	ماعِز (ج) مَواعِز	goat
فأر (ج) فِئْران	mouse	خِنْزير (ج) خَنازير	pig
جَرْذ (ج) جِرذان	rat	خَيْل (ج) خُيول	horse

الطُيور BIRDS

غُراب (ج) غِرْبان	crow	طائِر / طَيْر (ج) طيور	bird
نَسْر (ج) نُسور	eagle	عُصْفور (ج) عَصافير	small bird
صَقْر (ج) صُقور	falcon	دَجاجة (ج) دَجاج	chicken
بُومة (ج) بوم	owl	ديك (ج) دُيوك	rooster
طاووس (ج) طواويس	peacock	ديك رومي	turkey
نَعامة (ج) نَعام	ostrich	بَطّة (ج) بَطّ	duck
بَبّغاء (ج) بَبّغاوات	parrot	إوَزّة (ج) إوَزّ	goose
بَجَعة (ج) بَجَع	swan	حَمامة (ج) حَمام	pigeon
		يمامة (ج) يمام	dove

الثَّدْييات والحَيَوانات البَرِّيّة MAMMALS AND WILD ANIMALS

غَزال (ج) غِزلة	gazelle	أسَد (ج) أُسود	lion
ظَبْي (ج) ظِباء	deer, gazelle	نَمِر (ج) نُمور	tiger

فَهْد (ج) فُهود cheetah   حِمار وَحْشِيّ zebra (lit. wild donkey)

ذِئْب (ج) ذِئاب wolf   فيل (ج) فِيَلة elephant

ضَبْع (ج) ضِباع hyena   فَرَس النَّهْر (ج) أَفْراس النَّهْر hippopotamus (lit. river horse)

ثَعْلَب (ج) ثَعالِب fox   وَحيد القَرْن rhinoceros (lit. single horned)

دُبّ (ج) دِبَبة bear   كَنْغَر kangaroo

قِرْد (ج) قُرود monkey   سِنْجاب squirrel

زَرافة (ج) -ات giraffe   خُفّاش (ج) خَفافيش bat

<33> كَما قالَت العَرَب ... As the Arabs say ...
القِرْدُ في عَيْنِ أُمِّه غَزال
The monkey, in his mother's eye, is (as beautiful as) a gazelle.
Arabic proverb

الزَّواحِف REPTILES

زاحِف (ج) زواحِف reptile   سُلَحْفاة (ج) سَلاحِف turtle

ثُعْبان (ج) ثَعابين snake (1)   حَلَزون (ج) -ات snail

أَفْعى (ج) أَفاع snake (2)   سِحْلِيّة (ج) سِحال lizard

تِمْساح (ج) تَماسيح crocodile   بَرْمائِيّة (ج) -ات amphibian (this is a blend word combining بر land and ماء water)

ضِفْدَع (ج) ضَفادع frog

السَّمَك FISH

سَمَك (ج) أَسْماك fish   أُخْطُبوط (ج) -ات octopus

حوت (ج) حيتان whale   قِنْديل البَحْر jellyfish

قِرْش shark   حَبّار squid

أبو سيف	swordfish	روبيان	shrimp
دُلفين	dolphin	سَرطان بَحْريّ	lobster
نَجْمة البَحْر	starfish	سَرطان (ج) -ات	crab
حِصان البَحْر	seahorse	مَحَّار	oysters, clams
قَرْموط (ج) قَراميط	catfish		

الحشرات INSECTS

حَشَرة (ج) ات	insect	بَعوضة (ج) بَعوض	mosquito
عَنْكَبوت (ج) عَناكِب	spider	دودة (ج) دود	worm
نَحْلة (ج) نَحْل	bee	فَراشة (ج) فَراش	butterfly
نَمْلة (ج) نَمْل	ant	صُرْصور	cockroach
ذُبابة (ج) ذُباب	fly	خُنْفُساء (ج) خَنافِس	beetle

STUDY TIP

Try to associate the words you learn with pictures or situations. For instance, visualize:

a shy person drinking شاي/shaay/ i.e. *tea* or

a dog barking at a برق/barq/ i.e. *lightning*

Recreation and sports

التَّرْفيه والرِّياضة

In this unit you will learn essential vocabulary, organized as follows:

▸ Sport الرِّياضة
  ▷ Core vocabulary
  ▷ People الأشْخاص
  ▷ Individual sports الرِّياضات الفَرديّة
  ▷ Team sports الرِّياضات الجَماعيّة
▸ Hobbies and games الهِوايات والألْعاب
  ▷ Core vocabulary
  ▷ Performance and dancing الرَّقْص والأداء
  ▷ Outdoor activities الأنْشطة الخارجيّة
  ▷ Parties and celebrations الاحْتِفالات
  ▷ Useful verbs

Sport الرِّياضة

CORE VOCABULARY

رياضة (ج) -ات	sport	فَريق (ج) فِرَق	team
تَدْريب (ج) -ات	training, practice	مُنْتَخَب (ج) -ات	national team
تَمْرين (ج) تَمارين	exercise, drill	نادي (ج) نَوادي	club, society (student)
تَمارين رِياضيّة	sport exercises	مُباراة (ج) مُبارايات	match

لِياقة بَدَنية	fitness		مُدَرَّج (ج) -ات	stadium
مُنافَسة (ج) -ات	competition		مَلْعَب (ج) مَلاعِب	field
مُسابَقة (ج) -ات	race (1)		حَمّام سِباحة	swimming pool
سِباق (ج) -ات	race (2)		مِضْمار	racetrack
بُطولة	championship		كُرة (ج) كُرَر	ball
هَدَف (ج) أهْداف	goal		الأولَمْبياد	Olympics
ضَرْبة (ج) -ات	kick, shot		الاتِّحاد الدَّوْليّ لِكُرة القَدَم	FIFA (Fédération Internationale de Football Association)
كَأس العالَم	World Cup			

الأشْخاص PEOPLE

رِياضيّ	athlete, sportsperson		مُهاجِم	attacker
لاعِب	player		مُدافِع	defender
هاوٍ	amateur		مُدَرِّب	trainer, coach
مُحْتَرِف	professional		غَشّاش	cheat
قائِد الفَريق	team captain		بَطَل (ج) أبْطال	champion
حارِس مَرْمى	goalkeeper		حَكَم (ج) حُكّام	referee

● INSIGHT

With the exception of the last two words, all the nouns above have a sound plural form ending with ون-.

الرِّياضات الفَرْديّة INDIVIDUAL SPORTS

جَرْي/عَدْو	running		تَزَحْلُق عَلى الجَليد	ice skating
سِباحة	swimming		غولْف	golf
غَطْس	diving		جُمْباز	gymnastics
رُكوب الأمْواج	surfing		تَسَلُّق الجِبال	mountain climbing

رُكوب الدَّرَّاجات	cycling
رُكوب الخَيْل	horseback riding
تزحلق	skiing
رَفْع الأثْقال	weightlifting
رِماية	archery, shooting

الرِّياضات الجَماعيّة TEAM SPORTS

كُرة القَدَم	football (UK), soccer (US)
كُرة القَدَم الأمْريكيّة	(American) football
روكْبي\رُجْبي	rugby, American football
كُرة السَّلّة	basketball
الكُرة الطّائرة	volleyball
تنس أرضي	tennis
تنس طاولة	table tennis
بيْسبول (كُرة القاعدة)	baseball
كريكت\لُعْبة الكُرة والمَضْرِب	cricket
مُلاكَمة	boxing
ألْعاب القتال\الفُنون الحَرْبيّة	martial arts
مُصارَعة	wrestling
تَجْديف	rowing

● INSIGHT – YOU ALREADY SPEAK ARABIC!

Racket is actually an Arabic loanword from the term (راحَة, i.e. *palm of the hand*) and probably originally from a 'tennis-like game' played with open hand.

Hobbies and games الهِوايات والألْعاب

CORE VOCABULARY

جَمْع الطَّوابِع	stamp collecting	هِواية (ج) -ات	hobby
صَيْد	hunting	لُعْبة (ج) ألعاب	game
صَيْد السَّمَك	fishing	حِرْفة (ج) حِرَف	craft
خِياطة	sewing	وَقْت الفَراغ	spare time
لَعِب الألْواح	board game	قِراءة\مُطالَعة	reading
وَرَق اللَّعِب	cards	رَسْم	painting
قِمار	gambling	تَصْوير	photography
شِطْرَنْج	chess	رَقْص	dancing
		غِناء	singing

> ● **INSIGHT – YOU ALREADY SPEAK ARABIC!**
>
> The word *checkmate* is another Arabic loanword taken from the expression
> **الشّاه مات**, which is an alteration of the Persian phrase *Shaah Maat*, i.e. *the King is helpless, ambushed or defeated*. Many words are derived from *checkmate*, such as *to check*, *exchequer*, *checkout* and *chequered*.

PERFORMANCE AND DANCING الرَّقْص والأداء

رَقْص شَعْبيّ	folk dancing	رَقَص يَرْقُص رَقْص	to dance
رَقْص شَرْقيّ	belly dancing	رَقّاص (ج) -ون	dancer
باليه	ballet	حَلَبة الرَّقْص	dance floor
نُكْتة (ج) نُكَت	a joke	مَرْقَص (ج) مَراقِص	dance hall

OUTDOOR ACTIVITIES الأنْشِطة الخارِجيّة

مَدينة مَلاهي	fairground	بَسْتَنة	gardening
مَلْعَب أطْفال	playground	تَسْلية	entertainment

مُتَنَزَّه (ج) -ات	theme park	مُشاهَدة الطُّيور	birdwatching
نُزْهة	picnic	تَزَلُّج عَلى اللَّوح	skateboarding
سِحْر	magic	المَشْي لِمَسافات طَويلة	hiking
ساحِر/سُحّار	magician, sorcerer	تَخْييم	camping
سيرْك	circus	خَيْمة	tent
مُهَرِّج	clown	بَيْت مُتَنَقِّل	caravan

PARTIES AND CELEBRATIONS اِحْتِفالات

هَدِيّة (ج) هَدايا	gift, present	مُناسَبة (ج) -ات	occasion, event
دعا يَدْعو دَعْوة إلى	to invite (so.) to	حَفْلة (ج) -ات	party
نَظَّم يُنَظِّم تَنْظيم	to organize (an event)	مَهْرَجان (ج) -ات	fair, festival
		حَفْلة تَنَكُّريّة	costume party
		قِناع (ج) أَقْنِعة	mask

USEFUL VERBS

كَسَبَ يَكْسِب كَسْب	to win	لَعِب يَلْعَب لَعِب	to play
فاز يَفوز فَوْز	to win	قَضى يَقْضي قَضاء الوقْت	to spend (time)
خَسِر يَخْسَر خَسارة	to lose	اِسْتَمْتَع يَسْتَمْتِع اِسْتِمْتاع ب	to enjoy
سَجَّل يُسَجِّل تَسْجيل هَدَفا	to score (a goal)	تَسَلَّى يَتَسَلَّى تَسْلية	to be amused, to have a good time
جَرى يَجْري جَرْي	to run	فَضَّل يُفَصِّل تَفْضيل	to prefer
تَسَلَّق يَتَسَلَّق تَسَلُّق	to climb	تَنافَس يَتَنافَس تَنافُس	to compete
سَبَح يَسْبَح سِباحة	to swim	غَشَّ يَغُشّ غِشّ	to cheat
مَزَح يَمْزَح مَزْح	to joke		

12 *Recreation and sports* التَّرْفيه والرِّياضة   **175**

Arts and entertainment
الفُنون والتَّسْلِية

n this unit you will learn essential vocabulary, organized as follows:

- **Art** فَنّ
  ▷ *Core vocabulary*
  ▷ *The visual arts* الفُنون المَرْئِيّة
- **Books and literature** الكُتُب والأَدَب
  ▷ *Poetry* الشِّعْر
- **Music** الموسيقى
  ▷ *Popular music genres in the Arab world*

أَشْهَر أَنْواع الموسيقى في العالَم العَرَبيّ
- **Cinema and theatre** السّينما والمَسْرَح
  ▷ *Cinema* السّينما
  ▷ *Theatre* المَسْرَح
  ▷ *Film genres* أَنْواع الأَفْلام
  ▷ *Adjectives describing films*
  ▷ *Useful verbs*

Art فَنّ

CORE VOCABULARY

فَنّ (ج) فُنون	art	عَرْض (ج) عُروض	showing, performance
فَنّان (ج) -ون	artist	اِبْداع	creativity
فَنّيّ	artistic	اِبْتِكار (ج) -ات	innovation

177

تُحفة (ج) تُحَف	artefact, work of art	إلْهام	inspiration
مَتْحَف (ج) مَتاحِف	museum	جَدَل	controversy
مَهْرَجان (ج) -ات	festival	نَقْد	criticism
مَعْرِض (ج) مَعارِض	exhibition	ناقِد (ج) نُقّاد	critic
قاعة فُنون	art gallery		

الفُنون المَرْئيّة   THE VISUAL ARTS

صورة (ج) صُوَر	photo, picture, image	نَقّاش	painter, sculptor
مُصَوِّر (ج) -ون	photographer	زَيَّن يُزَيِّن تَزْيين	to decorate
رَسْم يَرْسُم رَسَم	to paint, draw	لَوْحة (ج) -ات	painting, picture (item)
رَسْم (ج) رُسوم\-ات	drawing, painting	فَخّار	pottery
رَسّام (ج) -ون	painter, artist	خَزَف	ceramics
مُصَمِّم (ج) -ون	designer	فُسَيْفِساء	mosaics
صَمَّم يُصَمِّم تَصْميم	to design	صَلْصال	clay
نَحَت يَنْحَت نَحْت	to sculpt	عَرْض أزْياء	modelling
تِمْثال (ج) تَماثيل	statue	مَعْرِض أزْياء	fashion show
نُصْب تَذْكاري	monument	موضة	fashion
نَقْش	sculpture	عالَم الأزْياء	the world of fashion

الكُتُب والأَدَب   Books and literature

كَما قالَت العَرَب ...   As the Arabs say ...

(37)

أعَزّ مَكانٍ في الدُّنْيا سِرْجُ سابِحٍ وخَيْرُ جَليسٍ
في الزَّمانِ كِتابُ

*The noblest place is on a noble steed; the best companion
is the book you read.*
Arabic poetry

أَدَب (ج) آداب	literature	إهْداء	dedication
الأدَب العَرَبيّ	Arabic literature	فَصْل (ج) فُصول	chapter
الأدَب المُقارَن	comparative literature	بِداية	beginning
أديب (ج) أُدَباء	author, literary figure	نِهاية	end
مُؤَلِّف (ج) -ون	author	قائمة المُحْتَوَيات	table of contents
كِتاب (ج) كُتُب	book	فَهْرَس (ج) فَهارِس	index
كاتِب (ج) كُتّاب	writer	صَفْحة (ج) -ات	page
رواية (ج) -ات	novel	كَلِمة (ج) -ات	word
روائيّ (ج) -ون	novelist	جُمْلة (ج) جُمَل	sentence
سيرة (ج) سِيَر	biography	سَطْر (ج) سُطور	line
سيرة ذاتيّة	autobiography	فَقْرة (ج) -ات	paragraph
مُذَكِّرة (ج) -ات	memoir	نَصّ (ج) نُصوص	passage, text
حكايّة (ج) -ات	story (1)	مَقال (ج) -ات	article (1)
حَكَواتي (ج) -ون	storyteller (1)	مَقالة (ج) -ات	article (2)
قصّة (ج) قِصَص	story (2)	شَخْصيّة (ج) ات	character, personality
قصّة قَصيرة (ج) قِصَص قَصيرة	short story	بَطَل (ج) أبْطال	hero, main character
		حِوار (ج) ات	dialogue
قَصّاص (ج) -ون	storyteller (2)	مَلْحَمة (ج) مَلاحِم	epic
سِلْسِلة (ج) سَلاسِل	series	انْطِباع (ج) ات	impression
سَرْد	narrative	ذِرْوة	climax
حَبْكة	plot (novel, story)	أُسْطورة (ج) أساطير	tale, legend
قراءة في كِتاب	book review	مأساة (ج) مَآس	tragedy
مُقَدِّمة (ج) -ات	introduction	سُخْرِيّة	satire
تَمْهيد	preface, foreword	ساخِر	satirical

كَما قالَت العَرَب ... As the Arabs say ...

(38)

الفَلَسْطينِيّون كُلّهم شُعَراء بالفِطْرة. قد لا يَكْتُبون شِعْرًا ولكنّهم شُعَراء، لأنّهم عَرَفوا شَيْئَيْن اثْنَيْن هامّين. جَمال الطَبيعة، والمَأساة.

ومن يَجْمَع بين هَذين، لا بدّ أن يكون شاعِرًا

All Palestinians are poets, by instinct. They may not write poetry, but they are poets because they intimately know two important things: Beauty of nature and tragedy; whoever has both must be a poet.
Arabic quote (Jabra Ibrahim Jabra)

شِعْر (ج) أشْعار	poetry
شَاعِر (ج) شُعَراء	poet
الشِّعْر الحَرّ	free poetry
الشِّعْر العَموديّ	metric poetry
الشِّعْر الجاهِليّ	pre-Islamic poetry
الغَزَل	romantic poetry
التَغَزُّل	flirtation
بَيْت (ج) أبيات	line, verse (poetry)
قطْعة (ج) قطَع	piece (several lines taken from a poem)
قَصيدة (ج) قَصائد	poem (narrative)
ديوان (ج) دَواوين	collection of poetry (often of a single poet)
أعْمال كامِلة	complete works
قافية (ج) قَواف	rhyme
وَزْن (ج) أوْزان	metre (of poetic lines) (1)
بَحْر (ج) أبْحُر ابُحور	metre (of poetic lines) (2)
طَوْر (ج) أطْوار	stage/phase
اسْتِعارة (ج).ات	metaphor
رَمْز (ج) رُموز	symbol
رَمْزِيّة	symbolism

الموسيقى Music

⟨39⟩ كَما قالَت العَرَب ... As the Arabs say
والأُذُن تَعْشَق قبل العَيْن أحْيانًا
The ear may fall in love before the eye.
Arabic proverb

موسيقي	musical	حَفْلة موسيقيّة	musical concert
أُغْنية (ج) أغان	song	جَوْلة غنائيّة	singing tour
مُغَنٍّ (ج) -ون	singer	صالة الموسيقى	concert hall
موسيقار	musician	آلة (ج) آلات موسيقيّة	musical instrument
مُطْرِب (ج) -ون	singer	كَمان	violin
مُلَحِّن (ج) -ون	composer	بيانو	piano
عازِف الجيتار	(guitar) player	طَبْلة (ج) طبل	drum
مُغَنٍّ رئيسيّ	lead singer	طَبْل (ج) طُبول	drum (traditional)
جُمْهور	audience	عود (ج) أعْواد	oud (lute)
مُعْجَب (ج) -ون بـ	fan	ناي (ج) -ات	flute
فِرْقة (ج) فِرَق	band	قيثارة (ج) قَياثير	guitar
جوقة (ج) -ات	choir	دُفّ (ج) دُفوف	tambourine
أوبرا	opera	غَنّى يُغَنّي غِناء	to sing
صَوْت (ج) أصوات	voice, sound	عَزْف يَعْزِف عَزْف على	to play (an instrument)
إيقاع	rhythm	ألبوم (ج) -ات	album
تَناغُم	harmony	شَريط (ج) شَرائط	tape
نَغْمة (ج) -ات	tone	أسطوانة (ج) -ات	record
لَحْن (ج) ألْحان	tune, melody	قُرْص (ج) أقْراص	disc/CD
نَغْم (ج) أنْغام	tune	كَلِمات أُغْنية	lyrics

POPULAR MUSIC GENRES IN THE ARAB WORLD

أَشْهَر أَنْواع الموسيقى في العالَم العَرَبيّ

موسيقى كلاسيكيّة عَرَبيّة	Arabic classical music
موسيقى البوب العَرَبيّة	Arabic pop music
الرّاب العَرَبيّ\الهيب هوب	Arabic rap/hip hop music
موسيقى الرّاي الجَزائريّة	Algerian rai music
الموسيقى الرّوحيّة	spiritual music
الموسيقى الصّوفيّة	Sufi music
التَّجْويد\تَرْتيل القُرْآن الكَريم	Tajwid (elocution or recitation of Qur'an readings)
موسيقى كناوة الإفريقيّة	Gnawa African music (popular in Morocco)
الموسيقى الأنْدَلُسيّة	Andalucian classical music (still popular in North Africa)
المَوّال	Mawwal music (vocal colloquial music)
المُوَشَّحات	Muwashshah (Arabic poetic form)
الموسيقى الشَعْبيّة	popular (mainstream) music

Cinema and theatre السّينما والمَسْرَح

CINEMA السّينما

سينما	cinema	أداء (ج) -ات	performance	
مُمَثِّل (ج) -ون	actor	تَجْسيد	portrayal, embodiment	
نَجْم (ج) نُجوم	star	مُراجَعة (ج) -ات	review	
نُجوميّة	stardom	دَوْر (ج) أدْوار	role, part	
مَشْهور (ج) مَشاهير	famous	بُطولة	starring	
شُهْرة	fame	دَوْر البُطولة	starring role	
مُخْرِج (ج) -ون	director	تُحْفة (ج) تُحَف سينمائيّة	cinematic masterpiece	
مُخْرِج سينمائيّ	film director			
مُنْتِج (ج) -ون	producer	شُبّاك التَّذاكِر	box office	

كاتِب السِّيناريو	scriptwriter	شاشة (ج) -ات	screen
سيناريو (ج)	script, screenplay	مَكْياج	make-up
سيناريوهات		تَصْميم الأزْياء	costume design
تَصْوير سينمائيّ	cinematography	مُؤَثِّرات تِقْنِيّة	special effects
تَحْرير	editing	مُؤَثِّرات صَوْتِيّة	sound effects
تَصْنيف	rating	مُؤَثِّرات بَصَرِيّة	visual effects

المَسْرَح THEATRE

مَسْرَحِيّة (ج) -ات	play
مَسْرَح (ج) مَسارِح	theatre
رواية غِنائيّة	musical (theatre)
رواية مَسْرَحِيّة	play (theatre)
فَصْل (ج) فُصول	act
مَشْهَد (ج) مَشاهِد	scene
خَشَبة المَسْرَح	stage
فِرْقة مَسْرَحِيّة	theatre group, company

أنْواع الأفْلام FILM GENRES

دراما	drama	رومانسيّ	romance
كوميديا	comedy	موسيقيّ	musical
فُكاهة	humour	حَرْبيّ	war
إثارة/أكشن	action	وَثائقي	documentary
الحَرَكة الحيّة	live action	تاريخي	historical
تَشْويق	thriller	عائلي	family
مُغامَرة	adventure	كَرْتون	cartoon
خَيالِيّ	fantasy	رُسوم مُتَحَرِّكة	animation
خَيال علميّ	science fiction	تَسْلِية	entertainment

رُعْب	horror	مَلْحَمِيّ	epic
لُغْز	mystery	شَعْبِيّ	popular
إجْرام	crime		

ADJECTIVES DESCRIBING FILMS

إيجابِيّ	positive	عادي	ordinary
سَلْبِيّ	negative	واقِعِيّ	realistic
مُثير	exciting	غامِض	mysterious
مَلِئٌ املي ءبِ	full of	عَظيم	magnificent, great
مُضْحِك	funny	عَجيب	amazing
مُمْتِع	enjoyable	رائِع	wonderful
مُسَلٍّ	entertaining	مُدَمِّر	devastating
رائِع	excellent	جَدَلِيّ/مُثير للجَدَل	controversial
بارِز	prominent	مُقَزِّز	disgusting
مَمَيَّز	distinguished, unique	مُمِلّ	boring
مُتَمَيِّز	special, distinguished	مُفْزِع	terrifying, frightening
فَريد	unique	سَخيف	silly, ridiculous
نادِر	rare	مُبالِغ	exaggerated
خارِق	marvellous, extraordinary	مُتَرْجَم	subtitled
مُذْهِل	astonishing	مُدَبْلَج	dubbed
جَذّاب	attractive		

USEFUL VERBS

لَعِب يَلْعَب لعب دَوْرًا	to play a role
أَدّى يُؤَدّي أداء	to perform
مَثَّل يُمَثِّل تمثيل	to act, represent

184

صَوَّر يُصَوِّر تَصْوير	to depict, photograph
انْتَقَد يَنْتَقِد انْتِقاد	to criticize
أَخْرَج يُخْرِج إِخْراج	to direct (film)
أَنْتَج يُنْتِج إِنْتاج	to produce
وَزَّع يُوَزِّع تَوْزيع	to distribute
عَرَض يَعْرِض عَرْض	to show (film, play, etc.)
أَبْدَع يُبْدِع إِبْداع	to create
حَقَّق يُحَقِّق تَحْقيق	to achieve, realize
دار يدور حولَ	to revolve around
تَدور أَحْداث الفيلم حول	the film's events revolve around ...
فاز يفوز فَوْز بجائزة أوسكار	to win (an Oscar)
تَناوَل يَتَناوَل تَناوُل	to deal with
أَلْهَم يُلْهِم إِلْهام	to inspire

As the Arabs say ... كَما قالَت العَرَب
الفَنّ واسِع ولكن عُيون النّاس ضَيِّقة
Art is wide, but people's eyes are narrow.
Arabic quote (Tawfiq Al-Hakim توفيق الحكيم)

STUDY TIP
Illustrate new words by creating visual diagrams, drawings, mind maps and flow charts to create meaningful visual illustrations and word associations. Annotate them in Arabic as you learn new words.

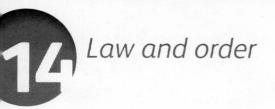

14 Law and order

القَانون والنِّظام

n this unit you will learn essential vocabulary, organized as follows:

▸ الإجْرام Crime

▷ Core vocabulary

▷ الأشْخاص People

▷ النِّظام القانونيّ The legal system

▷ نظام العُقوبات The punishment system

▸ حُقوق الإنْسان Human rights

▷ حُقوق وحُرِّيّات Rights and freedoms

▷ انْتِهاك حُقوق الإنْسان Human rights abuse

الإجرَام Crime

CORE VOCABULARY

حادِث (ج) حَوادث	incident	رَهينة (ج) رَهائن	hostage
جِناية (ج) جَنايا	felony	تَهْريب	smuggling
جَريمة (ج) جَرائم	crime	تَبْييض الأمْوال	money laundering
جَريمة (ج) جَرائم قَتْل	murder	تهْريب البَشَر	people smuggling
قَتَل يقْتُل قَتْل	to kill	تهْريب المُخدِّرات	drug trafficking
سَرق يسْرِق سَرِقة	to steal	حِيازة المُخدِّرات	drug possession

سَرِقة (ج) -ات	theft, robbery	مُتاجرة المُخدِّرات	drug trade
سَطْو على	burglary	تخريب مُتَعمَّد	vandalism
عُنْف	violence	إرْهاب	terrorism
عُنْف أسَريّ/منْزليّ	domestic/ family abuse	ارْتِشاء/رَشْوة	bribery
التَنَمُّر في المَدارِس	abuse in schools (bullying)	احْتيال/غِشّ	fraud
		خيانة	treason
عُنْف العِصابات	gang violence	تَزْوير	forgery
اعْتِداء (ج) -ات	assault	ارتَكَب جَريمة	to commit a crime
اخْتِطاف	abduction, kidnapping, hijacking	حاوَل يُحاوِل مُحاوَلة	to try, to attempt
تعرَّض يَتعرَّض تَعرُّض ل	to be subjected to	عانى يُعاني مُعاناة من	to suffer
ضَرَب يضْرِب ضَرْب	to hit, strike	كَسَّر يُكَسِّر تَكْسير	to break

الأشْخاص PEOPLE

مُجْرِم (ج) -ون	criminal	بلْطَجيّ (ج) بلْطَجية	gangster
جان (ج) جُناة	guilty, perpetrator	هارِب	runaway, fugitive
مُذْنِب (ج) -ون	guilty	قاضِي (ج) قُضاة	judge
ضَحيّة (ج) ضَحايا	victim	مُحامي (ج) -ون	solicitor, lawyer
بَريء (ج) أبْرِياء	innocent	مُسْتَشار قانونيّ	legal consultant
مُتَّهَم ب	accused, charged of/with	نائِب (ج) نُوّاب	prosecutor
مُشْتَبَه في	suspect in (a crime)	شاهِد (ج) شُهود	witness
		شاهِد عِيان	eyewitness

188

قاتِل (ج) قَتَلَة	killer	سَجين (ج) سُجَناء	prisoner (1)
سَفّاح (ج) -ون	murderer	أسير (ج) أسْرى	prisoner, captive (2)
لِصّ (ج) لُصوص	thief (1)	سَجين سِياسيّ	political prisoner
سارِق (ج) -ون	thief (2)	ظالِم (ج) -ون	unjust, despotic
إرهابيّ (ج) -ون	terrorist		

As the Arabs say ... كَما قالَتِ العَرَبُ

حاميها حَراميها

The guardian turned out to be the thief.
English equivalent: *Like a fox guarding the henhouse.*
Colloquial Arabic saying

النِّظام القانونيّ THE LEGAL SYSTEM

قانون (ج) قَوانين	law, canon	وِزارة العَدْل	ministry of justice
القانون المَدَنيّ	civil law	مَحْكَمة (ج) مَحاكِم	court of law, tribunal
القانون الجِنائيّ	criminal law	مَحْكَمة العَدْل الدُّوليّة	international court of justice
القانون الدُوَليّ	international law	المَحْكَمة الجِنائيّة الدُّوليّة	international criminal tribunal
قانونيّ	legal		
غير قانونيّ	illegal		
مَمْنوع	forbidden	مُحاكَمة (ج) -ات	trial
مَحْظور	banned	مَحْكوم بـ	sentenced to
مُخالَفة القانون	violation of the law	حَكَمَ يَحْكُمُ حُكْم	to rule, judge
القَضاء	legal system, jurisdiction	حُكْم (ج) أحْكام	sentence, judgement
تشْريع	legislation	اتَّهَمَ يَتَّهِمُ اتِّهام	to accuse, charge
عَدالة\عَدْل	justice	قِسْم (ج) أقْسام الشُّرْطة	police station (1)
تُهْمة (ج) تُهَم	accusation	مَرْكَز (ج) مراكِز الشُّرْطة	police station (2)

القانون والنِّظام **14** *Law and order* **189**

تَحْقيق (ج) -ات	investigation	اِدِّعاء	prosecution
اِسْتِجْواب (ج) -ات	questioning, interrogation	دِفاع	defence
قَضِيّة (ج) قَضايا	case, issue, lawsuit	اِسْتِئْناف	appeal
دَعْوى (ج) دَعاو	lawsuit	اِعْتَراف	confession
شَكْوى (ج) شَكاو	complaint	يَمين	oath (1)
اِشْتَكى يِشتِكي شَكْوى	to complain	قَسَم (ج) أَقْسام	oath (2)
أَثْبَت يُثْبِت إِثْبات	to prove	دَليل (ج) أَدِلّة	proof, evidence
اِعْتَرَف يَعْتَرِف اِعْتَراف ب	to confess to	تَقْرير الشُّرْطة	police report
		جَلْسة المُحاكَمة	court hearing
اِحْتَجَز يَحْتَجِز اِحْتِجاز	to detain	أدان يُدين إدانة ب	to convict
هَرَب يَهْرُب هَرَبا هُروب	to flee, escape	البوليس (coll.)\ الشُّرطة	the police (force)
		شُرْطِيّ (ة) (ج) شُرْطة	policeman/ woman
		ضابِط شُرْطة	police officer

THE PUNISHMENT SYSTEM نِظام العُقوبات

شَنْق	hanging	عِقاب	punishment (general)
عفا يَعْفو عَفْو عن	to pardon	عُقوبة (ج) -ات	a punishment, sanction
حُكْم بَراءة	acquittal	غَرامة (ج) -ات	fine
مُذَكِّرة تَوْقيف	arrest warrant	كَفالة	bail
اِعْتَقَل يعْتَقِل اعْتِقال	to arrest, detain (1)	حَبْس	imprisonment
أَلْقى يُلقي إلْقاء القَبْض على	to arrest (2)	سِجن مؤبَّد	life imprisonment
قَبَض يقبِض قَبْض على	to arrest (3)	سِجْن (ج) سُجون	prison
أَطْلَق يُطلِق إطْلاق سَراح	to release (so.)	حُكْم إعْدام	death penalty
		أعْدم يُعْدِم اعْدام	to execute (so.)

حُقوق الإنْسان Human rights

حُقوق وَحُريات RIGHTS AND FREEDOMS

حَقّ (ج) حُقوق	right (human)
حُرِّية (ج) -ات	freedom
مُنَظّمة حُقوقيّة	human rights organization
الحُرِّية الشَخْصيّة	personal freedom
الحَقّ في الدِّراسة	right to education
الحَقّ في العَمَل	right of employment
حَقّ الصِّحة والعلاج\التَطْبيب	right of health and treatment
حَقّ الهِجْرة	right of immigration
حَقّ المُحاكمة العادلة	right to fair trial
حَقّ الزَّواج	right of marriage
حَقّ التَصْويت	right of voting
حُرِّية التَعْبير	freedom of speech

حُرية التَمَلُّك	freedom of ownership
حُرِّية العِبادة	freedom of worship
الحَقّ في الحَياة	right to live
الحق في المُشاركة السِّياسية	right of political participation
حَقّ اللُّجوء السِّياسيّ	right of political asylum
حُرية تغيير الجِنْسيّة	right to a nationality (and the freedom to change it)
حَقّ الحِماية	right of protection
حَقّ العَيْش الآمِن	right to safety
الحَقّ في الأمان الشَخْصيّ	right to personal safety
حُقوق المَرْأة	women's rights

انْتِهاك حُقوق الإنْسان HUMAN RIGHTS ABUSE

اضْطِهاد	persecution
مُضْطَهد	persecuted

جَرائِم ضِدّ الإنْسانيّة	crimes against humanity
تَمْييز	discrimination
عُنْصُريّة	racism
جَريمة حَرْب	war crime
إبادة جَماعيّة	genocide
مَذْبَحة (ج) مَذابِح	massacre
عُنْف حُكوميّ	government abuse, brutality
العُنْف ضِدّ المُهاجِرين والأقَليّات	abuse against immigrants and minorities
كَراهِية العِرْق الآخَر	hatred of another race
اغْتِصاب جِنْسيّ	rape, sexual abuse
تَحَرُّش جِنْسيّ	sexual harassment
عَذَّب يُعَذِّب تعْذيب	to torture
انتَهك ينتَهك انْتِهاك	to contravene, abuse
كافَح يُكافِح كِفاح	to struggle
عامَل يُعامِل مُعامَلة	to treat (treatment)
طالب يُطالِب مُطالَبة ب	to demand
مُطالبات	demands

Arab society and religion
الدّين والمُجْتَمَع العَربيّ

In this unit you will learn essential vocabulary, organized as follows:

Arabic society المُجْتَمَع العَربيّ
▷ Core vocabulary

▷ *Social issues* قَضايا اجْتِماعيّة

Mankind and people البَشَريّة والنّاس
▷ Verbs

National holidays and festivals الأعْياد الوَطَنيّة والاحْتِفالات
▷ Core vocabulary

▷ *Holidays and festivals* الأعْياد والاحْتِفالات

▷ *International festivals* الاحْتِفالات العالَميّة

Religion الدِّين

▷ *People* الأشْخاص

▷ *Major religions* الأدْيان الرَّئيسية

▷ *Islam* الإسْلام

▷ *Religious scriptures* الكُتُب الدِّينيّة

▷ *Christianity* المَسيحيّة

▷ *Core vocabulary*

▷ *Judaism* اليَهوديّة

▷ *Useful verbs*

▷ *Useful adjectives*

Religious and ethnic groups in the Arab world
الجَماعات الدّينيّة والعِرْقيّة في العالَم العَربيّ
▷ Core vocabulary

▷ *Religious groups* الجَماعات الدّينيّة

▷ *Ethnic groups* الجَماعات العِرْقيّة

193

► Religious festivals and holidays الأَعْياد والعُطَل الدِّينيّة
  ▷ Muslim festivals الأَعْياد الإسْلاميّة
  ▷ Christian festivals الأَعْياد المَسيحيّة
  ▷ Jewish festivals and events الأَعْياد اليَهوديّة
  ▷ Festival greeting expressions

المُجْتَمَع العَرَبيّ Arabic society

CORE VOCABULARY

ثَقافة (ج) -ات	culture	سُلوك اجْتِماعيّ	social conduct
حَضارة (ج) -ات	civilization	آداب المُعاشَرة	etiquette
طَبَقة (ج) -ات	class	آداب العَلاقات	relationship etiquette
مُجْتَمَع (ج) -ات	society, community	آداب الاجْتِماعات	meeting etiquette
حَيّ (ج) أَحْياء	neighbourhood	آداب الأَعْمال	business etiquette
تَقْليد (ج) تَقاليد	tradition	آدابُ اللِّباس	dress etiquette
تَقْليديّ	traditional	آدابُ الطَّعام	dining etiquette
عادة (ج) -ات	custom	ضيافة\كَرَم	hospitality
ثَقافة فَرْعيّة	subculture	عِلْم الاجْتِماع	sociology
تَعَدُّد الثَّقافات\ تَعَدُّديّة ثَقافيّة	multiculturalism	عِلْم الإنْسان	anthropology
		الحُقوق المَدَنيّة	civil rights
أَخْلاق (ج) أَخْلاقيّات	manners	العَدالة الاجْتِماعيّة	social justice
		كرامة إنْسانية	human dignity
سُلوك (ج) سُلوكيّات	behaviour	الخَدَمات الاجْتِماعيّة	social services
		العَمَل الاجْتِماعيّ	social work
قِيَم أَخْلاقيّة	moral values	مُساعَدة (ج) -ات	help, assistance
مَعايير اجْتِماعيّة	social norms	تَطَوُّع	volunteering

194

كَما قالَت العَرَب ... As the Arabs say
الجَنَّة بلا ناس ما بتنْداس
Paradise without people is not worth setting foot in.
Colloquial Arabic saying

قَضايا اجْتِماعيّة SOCIAL ISSUES

رَفاهة	welfare
فَقْر	poverty
بَطالة	unemployment
أُمّيّة	illiteracy
هِجْرة	immigration
غَلاء المَعيشة	high cost of living
تَضَخُّم	inflation
تَفاوُت	inequality
عَدَم المُساواة الاجْتِماعيّة	social inequality
اكتِظاظ\ازْدِحام	overcrowding
ظُروف مَعيشيّة صَعْبة\سَيّئة	difficult living conditions
عُنْف مَنْزِليّ\أُسَريّ	domestic violence
إجْهاض	abortion
عَمالة الأَطْفال	child labour
استِعْباد\عُبوديّة	slavery
زَواج القاصِرات	child/minor marriage
عَدَم الأَمان	insecurity
تَخْريب	vandalism
جَرائِم الكَراهيّة	hate crimes

تَمْييز	discrimination
تَمْييز عُنْصُري	racial discrimination
التَّمْييز ضِدّ كِبار السِّنّ	ageism
التَّمْييز عَلى أَساس الجِنْس	gender discrimination, sexism
تَفْريق	differentiation
كُرْه النِّساء	misogyny
شُذوذ جِنْسيّ\مِثْليّة جِنسيّة	homosexuality (1)
لِواط	homosexuality, sodomy (2)
دَعارة	prostitution
تَحْديد النَّسْل	birth control
انْتِحار	suicide
إدْمان الكُحول	alcoholism
تَعاطي المُخَدِّرات	drug abuse
حُقوق الحَيَوان	animal rights
اضْطِرابات الطَّعام	eating disorder
تَنْميط	stereotyping
صورة نَمَطيّة	stereotypical image
عَمَل خَيْريّ\إنْسانيّ	charity/philanthropy
عُنْصُريّة	racism

فَرْد (ج) أفْراد	individual
شَخْص (ج) أشْخاص	person
نَسَمة (ج) -ات	person (e.g. in a census in statistics)
عُضْو (ج) أعْضاء	member
إنْسان	human
إنْسانيّة\بَشَريّة	humanity
بَشَر	human being, humankind
بَني آدَم	human being (lit. son of Adam)
ناس	people
شَعْب (ج) شُعوب	people (of a country/region)
قَبيلة (ج) قَبائل	tribe

VERBS

تَطَوَّع يَتَطَوَّع تَطَوُّع	to volunteer
قام يَقوم قيام بعَمَل خَيْريّ	to do charity work
ساعَد يُساعِد مُساعَدة	to assist

National holidays and festivals

الأعْياد الوَطَنيّة والاحْتِفالات

CORE VOCABULARY

عيد (ج) أعْياد	festival, feast, festivity
عَيَّد يُعَيِّد تَعْييد	to celebrate a feast
ذكْرى (ج) ذِكْرَيات	commemoration, anniversary
إحْياء	celebrating, reviving
احْتِفال (ج) -ات	celebration
احْتَفَل يَحْتَفِل احْتِفال ب	to celebrate
عُطْلة (ج) -ات\إجازة (ج) -ات	holiday, vacation, permission, licence
عُطْلة مَصْرِفيّة	bank holiday

HOLIDAYS AND FESTIVALS الأَعْياد والاحْتِفالات

العيد الوَطَنيّ	National Day (in most Arab countries)
عيد الشُّهَداء	Martyrs' Day (in some Arab countries)
عيد الإسْتِقلال	Independence Day (in most Arab countries)
عيد العُمّال	Labour Day (in most Arab countries)
يَوم تَحْرير سيناء	Sinai Liberation Day (Egypt)
عيد الثَّوْرة	Revolution Day (Egypt, Libya, Algeria)
عيد القُوّات المُسَلَّحة	Armed Forces Day (Egypt, Iraq, Lebanon)
عيد المُقاوَمة والتَّحْرير	Resistance and Liberation Day (Lebanon)
عيد العَرْش	Enthronement (Morocco)
ثَوْرة المَلِك والشَّعْب	Revolution of the King and the People (Morocco)
ثَوْرة 25 يَناير	January 25 Revolution Day (Egypt)
شَمّ النَّسيم	Sham el-Nassim (celebrated in Egypt to mark the beginning of spring)
اليَوْم الرِّياضيّ لِلدَّوْلة	National Sports Day (Qatar)

INTERNATIONAL FESTIVALS الاحْتِفالات العالَميّة

عيد الأُمّ	Mother's Day (15 March)
عيد الأب	Father's Day (21 June)
عيد الحُبّ/عيد العُشّاق	Valentine's Day (14 February)
يَوْم المَرأة	International Women's Day (8 March)
اليَوْم العالَميّ لِلُّغة العَرَبيّة	World Arabic Language Day (18 December)
اليَوْم العالَميّ لِلمُعَلِّم	World Teachers' Day (5 October)
اليَوْم العالَميّ لِلتَّضامُن مَع الشَّعْب الفِلَسْطينيّ	International Day of Solidarity with the Palestinian People (29 November)
يَوْم حُقوق الإنْسان	Human Rights Day (10 December)
يَوْم السَّعادة العالَميّ	International Day of Happiness (20 March)

Religion الدِّين

MAJOR RELIGIONS الأَدْيان الرَّئيسيّة

الأَدْيان السَّماويّة	the Abrahamic religions	الهِنْدوسيّة	Hinduism
اليَهوديّة	Judaism	البوذيّة	Buddhism
المَسيحيّة	Christianity	السّيخيّة	Sikhism
الإسْلام	Islam	الزَّرادشْتيّة	Zoroastrianism

RELIGIOUS SCRIPTURES الكُتُب الدِّينيّة

التَّوْراة	the Torah	العَهْد الجَديد	the New Testament
الكِتاب المُقَدَّس	the Bible	الإنْجيل	the Gospels
العَهْد القَديم	the Old Testament	القُرْآن الكَريم	the Holy Qur'a

CORE VOCABULARY

دين (ج) أَدْيان	religion (1)	طَقْس (ج) طُقوس دينيّة	religious rite, ritual
ديانة (ج) -ات	religion (2)	ضَحيّة (ج) ضَحايا	sacrifice (or victim)
عَقيدة (ج) عَقائد	creed, belief, dogma	مَوْسِم (ج) مَواسِم	season
الإلهيّات	theology	اخْتِبار (ج) -ات	test, trial
وَثَنيّة	paganism	قَدَر (ج) أَقْدار	fate, destiny
إلْحاد	atheism	مَكْتوب،مُقَدَّر	destined (lit. written)
تَوْحيديّة	monotheism	روح (ج) أَرْواح	soul, spirit
شِرْك	polytheism	خُرافة (ج) -ات	fairy tale, fable, superstition
إله (ج) آلِهة	a god (in polytheistic context), deity, divinity	تَقْوى	devotion, piety
الله	God (in Islam/ Christianity)	بَرَكة (ج) -ات	blessing
رَبّ (ج) أَرْباب	Lord	تَجْديف	blasphemy

مَلاك (ج) مَلائِكة	angel	ذَنْب (ج) ذُنوب	guilt
شَيْطان (ج) شَياطِ	Satan, the devil	خَطيئة (ج) خَطايا	sin
خَيْر	good	جَزاء	reward
شَرّ	evil	عَذاب	punishment, torture
الدُّنْيا	world	مُعاناة\آلام	suffering
الآخِرة	the hereafter	مُعْجِزة (ج) -ات	miracle
الجَنّة	heaven, paradise	مَزار (ج) -ات	shrine
النّار	hellfire	تَوْبة	repentance
الجَحيم\جَهَنَّم	hell	اِسْتِغْفار	asking forgiveness (from God)
قيامة	resurrection	رَحْمة	mercy
يَوْم القيامة	Judgement Day	تَضْحِية	sacrifice

كَما قالَتِ العَرَب ... As the Arabs say ...

الدّين المُعامَلة

Religion is judged by your treatment of others.
Arabic proverb

EFUL VERBS

آمَنَ يُؤْمِن إيمان ب	to believe in (st.)
عَبَدَ يَعْبُد عِبادة	to worship
تَدَيَّن يَتَدَيَّن تَدَيُّن	to practise a religion
صَدَّق يُصَدِّق تَصْديق	to believe
مَثَّل يُمَثِّل تَمْثيل	to represent
أَنْقَذ يُنْقِذ إِنْقاذ	to save
أَلْحَد يُلْحِد إلْحاد	to renounce religion (apostatize)
صام يَصوم صِيام\صَوْم	to fast
صَلَّى يُصَلّي صَلاة	to pray
اِرْتَكَب يَرْتَكِب اِرْتِكاب خَطيئ	to commit a sin

تاب يَتوب تَوْبة	to repent
اسْتَغْفَر يَسْتَغْفِر اسْتِغْفار	to ask forgiveness
غَفَر يَغْفِر غُفْران لـ	to grant forgiveness to (so.)
رَحِم يَرْحَم رَحْمة	to have mercy
بارَك يُبارِك مُبارَكة	to bless
اعْتَرَف يَعْتَرِف اعْتِراف ب	to confess
ضَحَّى يُضَحِّي تَضْحية ب	to sacrifice (st. or so.)
ذَبَح يَذْبَح ذَبْح	to slaughter

USEFUL ADJECTIVES

دِيني	religious (for objects, things and concepts)
مُتَدَيِّن	religious (for people)
مُقَدَّس	holy
سَماويّ/إلَهيّ	celestial, divine
تَوْحيديّ	monotheistic

الأشْخاص PEOPLE

نَبيّ (ج) أَنْبياء	prophet	مُبَشِّر (ج) -ون	missionary (Christianity)
رَسول (ج) رُسُل	messenger (e.g. Messenger of God	مُلْحِد (ج) -ون	atheist, apostate
(رسول الله		عَلْمانيّ (ج) -ون	secular
مُؤْمِن (ج) -ون	believer	دُنْيويّ (ج) -ون	secular
تَقيّ (ج) أَتْقِياء	pious, devout	كافِر (ج) كُفّار	unbeliever, disbeliever
داعِية (ج) دُعاة	missionary, caller (to Islam)	وَثَنيّ (ج) -ون	pagan
واعِظ (ج) وُعّاظ	preacher	مُشْرِك (ج) -ون	idolater

200

كَما قالَتِ العَرَب ... As the Arabs say

ما عَلى الرّسولِ إلاّ البَلاغ

The messenger has only to convey.
Arabic proverb

الإسلام ISLAM

مُسْلِم (ج) -ون	Muslim
مَسْجِد (ج) مَساجِد	mosque (lit. place of prostration)
جامِع (ج) جَوامِع	mosque (lit. place of congregation)
مُصَلّى (ج) مُصَلّيات	prayer place or room
مِئْذَنة (ج) مآذِن	minaret
أَذان	call to prayer
مُؤَذِّن (ج) -ون	muezzin (caller to prayer)
مِنْبَر (ج) مَنابِر	minbar (pulpit)
خُطْبة (ج) خُطَب	sermon
إمام (ج) أَئِمّة	Imam (prayer and/or community leader)
مُفْتي	Mufti (scholar who is an interpreter of Islamic law)
فَتْوى	fatwa (religious verdict)
عالِم (ج) عُلَماء	scholar/alim, ulama
حاجّ (ج) حُجّاج	pilgrim
خَليفة (ج) خُلَفاء	Caliph
سُورة (ج) سُوَر	Sura (i.e. chapter from the Qur'an)
آية (ج) -ات	verse from the Qur'an
حافِظ (ج) حُفّاظ	Hafiz (i.e. one who has memorized the Qur'an by heart)
قارِئ (ج) قُرّاء	reciter (of the Qur'an)

أُصول الدِّين	principles of the religion
أَرْكان الإسْلام	the pillars of Islam
الشَّهادة	testimony of faith
الصَّلاة	prayer
الصَّوْم	fasting
الحَجّ	the Hajj (pilgrimage to Mecca, Saudi Arabia)
رَمَضان	Ramadan (the month of fasting)
الزَّكاة	alms giving (zakat)
دُعاء (ج) أَدْعية	invocation of God
وُضوء	ablution (before prayer)
العُمْرة	minor pilgrimage (pilgrimage outside the hajj season)
حَلال	permitted
حَرام	forbidden
القَضاء والقَدَر	fate and destiny
سَبْحَة (ج) -ات	prayer beads
هِلال	crescent
أَفْطَر يُفْطِر إفْطار	to break the fast (after sunset)
أَسْلَم يُسْلِم إسْلام	to convert to Islam
اعْتَنَق يَعْتَنِق اعْتِناق	to convert to (lit. embrace)
ارْتَدّ يَرْتَدّ ارْتِداد (عن الإسلام)	to leave Islam

المَسيحيّة CHRISTIANITY

مَسيحيّ (ج) -ون	Christian	أُسْقُف (ج) أَساقِف	bishop
المَسيح	the Messiah, the Anointed	البابا	the Pope
		الوَصايا العَشْر	the Ten Commandme

عظة	sermon (Christian)	اليَسوع\عيسى	Jesus
تَبْشير	preaching (of the Gospel)	الرّوح القُدُس	the Holy Ghost/Spirit
اعْتِراف	confession	مَرْيَم العَذْراء	the Holy Virgin Mary
ابْتِهال (ج) -ات	supplication, prayer	الصَّلاة الرَّبّانِيّة	the Lord's Prayer
تَعْميد	baptism	كَنيسة (ج) كَنائس	church
الحَياة الأَبَدِيّة	eternal life	كاثِدْرائِيّة	cathedral
خَلاص	redemption	صَليب (ج) صُلْبان	cross
تَنَصَّر يَتَنَصَّر تَنَصُّر	to convert to Christianity	راهِب (ج) رُهْبان	monk
بَشَّر يُبَشِّر تَبْشير	to engage in missionary work (Christianity)	راهِبة (ج) -ات	nun
		قِسّيس (ج) قَساوِس	priest, minister

اليَهودِيّة JUDAISM

شَمْعَدان	candlestick, menorah	يَهوديّ (ج) يَهود	Jew
حاخام (ج) -ات	rabbi	اليَهوديّة الأُرْثوذوكْسِيّة	Orthodox Judaism
دير (ج) أَدْيار	monastery	كَنيس (ج) كُنُس	synagogue
كوشير	kosher	مَعْبَد (ج) مَعابِد	temple (1)
تَهَوَّد يَتَهَوَّد تَهَوُّد	to convert to Judaism	هَيْكَل سُلَيْمان	temple (2) (e.g. Solomon's Temple)
المَسيح المُخَلِّص	Messiah	نَجْمة داوود	Star of David

As the Arabs say ... كَما قالَت العَرَب

كُلُّ شَيْءٍ عادة حَتَّى العِبادة

Everything including worship becomes a habit.
Arabic proverb

Religious and ethnic groups in the Arab world
الجَماعات الدينيّة والعِرْقيّة في العالَم العَرَبيّ

CORE VOCABULARY

مَذْهَب (ج) مَذاهِب	doctrinal school, denomination	أَقَلّيّة (ج) -ات	minority
عِرْق (ج) أَعْراق	race, ethnicity	أَغْلَبيّة\أَكْثَريّة	majority
عِرْقيّ	racial, ethnic	طائفة (ج) طوائف	sect
تَطْهير عِرْقيّ	ethnic cleansing	طائفيّة	sectarianism

RELIGIOUS GROUPS — الجَماعات الدينيّة

كاثوليكيّ (ج) الكَثْلَكة	Catholic	سُنّيّ (ج) السُّنّة	Sunni
بُروتِسْتانيّ (ج) -ون\ البُروتِسْتان	Protestant	شيعيّ (ج) الشّيعة	Shi'ite, Shi'a
قِبْطيّ (ج) الأَقْباط	Copt	الصّوفيّة	Sufism
مارونيّ (ج) المَوارنة	Maronite	دُرْزيّ (ج) دُروز	Druze
أُورْثودوكسيّ (ج) الأُورْثودوكس	Orthodox	عَلَويّ (ج) العَلويّون	Alawite
أَرْمانيّ (ج) الأَرْمان	Armenians	آشوريّ (ج) الآشوريّون	Assyrian
الأَرْثوذِكْسيّة اليونانيّة	Greek Orthodox (in Levant)	إسْماعيليّ (ج) الإسْماعيليّون	Ismailis
إيزيديّ\يَزيديّ (ج) -ون	Yazidi	البَهائيّة	Baha'ism

ETHNIC GROUPS — الجَماعات العِرْقيّة

تُرْكُمانيّ (ج) تُرْكُمان	Turkmen	البَرْبَر\الأَمازيغ	Berbers, Amazigh
شيشانيّ (ج) شيشان	Chechens	تُرْكيّ (ج) أَتْراك	Turks
آشوري (ج) -ون	Assyrians	كُرْديّ (ج) أَكْراد	Kurds

سِريانيّ (ج) سِريانيّة Syrians   كَلْدانيّ (ج) -ون Chaldeans

شِرْكِسيّ (ج) شِرْكِس\شَراكِس Circassians

eligious festivals and holidays
الأَعْياد والعُطَل الدّينيّة

USLIM FESTIVALS الأَعْياد الإسْلاميّة

العيد الصَّغير\عيد الفطْر	Eid al-Fitr (feast of end of Ramadan/the small feast)
العيد الكَبير\عيد الأَضْحى	Eid el-Ad'ha (feast of the sacrifice/the big feast)
لَيْلَة القَدْر	Leilat al-Qadr (the Night of Power during Ramadan)
مَوْلِد النَّبيّ\المولِد النَّبويّ الشَّريف	the Prophet Muhammad's Birthday
رَأْس السَّنة الهِجْريّة	Islamic New Year
عاشوراء	Ashura (10th of the month of Muharram)
لَيْلَة الإسْراء والمِعْراج	al-Isra wal-Mi'raj (the Prophet Muhammad's Night Journey)

HRISTIAN FESTIVALS الأَعْياد المَسيحيّة

عيد الميلاد المَجيد	Christmas
عيد ميلاد المَسيح	birthday of Jesus
رَأْس السَّنة الميلاديّة	New Year's Day
عيد الفصْح\عيد القيامة	Easter
أَحَد الفصْح	Easter Sunday
عيد البِشارة	Annunciation
جُمُعة الآلام\الجُمُعة العَظيمة	Good Friday
عيد انْتِقال العَذْراء	Feast of the Assumption of Mary
حُلول الرّوح القُدُس	Pentecost
العَنْصَرة	Ascension
عيد الشُّكْر	Thanksgiving Day

JEWISH FESTIVALS AND EVENTS الأَعْيَاد اليَهوديّة

عيد الرُّقاق *Passover*

عيد الغُفْران *Yom Kippur (Day of Atonement)*

FESTIVAL GREETING EXPRESSIONS

Having a good knowledge of Arabic greetings and knowing when to use them is a unique skill you should develop over time. This will help you to build a fine cultural awareness of how people celebrate across the Arab world.

Here are some popular greetings Arabs use for the celebrations above:

عيد مُبارَك *Blessed feast/festivity (usually said by Muslims at the end of Ramadan (to celebrate Eid al-Fitr) and during the day of Eid el-Ad'ha, i.e. feast of the sacrifice)*

رَمضان كَريم\مُبارَك *Happy/Blessed Ramadan*

كلُّ عامٍ وأَنْت بِخَيرٍ\كلُّ سَنةٍ وأَنْت طَيّب *May you be well every year/Best wishes for a happy new year (This particular greeting is very popular and can be used for most annual occasions, main birthdays, most Muslim festivals, Christmas, New Year (both Christian and Islamic) and Easter.)*

عيد ميلاد مَجيد *Merry Christmas*

عيد ميلاد سَعيد *Happy Birthday*

كَما قالَت العَرَب ... As the Arabs say

أَنْت تُريد وَهُوَ يُريد وَاللهُ يَفْعَل ما يُريد

You want what you want and he wants what he wants, but God does what He wants.

(Man proposes, God disposes.)

Arabic saying

16 Politics and the military
السِّياسْة والشُّؤون العَسْكَريّة

this unit you will learn essential vocabulary, organized as follows:

207

Politics السِّياسة

POLITICAL SYSTEMS الأَنْظِمة السِّياسيّة

دُسْتور (ج) دَساتير	constitution	سِياسة (ج) -ات	politics, policy
بَرْلَمان (ج) -ات	parliament	سِياسيّ	politician, political
جَلْسة برلمان	parliamentary session	دَوْلة (ج) دُوَل	state, nation, country
لَجْنة (ج) لِجان	committee	وَطَن (ج) أَوْطان	nation, homeland
سِيادة	sovereignty	وِلاية (ج) -ات	state, province
نُفوذ	power, autho	مَمْلَكة (ج) مَمالك	kingdom
شَعْبيّة	popularity	مَحَلّي	local
اسْتِقلال	independen	حُكومة (ج) -ات	government
اسْتِعمار	colonization	نظام (ج) أَنْظمة	regime
فَساد	corruption	حُكومة ائْتِلافيّة	coalition government
فَضيحة (ج) فَضائح	scandal	حُكومة اتِّحاديّة	federal government
رَشْوة	bribery	إدارة (ج) -ات	administration
احْتِيال	fraud	دائرة (ج) دَوائر	government office
اخْتِلاس	embezzleme	قُنْصُليّة (ج) -ات	consulate
ابْتِزاز	blackmail	جُمْهوريّة (ج) -ات	republic
اسْتِغلال	exploitation	سَلْطنة (ج) -ات	sultanate

تَراجُع	decline	إمارة (ج) -ات	emirate
حَظْر، حِصار	blockade, embargo	سُلْطة (ج) -ات	power, authority
مَحْظور	prohibited, forbidden	امْبراطوريّة (ج) -ات	empire
جدل	controversy	مُسْتَعْمرة (ج) -ات	colony
انْتَقَد يَنْتَقِد انْتِقاد	to criticize	العائلة الحاكمة	ruling party (1)
أَصْلَح يُصْلِح إصْلاح	to reform	الحِزْب الحاكم	ruling party (2)
إصْلاح (ج) -ات	reform	الأُسْرة المَلَكيّة	royal family
إصْلاحات سياسيّة	political reforms	عَرْش (ج) عُروش	throne
تَعْديل (ج) -ات	amendment	رِئاسة	presidency
تَغْيير وِزاريّ	cabinet reshuffle	السُّلُطات	the authorities
صِياغة الدُّسْتور	drafting or writing of the constitution	تَشْريع	legislation
تَأْميم	nationalization	تَشْريعيّ	legislative
		تَنْفيذيّ	executive
		قَضائي	judicial

الأَيْديولوجيات السّياسيّة   OLITICAL IDEOLOGIES

كَما قالَتِ العَرَب ...   As the Arabs say ...

إذا أَرَدْتَ أَنْ تُطاع فَسْل المُسْتَطاع

If you wish to be obeyed, demand what is possible.
Arabic proverb

ديموقْراطيّة	democracy	اليَمين	the right
وَطَنيّة	patriotism	اتّحاديّ	federal
وَطَنيّ	national, nationalist	مَرْكَزيّ	centralized, central
قَوْميّة	nationalism	ليبراليّة	liberalism
القَوْميّة العَرَبيّة	pan-Arab nationalism	سِياسة مُحافِظة	conservatism
عُروبة	Arabism, Arab nationalism	الإسْلام السّياسيّ	political Islam

قَبَلِيّة	tribalism	جَذْرِيّة\رادِكالِيّة	radicalism
يَسارِيّ	left wing	أُصولِيّة	fundamentalism
يَمينِيّ	right wing	بيروقراطيّة	bureaucracy
اليَسار	the left	دِكْتاتوريّة	dictatorship

٥٣

كَما قالَتِ العَرَب ... As the Arabs say ...

أُمَّتُنا تَرْفُض الدِّيكْتاتور وتَكْرَهُه وتُعاديه، سَواءً كان يَلْبَس عَمامة
الشَّيْخ، أو طَرْبوش الأَفَنْدي، أو بَرْنيطة الخَواجة، أو طاقيّة الفَلاَّح
أو خوذة الجُنْدِيّ، أو لا يَلْبَس شَيْئًا فَوْق رَأْسِه

Our nation despises and opposes the dictator, whether he wears the scholar's turban, the aristocrat's fez, the foreigner's bowler hat, the farmer's cap, the soldier's helmet, or leaves his head bare.

(د. يوسف القرضاوي)
Dr Yousef Al-Qaradawi

أَبَوِيّة\بابَوِيّة	patriarchism	اِشْتِراكِيّة	socialism
تَطَرُّف\تَطَرُّفيّة	extremism	فاشيّة	fascism
حُكومة مُطْلَقة\أوتوقْراطيّة	autocracy	إمْبْرِيالِيّة	imperialism
اسْتِعْماريّة	colonialism	صُهْيونيّة	Zionism
رَأْسْماليّة	capitalism	فَوْضَويّة	anarchism
شُموليّة	totalitarianism	اِنْفِصاليّة	separatism
شُيوعيّة	communism	تَعَدُّديّة	pluralism

● INSIGHT

To turn these nouns into adjectives, simply remove the feminine ending (ة). The feminine adjective is written and pronounced in exactly the same way as the noun.

For example:

ديموقْراطيّ\ة *democratic*   رَأْسْماليّ\ة *capitalist*

شُيوعيّ\ة *communist*

كَما قالَت العَرَب ... As the Arabs say

حَكَمْتَ فَعَدِلْتَ فَأَمِنْتَ فَنِمْتَ

*You have ruled justly, therefore felt secure and
thus slept peacefully.*
Arabic quote
The messenger of Persian Emperor Kisra said this
of Umar Ibn Al-Khattab, an influential caliph and close companion of
the Prophet Muhammad.

مَنْصِب (ج) مَناصِ	position	دِبْلوماسِيّ (ج) -ون	diplomat
سِياسِيّ (ج) -ون	politician	سَفير (ج) سُفَراء	ambassador
مَسْؤُول (ج) -ون	official	قُنْصُل (ج) قَناصِل	consul
رَئيس (ج) رُؤَساء	president, head, leader	مَبْعوث (ج) -ون	delegate, envoy
زَعيم (ج) زُعَماء	leader (1)	وَفْد (ج) وُفود	delegation (1)
قائِد (ج) قادة	leader (2)	بِعْثة (ج) -ات	delegation (2)
مَلِك (ج) مُلوك	king	مَنْدوب (ج) -ون	delegate
حاكِم (ج) حُكّام	ruler, governor	طَرَف (ج) أطْراف	party, side (1)
وَزير (ج) وُزَراء	minister	جانِب (ج) جَوانِب	party, side (2)
رَئيس وُزَراء	PM (Prime Minister)	مُشارِك (ج) -ون	participant
وال (ج) وُلاة	governor, mayor, ruler	ناشِط (ج) -ون	activist
نائِب (ج) نُوّاب	deputy, vice	مُتَظاهِر (ج) -ون	protestor (1)
عاهِل (ج) عَواهِل	monarch	ثَوْرِيّ (ج) ثُوّار	revolutionary
أمير (ج) أُمَراء	prince	مُحْتَج (ج) -ون	protester (2)
عُضْو (ج) أعْضاء	member	مُعْتَصِم (ج) -ون	protester (3)
مُمَثِّل (ج) -ون	representative	مُحافِظ (ج) -ون	conservative
مُتَحَدِّث\ناطِق باسْ	spokesperson	طالِب لُجوء	asylum seeker

مُوَظَّف مَدَنيّ حُكوميّ	civil servant		وَسيط (ج) وُسَطاء	intermediary
مُواطِن (ج) -ون	citizen		مَجْلِس (ج) مَجالِس	council
مستشار (ج) -ون	councillor, advisor		لَجْنة (ج) لِجان	committee
أمين عامّ	general secretary			

POLITICAL TITLES AND FORMS OF ADDRESS
أَشْكال التَّخاطُب السِّياسيّة

سِيادة	His/Her Majesty	to address a head of state
جَلالة	His/Her Majesty	to address a king
فَخامة	His/Her Majesty	to address a head of state (Lebanon)
مَعالي	His/Her Excellency	to address a high-ranking official
سَعادة	Your Excellency/Grace	to address a high-ranking official
مَوْلاي\ة	My Lord	to address a king
سُمُوّ\ة	His/Her Highness	to address a prince or a member of the royal family
صاحِب الغِبْطة نيافة	Your Grace	to a Christian patriarch

الأَحْداث الجَارِية CURRENT AFFAIRS

حَدَث (ج) أَحْداث	event, happening		أَزْمة (ج) -ات	crisis
قَضيّة (ج) قَضايا	case		أَزْمة إِنْسانيّة	humanitarian crisis
مَسْأَلة (ج) مَسائِل	issue		هُجوم (ج) هَجَمات	attack
شَأْن (ج) شُؤون	affair, issue		مواجَهة (ج) -ات	confrontation
وَضْع (ج) أَوْضاع	situation, state of affairs		تَهْديد (ج) -ات	threat
حال (ج) أَحْوال	status/condition		عُنْف	violence
الوَضْع الرّاهِن	status quo		انقِلاب (ج) -ات	coup
الرَّأي العامّ	public opinion		انْقِلاب أَبْيَض	bloodless coup

قَرار (ج) -ات	resolution, decision	عُقوبات	sanctions
جَلْسة (ج) -ات	session	مُؤامَرة	conspiracy, plot
بَيان (ج) -ات	statement, report	صِراع (ج) -ات	conflict
تَصْريح (ج) -ات	statement, declaration	نِزاع (ج) -ات	dispute
حَقيقة (ج) حَقائِق	truth, fact	نِضال\كِفاح	fight, struggle
تَعْميم	generalization	مُقاوَمة	resistance
إجْماع	consensus, unanimity	عِصْيان مَدَنيّ	civil disobedience
دافِع (ج) دَوافِع	incentive, motive	تَمَرُّد	rebellion
ذَريعة (ج) ذَرائِع	excuse, pretext	حُرِّية (ج) -ات	freedom, liberty

HE ARAB SPRING الرَّبيع العَرَبيّ

ثَوْرة (ج) -ات	revolution	ثَوْرة الكَرامة	revolution of honour
الثَّوْرة العَرَبيّة	Arab revolt	إرادة الشُّعوب	the will of the people
الرَّبيع العَرَبيّ	Arab Spring	اسْتِبْداد	tyranny, oppression
الخَريف الإسْلاميّ	Islamic Winter	قَمْع	repression
ثَوْرة الياسْمين	the Jasmine revolution (Tunisia)	ظُلْم\اضْطِهاد	oppression, tyranny
ثَوْرة الشَّباب العَرَبيّ	revolution of Arab youth	اضْطَهَد يضطهد اضْطِهاد	to persecute, oppress
ثَوْرة التَّغْيير	revolution of change	مُضْطَهَد	persecuted
ثَوْرة الغَضَب	revolution of anger	اِحْتِجاج (ج) -ات	protest, objection
ثَوْرة الجِياع	revolution of hungry	اِحْتَجّ يَحْتَجّ اِحْتِجاج	to protest, to object
مُحْتَجّ	protestor	مُشارَكة	participation
مُعارَضة	opposition	فَوْضى عارِمة	utter chaos
تظاهَر يتظاهر تظاهُر	to demonstrate	حالة تَأَهُّب	state of alert

مُظاهرة (ج) -ات	demonstration, protest	شُرْطة مُكافَحة الشَّغَب	riot police
اِشْتِباك (ج) -ات	clash	فِكْر اِنْقِلابيّ	revolutionary thought
اِعْتِصام (ج) -ات	sit-in	صُعود التّيار الإسْلاميّ	the rise of the Islamic movement
تَمَرُّد	riot, political unrest	أَسْلَمة	Islamization
شَغَب	riot	شَيْطَنة	demonization
حِياديّ\مُحايد	neutral		

النّزاع العَرَبيّ - الاِسْرائيليّ
THE ARAB–ISRAELI CONFLICT

كَما قالَت العَرَب ... As the Arabs say

لِكُلِّ النّاس وَطَنٌ يَعيشون فيه إلاّ نَحْنُ فَلَنا وَطَنٌ
يَعيشُ فينا

All people have a homeland in which they live, except us; we have a homeland which lives within us.
Arabic quote

النّزاع الفِلَسْطيني - الاِسْرائيلي	Palestinian–Israeli conflict
القَضيّة الفِلَسْطينيّة	the Palestinian issue
فِلَسْطين المُحْتَلّة	occupied Palestine
الأَراضي المُحْتَلّة	the occupied land
الضفّة الغَرْبيّة	the West Bank
قِطاع غَزّة	the Gaza Strip
مُسْتَوْطَنة (ج) -ات	settlements
مُسْتَوْطِن (ج) -ون	settler
مُطالَبة إقْليميّة	territorial claim
نِزاع إقْليميّ	territorial dispute
لاجِئ (ج) -ون	refugee

مُخَيَّم (ج) مُخَيَّمات اللّاجِئين	refugee camps
اِنْتِفاضة	intifada, uprising
النَّكْبة	the Nakba (catastrophe of 1948)
هَرَب يَهْرَب هُروب	to flee
طَرْد	expulsion
حَقّ العَوْدة	the Right of Return
حاجِز (ج) حَواجِز	barrier
نقطة تفتيش	checkpoint
مذبحة (ج) مذابح	massacre (1)
مَجْزَرة (ج) مَجازِر	massacre (2)
إبادة جَماعيّة	genocide
تَطْهير عِرْقيّ	ethnic cleansing
العُدْوان الاسْرائيليّ	Israeli aggression
حُقوق مَشْروعة	legitimate rights
تَهْويد	Judaization
فلَسْطينيو الشَّتات	the Palestinian diaspora
فلَسْطينيو الدّاخل	Arab-Israelis
تَقْرير المَصير	self-determination
الجِدار العازِل	the Separation Wall
وَعْد بَلْفور	the Balfour Declaration
دَوْلة ثنائيّة القَوْميّة	bi-national state
حُكْم ذاتيّ	self-rule
مَشْروع التَّقْسيم	the Partition Plan
الحَرَكة الصُّهْيونيّة	the Zionist Movement
مُعاداة السّاميّة	anti-Semitism
العاصمة الأبَديّة	the eternal capital
الميثاق الوَطَنيّ الفِلَسْطينيّ	the National Palestinian Charter

عَلاقة (ج) -ات	relation, relationship
عَلاقات عامّة	public relations
المُجْتَمَع الدُّوَليّ	the international community
السّاحة الدُّوَليّة	the international stage
دِبْلوماسْيّة	diplomacy
سِفارة (ج) -ات	embassy
قُنْصُلِيّة (ج) -ات	consulate
مُلْحَق ثَقافيّ	cultural attaché
مُعاهَدة (ج) -ات	treaty, accord
اتِّفاقيّة (ج) -ات	agreement, treaty, convention
اتِّفاق (ج) -ات	agreement
ميثاق (ج) مَواثيق	charter, treaty
مُؤْتَمَر (ج) -ات	conference
اِجْتِماع (ج) -ات	meeting
حِوار (ج) -ات	dialogue
مُحادَثة (ج) -ات	talk
مُباحَثات	talks
قِمّة (ج) قِمَم	summit
مُفاوَضة (ج) -ات	negotiation
إجْماع	unanimity, agreement
حَلّ (ج) حُلول	solution
حَلّ وَسَط	compromise

تَطْبيع العَلاقات	normalization of relations
تَعايُش	coexistence
ائتِلاف	coalition
تَحالُف	alliance
تَعاوُن	cooperation, collaboration
اتِّحاد\وِحْدة	unity
مُساعَدات إنْسانيّة	humanitarian aid
مُساعَدات دُوَليّة	international aid
عَمَليّة السَّلام	the peace process
مُخَطَّط السَّلام	the peace plan
مَصْلَحة (ج) مَصالِح	interest, benefit
حَسَّن يُحَسِّن تَحْسين	to improve
أساء يُسيء اساءة	to worsen
قَطَع يَقْطَع قَطْع العَلاقات الدِّبْلوماسيّة	to sever diplomatic relations
تَبادَل يتبادل تَبادُل	to exchange
ناقَش يُناقِش مُناقَشة	to discuss
اتَّفَق يَتَّفِق اتِّفاق على	to agree upon

POLITICAL PARTIES AND ORGANIZATIONS
أَحْزاب ومُنَظّمات سِياسيّة

مُنَظّمة (ج) -ات	organization	جَمْعيّة (ج) -ات	group, association (2)
عُضْو (ج) أعْضاء	member	جَمْعيّة خَيْريّة	charitable organization
عُضْويّة\انْتِماء إلى	membership of	جَمْعيّة تَعاوُنيّة	cooperative organization
مُنَظّمة دُوَليّة	international organization	حِزْب (ج) أحْزاب	(political) party
مُنَظّمة حُكوميّة	governmental organization	وَكالة (ج) -ات	agency

مُنَظَّمة غير حُكوميّة	non-governmental organization	حَرَكة (ج) -ات	movement
مُؤَسَّسة (ج) -ات	institution, foundation	حَرَكة نِسائيّة	feminist moveme
جَماعة (ج) -ات	group, association (1)		

POLITICAL ORGANIZATIONS IN THE ARAB WORLD

جَماعات سِياسيّة في العالَم العَرَبيّ

جامعة الدُّوَل العَرَبيّة	the Arab League
حِزْب الله	Hizbollah (lit. Party of God)
حِزْب التَّحْرير	HT (Liberation Party)
مُنَظَّمة التَّحْريرِ الفِلَسْطينيّة	PLO (Palestinian Liberation Organization)
السّلْطة الوَطَنيّة الفِلَسْطينيّة	PNA (Palestinian National Authority)
الجَبْهة الشَّعْبيّة لتَحْرير فِلَسْطين	PFLP (Popular Front for the Liberation of Palestine)
حَماس\حَرَكة المُقاوَمة الإسْلاميّة	Hamas (Movement of Islamic Resistance)
الجَبْهة الدّيموقراطيّة لتَحْرير فِلَسْطين	The Democratic Front for the Liberation of Palestine
حَرَكة فَتْح	the Fatah movement
الفَصائِل الفِلَسْطينيّة	Palestinian factions
المَجْلِس الوَطَنيّ الفِلَسْطينيّ	the National Palestinian Council
الرّابِطة الإسْلاميّة	the Muslim League
مُنَظَّمة المُؤْتَمَر الإسْلاميّ	OIC (the Organization of the Islamic Conference)
الإخْوان المُسْلِمون	the Muslim Brotherhood
تَنْظيم القاعدة	Al-Qaeda
الجِهاد الإسْلاميّ	Islamic Jihad
الدَّوْلة الإسْلاميّة في العِراق والشّام (داعِش)	ISIS/IS (Islamic State of Iraq and the Levant/Sham)

جَبْهة الإنْقاذِ الإسْلاميّ	the Islamic Salvation Front
مَجْلِس التّعاوُن الخَليجيّ	GCC (Gulf Cooperation Council)
مُنَظّمة الأقْطار العَربيّة المُصِّدِرة للنّفط	OAPEC (the Organization of Arab Petroleum Exporting Countries)

INTERNATIONAL ORGANIZATIONS مُنَظّمات دُوَليّة

الأُمَم المُتَّحدة	UN (United Nations)
الجَمْعيّة العامّة	UN (General Assembly)
مَجْلِس الأمْن	UN (Security Council)
قَرار مَجْلِس الأمْن التّابِع للأُمَم المُتَّحدة	UN (Security Council) resolution
يونسكو	UNESCO (United Nations Educational, Scientific and Cultural Organization)
مُنَظّمة الاتِّحاد الأوُروبيّ	EU (European Union)
المُفَوَّضيَة الأوُروبيّة	EC (European Commission)
مَجْموعة الثّماني	G8 (Group of Eight)
البَنْك الدُوَليّ	World Bank
مُنَظّمة الصِّحة العالَميّة	WHO (World Health Organization)
صُنْدوق النّقد الدُوَليّ	IMF (International Monetary Fund)
مُنَظّمة التّجارة العالَميّة	WTO (World Trade Organization)
مُنَظّمة العَفْو الدُوَليّة	Amnesty International
مُراقَبة حُقوق الإنْسان	Human Rights Watch
مُنَظّمة أطبّاء بلا حُدود	Doctors Without Borders
جَماعة السّلام الأخْضَر	Greenpeace

الحِزْب الدّيموقراطيّ	the Democratic Party
الحِزْب الجُمْهوريّ	the Republican Party
حِزْب العُمّال	the Labour Party
حِزْب المُحافظين	the Conservative Party
مُنَظّمة حِلْف شَمال الأَطْلَسيّ	NATO (North Atlantic Treaty Organization)
الوكالة الدُّوَليّة للطاقة الذَّرِّيّة	IAEA (International Atomic Energy Authority)
مِحْوَر الشَّرّ	axis of evil

NAMES OF MINISTRIES أَسْماء الوِزارات العَرَبيّة

الدِّفاع	defence	وِزارة (ج) -ات	ministry of ...
الأَوْقاف والشُّؤُون الإسْلاميّة	Islamic affairs and endowments	الخارجيّة	foreign affairs
		الدّاخليّة	the interior
الثَّقافة	culture	التَّربيّة والتَّعليم	education
الزِّراعة	agriculture	التَّعليم العالي	higher education
الصِّحة العُموميّة	public health	العَدْل	justice
الصِّناعة والتِّجارة	industry and trade	الماليّة	finance

● INSIGHT

In certain Arab countries the names of ministries might vary. For instance, in لبنان, the Ministry of Justice is locally referred to as قَصْر العَدْل, lit. *Palace of Justice*.

ELECTIONS الإنْتِخابات

صُنْدوق (ج) صَناديق	ballot box	انْتِخاب (ج) -ات	election
الاقْتِراع		حملة انْتِخابيّة	election campaign
مَرْكَز اقْتِراع	polling station	صَوْت (ج) أصوات	vote
شَفافيّة	transparency	ناخِب (ج) -ون	voter

مُرَشَّح (ج) -ون	candidate	انْتِخابات حُرّة وَنَزيهة	free and fair elections
مُنافِس (ج) -ون	competitor	تَزْوير/تَزْييف الانْتِخابات	election rigging
حَمْلة (ج) -ات	campaign	اسْتِفْتاء (ج) -ات	referendum
شِعار (ج) -ات	slogan	اسْتِطْلاع (ج) -ات	poll
دِعاية (ج) -ات	propaganda	أصْدَر يُصْدِر إصْدار	to issue, release
تَصْريح (ج) -ات	statement, declaration	نافَس يُنافِس مُنافَسة	to compete
اسْتِطْلاع رَأْي	opinion poll	فاز يفوز فَوْز	to win
اسْتِبْيان (ج) -ات	poll, survey	خَسِر يَخْسَر خَسارة	to lose
أحْصاءات	statistics	دَعَّم يُدَعِّم دَعْم مع	to support with (a) candidate
نَتيجة (ج) نتائج	result	عارَض يُعارِض مُعارَضة	to oppose
أغْلَبيّة	majority	ضِدّ	against
الأغْلَبيّة السّاحِقة	the overwhelming majority		
صَوَّت يُصَوِّت تَصْويت	to vote		
أعْلَن يُعْلِن إعْلان	to announce		
خاض يَخوض خَوْض	to run (for office)		

النّشاط السّياسيّ عبر الإنْتِرْنِت ONLINE POLITICAL ACTIVISM

حُكومة إلِكْترونيّة	e-government
ديمقْراطيّة إلِكْترونيّة	e-democracy
حَوْكَمة الإنْتِرْنِت	internet governance
مُدَوّنة صَحَفيّة	journalist blog
مُدَوّنة شُؤون حَرْبيّة	warblog, milblog
ثوْرة إلِكْترونيّة 2.0	revolution 2.0

ثَوْرة إِعْلاميّة	media revolution
ثَوْرة فيسبوكيّة	Facebook™ revolution
حَمْلة فيْسبوكيّة	Facebook™ campaign
ثَوْرة الإِعْلام الإِجْتِماعي	social networking revolution
ذَكاء جَماعيّ	collective intelligence
صَحافة شَعْبيّة	citizen journalism (1)
صَحافة المُواطن	citizen journalism (2)
صَحافة إِلِكْترونيّة	online journalism
صَحيفة إِلِكْترونيّة	e-paper
مَجَلّة إِلِكْترونيّة	e-magazine, e-zine
نَشْر إِلِكْترونيّ	online publishing
مُحْتَوى عُموميّ	public content
مُحْتَوى حُرّ	free content
مُحْتَوى عِنْد الطَلَب	content on demand
تَغْريدة (ج) -ات	Tweet™ (message)
تَغْريد	Tweeting™ (using Twitter™)
تَصْويت إِلِكْترونيّ	electronic voting, e-voting
عَريضة إِلِكْترونيّة	e-petition

Military and defence الجَيْش والدِّفاع

الشُّؤُون العَسْكَريّة	military affairs	مَعْسْكَر إعْتِقال	concentration camp
المُؤَسَّسة الْعَسْكَريّة	the military (institution)	قُوّة (ج) -ات	force
جَيْش (ج) جُيوش	army, military	قُوّات مُسَلّحة	armed forces
قُوّات الأَمْن	security forces	قُوّات جَوّيّة	air force
دِفاع	defence	قُوّات بَرّيّة	ground forces
قِيادة (ج) -ات	command (centre)	البَحْريّة	navy
قاعدة (ج) قواعد	base	قُوّات خاصّة	special forces
قاعدة عَسْكَريّة	military base	قُوّات التّحالف	the allied forces
مَعْسْكَر (ج) -ات	military camp	قُوّات حفظ السّلام	peacekeeping forces
مُعْتَقل (ج) -ات	detention camp	قُوّات تَحالُف	coalition forces

في حالةِ الحَرْب AT WAR

حَرْب (ج) حُروب	war	مَوْقِع اسْتراتيجيّ	
الحَرْب الباردة	the Cold War	(ج) مَواقِع	strategic point
حَرْب أَهْليّة	civil war	اسْتراتيجيّة	strategy
حَرْب عصابات	guerrilla warfare	مُخَطَّط (ج) -ات	plan, blueprint, strategy
حَرْب إلِكْتْرونيّة	electronic warfare	حالة الطَّوارئ	state of emergency
حَرْب نَفْسيّة	psychological warfare	مَعْرَكة (ج) مَعارك	battle
حالة حَرْب	state of war	غَزْو (ج) -ات	invasion
في حالة الحَرْب	at war	غارة (ج) -ات	raid
تَدَخُّل عَسْكَريّ	military intervention	غارة جَوّيّة	air raid

ضَرْبة عَسْكَرِيّة	military strike	مَيْدان العَمَلِيّات	field of operations
عُدْوان	aggression	مِنْطَقة القِتال	combat zone
حِصار	siege, blockade	قِتال	fighting
قَصْف	bombing, shelling	تَكْتيكات عَسْكَرِيّة	military tactics
تَدْمير	destruction	سَفْك الدِّماء	bloodshed
انْتِشار الأسْلِحة النَّوَوِيّة	nuclear proliferation	هاجَمَ يُهاجِم هُجوم	to attack
إرْهاب	terrorism	اعْتِداء (ج) -ات	attack, aggression
هُجوم إرْهابيّ	terrorist attack	عَمَلِيّة انْتِحارِيّة\ اسْتِشْهادِيّة	suicide/martyrdom attack or mission
تَهْديد إرْهابيّ	terrorist threat	اغْتِيال (ج) -ات	assassination
الحَرْب على الإرْهاب	war on terror	انْفِجار (ج) -ات	explosion (1)
جَرائِم الحَرْب	war crimes		
احْتِلال\اسْتِعْمار	occupation, colonization	تَفْجير (ج) -ات	explosion (2)

في حالةِ السِّلم AT PEACE

كَما قالَتِ العَرَب ... As the Arabs say ... 〈59〉

وَإنْ جَنَحوا لِلسِّلْمِ فاجْنَحْ لَها وَتَوَكَّلْ عَلى الله

But if the enemy incline towards peace, do also incline towards it and trust in God.

Qur'anic verse (al-Anfal 8:61 الأنْفال)

مَنْع التَّجَوُّل	curfew	سِلْم\سَلام	peace
وَقْف إطْلاق النّار	ceasefire	انْسِحاب	withdrawal
نَزْع السِّلاح	disarmament	تَحْرير	liberation
حَلّ النِّزاعات	conflict resolution	هُدْنة (ج) -ات	truce
تَبادُل الأسْرى	prisoner exchange	اسْتِسْلام	surrender

انْتِصار (ج) -ات	victory	عَفْو عامّ	amnesty
هَزيمة (ج) هَزائِم	defeat		

WEAPONS الأَسْلِحة

سِلاح (ج) أسْلِحة	weapon	سِلاح ناريّ	firearm
سِلاح الجَوّ	air force	أسْلِحة خَفيفة	small arms
أسْلِحة بَيْضاء	non firearms weapons (e.g. knives, batons, etc.)	أسْلِحة مُتَوَسِّطة	medium-range weapons
أسْلِحة الدَّمار الشَّامِل	weapons of mass destruction (WMD)	غاز مُسيل للدُّموع	tear gas
أسْلِحة كيماويّة	chemical weapons	كَمين\شرك مَلْغوم	booby trap
أسْلِحة نَوَويّة	nuclear weapons	صاروخ (ج) صَواريخ	missile, rocket
بُنْدُقيّة (ج) بَنادِق	rifle, gun	لُغْم (ج) ألْغام أرْضيّة	landmine
مُسَدَّس (ج) -ات	pistol, revolver	قَذيفة (ج) قَذائِف	missile
رَصاصة (ج) -ات	bullet	سَيّارة مُفَخَّخة	car bomb
رَصاص مَطّاطي	rubber bullets	غَوّاصة (ج) -ات	submarine
سَيْف (ج) سُيوف	sword	سَفينة حَرْبيّة (ج) سُفُن حَرْبيّة	warship
مُتَفَجِّرات	explosives	طائِرة مُقاتِلة (ج) -ات	fighterplane
قُنْبُلة (ج) قَنابِل	bomb	طائِرة مِنْ دون طَيّار	drone

قُنْبُلة ذَرّيّة	atomic bomb	قاذِفة الصَّواريخ	rocket/missile launcher
قُنْبُلة ذَكِيّة	smart bomb	دَبّابة (ج) -ات	tank
قُنْبُلة مَوْقوتة	time bomb	حامِلة طائرات	aircraft carrier

الأشْخاص PEOPLE

عَسْكَريّ	military, martial	ضَحيّة (ج) ضَحايا	victim
جُنْدي (ج) جُنود	soldier, serviceman	شَهيد (ج) شُهَداء	martyr
الشُّرطة العَسْكَريّة	the military police	جَريح (ج) جَرْحى	injured person, wounded person
ضابِط (ج) ضُبّاط	officer	جُرْح (ج) جِراح	injury, wound
مَفَتِّش (ج) -ون	inspector, detective	قَتيل (ج) قَتْلى	killed, dead
قائِد (ج) قادة	commander	مَدَنيّ (ج) -ون	civilian
مُسَلَّح (ج) -ون	gunman	حَليف (ج) حُلفاء	ally
انْتِحاري (ج) -ون	suicide bomber	عَدُوّ (ج) أعْداء	enemy
خاطِف\مُخْتَطِف	kidnapper	أسير حَرْب (ج) أسْرى حَرْب	POW (prisoner of war)
خاطِف طائرات	hijacker		
رَهينة (ج) رَهائن	hostage	مُجْرِم حَرْب (ج) مُجْرِمو حَرْب	war criminal

---

<61> **كَما قالَتِ العَرَب ... As the Arabs say ...**

أصْدِقاؤك ثَلاثة: صَديقُك، وصَديقُ صَديقِك، وعَدُوُّ عَدُوِّك

Your friends are three: Your friend, your friend's friend, and your enemy's enemy.
Imam Ali

226

USEFUL VERBS

خَطَّطَ يُخَطِّط تَخْطِيط	to plan
شَنَّ يشُنَّ شَنَّ الحَرْب على	to wage war
شَنَّ يشُنَّ شَنَّ هُجومًا على	to launch an attack on
أَطْلَقَ يُطْلِق إطْلاق النَّار على	to fire on (so.)
اقْتَحَم يَقْتَحِم اقْتِحام	to assault
ضَرَب يَضْرِب ضَرْب	to hit, strike
اسْتَوْلى يَسْتَوْلي اسْتِيلاء على	to seize, to take control of
احْتَلَّ يَحْتَلّ احْتِلال	to occupy
حَرَّر يُحَرِّر تَحْرير	to liberate
قَتَل يَقْتُل قَتْل	to kill
قاتَل يُقاتِل قِتال	to fight
أطاح يَطوح إطاحة	to overthrow
انْدَلَع يَنْدَلِع انْدِلاع	to break out
أصاب يُصيب إصابة	to injure, wound
أُصيب يُصاب بـ	to be injured, wounded
هَزَم يَهْزِم هَزْم	to defeat
هَجَم يَهْجُم هُجوم عَلى	to attack
غزا يَغْزو غَزْو	to attack, invade
فَجَّر يُفَجِّر تَفْجير	to explode (v.t.) (1)
تَفَجَّرَ يَتَفَجَّر تَفَجُّر	to explode (v.i.) (2)
دَمَّرَ هَدَّم	to destroy

أَبادَ\أَفْنى	to annihilate
أَعْلَنَ الحَرْب	to declare war
قاوَمَ يُقاوِم مُقاوَمة	to resist
اِسْتَسْلَمَ يَسْتَسْلِم اِسْتِسْلام	to surrender (v.i)
اِنْسَحَبَ يَنْسَحِب اِنْسِحاب من	to withdraw (v.i)
حارَبَ يُحارِب مُحارَبة	to battle (against), combat, fight

الأَمْن والاِسْتِخْبارات Security and intelligence

مُخابَرات	intelligence/secret service (organization)
اِسْتِخْبارات	intelligence (information)
مَصْدَر اِسْتِخْباراتي	intelligence source
اِسْتِخْبارات الاتِّصالات	communication intelligence
جاسوسيّة	espionage
جاسوس (ج) جَواسيس	spy
عَميل (ج) عُمَلاء	agent
إجْراءات أَمْنيّة مُشَدَّدة	heightened security measures
أمان	safety
الأَمْن العالَميّ\الدُّوَليّ	global security
أَمْن داخِليّ	internal security
قُوّات الأَمْن	security forces
إجْراءات أَمْنيّة	security measures
تَصْريح أَمْنيّ	security clearance

حَصانة دِبْلوماسيّة	diplomatic immunity
أمْن قَوْميّ	national security
سريّة	confidentiality
مهمة (ج) -ات	mission, assignment
سِرّيّ للغايّة	top secret
عَمَليّة سِرّيّة	covert operation
تَسْريب مَعْلومات	leak of information
وَثائِق مُصَنَّفة/سِرّيّة	classified documents
شُرْطة الحُدود	border police
رِقابة الجُمْرُك	customs control
قائِمة مُراقَبة	watch list

As the Arabs say ... كَما قالَتِ العَرَب

إنْ كانَ بَيْني وَبَيْنَ النّاس شَعْرَة

لَما قُطِعَت. إذا أَرْخوا شَدَدْت، وَإنْ شَدّوا أَرْخَيْت

Should there be but one hair between me and the others, I would not have it cut: for if they slacken it I would pull, and if they pull I would slacken it some.
Arabic quote (Muawiya)

17 Media

الإعْلام

In this unit, you will learn essential vocabulary, organized as follows:

- **Media** الإعْلام
  - ▷ Core vocabulary
  - ▷ *Print media and the press* الإعْلام المَكْتوب والصَّحافة
  - ▷ *Visual media* الإعْلام المَرْئِيّ
  - ▷ *Audio media* الإعْلام المَسْموع
  - ▷ *Multimedia* الإعْلام المُتَعَدِّد الوَسائط
  - ▷ *Digital and social media* الإعْلام الرَّقْميّ والإجْتِماعيّ
  - ▷ *People* الأشْخاص
  - ▷ *News items* الأخْبار
  - ▷ How frequent?
  - ▷ Useful verbs and nouns

الإعْلام Media

CORE VOCABULARY

وَسائِل الإعْلام	the media
اتِّصال (ج) -ات	communication
شَبَكة (ج) -ات	network
شَبَكة أخْبار	news network
وكالة أنْباء	news agency

231

PRINT MEDIA AND THE PRESS الإعْلام المَكْتوب والصِّحافة

جَريدة (ج) جَرائد	newspaper (1)	طَبَع يَطْبَع طَبْع	to print
صَحيفة (ج) صُحُف	newspaper (2)	نَشَر يَنْشُر نَشْر	to publish
مَجَلّة (ج) -ات	magazine, journal	الصِّحافة	the press, journalism
حَدَث (ج) أحداث	incident, event	وكالة صَحَفيّة	press agency
سلسلة أحْداث	chain of events	مُؤْتَمَر صَحَفيّ	press conference
الرَّأي العامّ	public opinion	حَمْلة صَحَفيّة	press campaign
رَقابة	censorship	تَحْقيق صَحَفيّ	reportage (1)
حُقوق النَّشْر والطَّبْع	copyright	ريبورتاج\روبورتاج	reportage (2)
عَدَم كَشْف الهُويّة	anonymity	بَيان صَحَفيّ	press release, statement
مَصادِر مَوْثوق بها	reliable sources	خَبَر (ج) أخْبار	a piece of news
مَصادِر مُطَّلِعة	informed source	الأخْبار	the news
مَصادِر مُقَرَّبة من	sources close to	أخْبار مَحَلّيّة	local news
دار النَّشْر	publishing house	أخْبار جارية\حالية	current affairs
مَطْبَعة (ج) مَطابِع	printing press	أخْبار دُوَليّة	international news
كشْك (ج) أكْشاك		واقِعة (ج) -ات	incident, happening
الجَرائد	news-stand		

VISUAL MEDIA الإعْلام المَرْئيّ

صورة (ج) صُوَر	picture, photograph
صورة رَقْميّة	digital photo
تَصْوير	photography
صَوَّر يُصَوِّر تَصْوير	to take a photo, record a film
مَرْئيّ\بَصَريّ\صُوَرِيّ	visual
كاميرا (ج) -ت	camera

كاريكاتير\كاريكاتور	caricature, cartoon
جرافيتي\خَرْبَشات	graffiti
لافتة (ج) -ات	poster
مَنْشور (ج) -ات	leaflets, handouts
مُلْصَقات\الوّحات إعْلانيّة	advertising signboards
إعْلانات الحافلات\التّاكسيات	bus/taxi advertising

الإعْلام المَسْموع AUDIO MEDIA

إذاعة (ج) -ات	broadcast	سَمِعَ يَسْمَعَ سَماع	to hear
راديو (ج) راديوهات	radio (1)	اسْتَمَعَ يَسْتَمِعِ اسْتِماع إلى	to listen
مِذْياع	radio (2)	سَجِّل يُسَجِّل تَسْجيل	to record
		أذاع يُذيع إذاعة	to broadcast

● INSIGHT

مِذْياع is an Arabized version of the word راديو, but it is less commonly used for *radio* in day-to-day communication.

مَحَطّة إذاعيّة	radio station
بَرْنامَج إذاعيّ	radio programme
بَثّ إذاعيّ	radio broadcast
تَرَدُّد	frequency
خُطْبة (ج) خُطَب	sermon (religious)
مُحاضَرة (ج) -ات	lecture, seminar
كِتاب مَسْموع	audiobook
تَسْجيل صَوْتيّ	audio recording
تَسْجيل مُباشِر	live broadcast, recording

الإِعْلام المُتَعَدِّد الوَسائط MULTIMEDIA

شاهَد يُشاهِد مُشاهَدة	to watch
عَرَض يَعْرِض عَرْض	to show
وَسائط سَمْعيّة وَبَصَريّة	audio-visual media
سينما	cinema
تليفزيون (ج) -ات	television
تلفاز	television
قَناة (ج) قَنَوات	channel (TV)
قَناة فَضائيّة	satellite channel
فَضائيات	satellite channels
تَغْطية	TV coverage
تَغْطية تلفزيونيّة	television coverage
بَرْنامَج (ج) بَرامِج	programme
فيديو (ج) فيديوهات	video
مَقْطَع فيديو (ج) مَقاطِع فيديو	video clip
فيلم (ج) أفلام	film
مُسَلْسَل (ج) -ات	TV show, series
حَلْقة (ج) -ات	episode
مُسابَقة (ج) -ات	quiz
نَشْرة أحْوال الطَّقْس	weather forecast (1)
نَشْرة جَوِّيّة	weather forecast (2)

الإِعْلام الرَّقْميّ والإِجْتِماعيّ DIGITAL AND SOCIAL MEDIA

● INSIGHT

الشّابكة is a new terminology coined by the Arabic Language Academy (مجمع اللغة العربيّة بدمشق) in Damascus, Syria, in an attempt to Arabize the term Internet.

الشّابِكة\الإنْتِرْنِت\الشّبَكة	the Internet
الشّبَكة العالَمِيّة العَنْكبوتيّة	World Wide Web (WWW)
مُدَوّنة (ج) -ات	blog
تَدْوين	blogging
مُدَوّن (ج) -ون	blogger
مُدَوّنة صَوْتيّة	podcast
تَدْوين صَوْتيّ	podcasting
مُدَوّنة صوريّة	photoblog
مُشارَكة الصُّوَر على الإنْتِرْنِت	online photo sharing
مُنْتَدى للمُناقَشة	discussion forum (1)
مُنْتَدى للدردشة	discussion forum (2)
مُنْتَدى للحِوار	discussion forum (3)
تَدْوين	micro-blogging
إعْلانات الإنْتِرْنِت	online advertising
تلفزيون رَقْميّ	digital TV
الإنْتِرْنِت الاجْتِماعيّ	the social web
إعْلام اجْتِماعيّ	social media
تَفاعُل اجْتِماعيّ عَبْرَ الإنْتِرْنِت	online social interaction
شَبَكة اجْتِماعيّة	social network
شَبَكات التَّواصُل الاجْتِماعيّ	social media network
تَواصُل\تَشْبيك اجْتِماعيّ	social networking
مُجْتَمَع إلِكْترونيّ	online community
تَحْديث الحالة الشَخْصِيّة	status update
أعْجَبَني	I like (Facebook™)
تابِعونا عَلى الفيْسْبوك	follow us on Facebook™
مُتابَعة	follow (so.)
كَلِمة مِفْتاحيّة (ج) كَلِمات مِفْتاحيّة هاشتاغ #	# hashtag

الأشخاص PEOPLE

صَحَفيّ (ج) -ون	journalist
مُحَرِّر (ج) -ون	editor
رئيس تَحْرير	chief editor
مُصَوِّر (ج) -ون	photographer
مُذيع (ج) -ون	broadcaster
مُعَلِّق (ج) -ون	commentator
مُراسِل (ج) -ون	correspondent
كاتب عَمود (ج) كُتّاب أعْمدة	columnist
مُراسِل خَاصّ	special correspondent

مُراسِل حَرْبيّ	war correspondent
مُراسِل رِياضيّ	sports correspondent
مُقابِل (ج) -ون	interviewer
ناقد (ج) -ون انُقّاد	critic
مُقَدِّم (ج) -ون	presenter
ناشر (ج) -ون	publisher
قارِئ أخْبار	newsreader
مُشاهِد (ج) -ون	viewer

الأخْبار NEWS ITEMS

نَشْرة (ج) -ات	publication, broadcast, leaflet
نَشْرة أخْباريّة	newscast
مَنْشور رَسْميّ	official publication, bulletin
الصَّفْحة الرئيسيّة	front page
مَقالة (ج) -ات	article
عَدَد (ج) أعْداد	issue
إصْدار	version
افتتاحيّة (ج) -ات	editorial
عُنْوان (ج) عَناوين	title/headline
عَمود (ج) أعْمدة	column
الوَفَيات	obituaries

أخْبار عاجِلة	breaking news (3
بعد قَليل	coming up
بعد الفاصِل	after the break
برعاية	sponsored by
بَيان (ج) -ات	statement
إعْلان (ج) -ات	statement, declaration, announcemer
تَحْليل (ج) -ات	analysis
سِياق	context
نطاق (ج) نُطُق	scope
تَعْليق (ج) -ات	commentary
بدون تَعْليق	no comment

236

كَلِمات مُتَقاطِعة	crosswords	تَقْرير (ج) تَقارير	report
تَرويج	promotion	مُقابَلة (ج) -ات	interview
إعْلان (ج) -ات	advertisement, announcement	مَوْضوع (ج) مَواضيع	topic
إعْلانات مُبَوَّبة	classified ads	مَسألة (ج) مَسائل	issue
موجَز	summary	مُشْكلة (ج) مَشاكل	problem
خَطأ مَطْبَعيّ	misprint	قَضيّة (ج) قَضايا	case, issue
على الهَواء	on the air	طَريقة (ج) طُرُق	means, way (lit. path)
مُباشِر	live, direct (1)	سَبيل (ج) سُبُل	way
بَثّ حَيّ	live (2)	جَدْوَل أعْمال	agenda
أخْبار عاجِلة	breaking news (1)	ميثاق (ج) مَواثيق	charter
عاجِل	breaking news (lit. urgent) (2)		

HOW FREQUENT?

يَوْميّ	daily
صَباحيّ	morning
مَسائيّ	evening
أسْبوعيّ	weekly
شَهْريّ	monthly
نِصْف شَهْريّ	bi-monthly
فَصْليّ	quarterly
مَوْسِميّ	periodically
سَنَويّ	yearly
نِصْف سَنَويّ	bi-yearly

USEFUL VERBS AND NOUNS

أفاد يُفيد إفادة	to report
قال يَقول قَوْل	to say
أكَّد يُؤَكِّد تأكيد	to confirm

ذَكَر يَذْكُر ذِكْر	to mention
أَشار يُشير إِشارة إلى	to indicate
سَأَل يَسْأَل سُؤَال	to ask
رَدَّ يَرُدُّ رَدّ	to respond
دعا يَدْعو دَعْوة	to invite, call for
أَعْلَن يُعْلِن إِعْلان	to announce
اِعْتَرَف يَعْتَرِف اِعْتِراف	to acknowledge, recognize
اِعْتَبَر يَعْتَبِر اِعْتِبار	to consider, regard
أَوْضَح يُوَضِّح إِيضاح	to clarify (1)
وَضَّح يُوَضِّح تَوْضيح	to clarify (2)
نَقَل يَنْقُل نَقْل	to quote
عَبَّر يُعَبِّر تَعْبير	to express (1)
أَعْرَب يُعْرِب إِعْراب	to express (2)
حَذَّر يُحَذِّر تَحْذير	to warn
ناقَش يُناقِش نِقاش\مُناقَشة	to debate
حادَث يُحادِث مُحادَثة	to discuss

Science, technology and communication

العُلوم والتِّكْنولوجيا وَالاتِّصالات

In this unit you will learn essential vocabulary, organized as follows:

Science and technology العُلوم والتِّكْنولوجيا
▷ *Core vocabulary*
▷ *Computers and gadgets* الكُمْبْيوتِر والآلات

Information and communication technology (ICT)

تِكْنولوجيا المَعْلومات وَالاتّصالات
▷ *The Internet* الإِنْتِرْنِت
▷ *Searching and browsing* البَحْث والتَصَفُّح
▷ *Searching the Internet* البَحْث والتَصَفُّح في الإِنْتِرْنِت

Online communication and social networking

التَواصُل الاجتماعي على الإِنترنت
▷ *Email communication* التَواصُل بالبَريد الإِلِكْتْرونيّ
▷ *Instant messaging* المُراسَلة الفَوْرِيّة
▷ *Social networking* التَواصُل الاِجْتِماعيّ
▷ *Blogging* التَدْوين
▷ *Text processing and file management*
تَحْرير النُصوص وَإدارة المِلَفّات
▷ *My digital identity* هُوِيَّتي الرَقْميّة

239

Science and technology العُلوم والتِّكْنولوجيا

CORE VOCABULARY

عِلْم (ج) عُلوم	science	بَحْث عِلْميّ	scientific research
تِكْنولوجيا	technology	اِرْتِياد الفَضاء	space exploration
تَجْرِبة (ج) تَجارِب	experiment, trial	قَمَر اصْطِناعيّ	satellite
تِكْنولوجيا رَقْميّة	digital technology	رائِد (ج) رُوّاد	pioneer
رائِد فَضاء	astronaut	طِفْل أنابيب	a test-tube baby
اِتِّصالات الأَقْمار الصِّناعيّة	satellite communication	القَرْية العالَميّة	global village
تِكْنولوجيا النّانو	nanotechnology	الطّاقة المُتَجَدِّدة	renewable energy
تِكْنولوجيا حَيَويّة	biotechnology	الطّاقة الشَّمْسيّة	solar energy
ذَكاء اِصْطِناعيّ	artificial intelligence (AI)	الطّاقة النَّوَويّة	nuclear energy
		الطّاقة الحَيَويّة	bioenergy
الحِمْض النَّوَويّ	DNA	مَواد خام	raw materials
جين (ج) -ات	gene	خَطَر نَوَويّ	nuclear risk
عِلْم الوِراثة	genetics	نَشاط إِشْعاعيّ	radioactivity
هَنْدَسة وِراثيّة	genetic engineering	اِنْبِعاثات	emissions
اِسْتِنْساخ	cloning	تَدْوير النُّفايات	recycling
أُنْبوب اِخْتِبار	a test tube	عُضْويّ	organic

● INSIGHT – YOU ALREADY SPEAK ARABIC!

Algorithm is an Anglicized form of the surname of a well-known Muslim mathematician known by the name of Muhammad al-Khwarizmi (الخوارِزْمي) who pioneered sophisticated mathematics, including algebra. Algorithm is a term currently used in computer science and many other related fields.

الكُمْبْيوتِر والآلات COMPUTERS AND GADGETS

computer hardware	عَتاد الحاسوب
computer (1)	حاسوب (ج) حَواسيب
computer (2)	كُمْبْيوتِر (ج) -ات
personal computer	حاسوب شَخْصيّ (ج) حَواسيب شَخْصيّة
desktop computer	حاسوب المَكْتَب
notebook	حاسوب دَفْتَريّ
laptop	حاسوب مَحْمول
portable PC	حاسوب نَقّال\حاسوب
netbook	حاسوب لِتَصَفُّح الإنْتَرْنِت
tablet PC	حاسوب لَوْحيّ
mouse (computer)	فَأْرة حاسوب
keyboard	لَوْحة مَفاتيح
digital versatile disc (DVD)	قُرْص رَقْميّ (ج) أَقْراص رَقْميّة
memory (computer)	ذاكِرة حاسوب
printer	طابِعة (ج) -ات
scanner	ماسِح ضَوْئيّ

virtual keyboard	لَوْحة مَفاتيح افْتِراضيّة
key	زِرّ (ج) أَزْرار
screen	شاشة (ج) -ات
touchscreen	شاشة لَمْس
digital pen	قَلَم رَقْميّ
touchpad	لَوْحة لَمْسيّة
speakers	سَمّاعات
hard disk	وَسيط تَخْزين (ج) وَسائِط تَخْزين
compact disc (CD) (1)	قُرْص جامِد (ج) أَقْراص جامِدة
compact disc (CD) (2)	أُسْطُوانة مَضْغوطة
compact disc – read-only memory (CD-ROM)	قُرْص مُدْمَج\ق. م
webcam	كاميرا الإنْتَرْنِت
microphone	ميكروفون\لاقِط الصَّوت\مكبر صوت
plug and play (PnP)	رَكِّب وَشَغِّل
wireless	لاسِلْكيّ

تِكْنولوجيا المَعْلومات وَالاتِّصالات ICT

الإِنْتِرْنِت THE INTERNET

الإِنْتِرْنِت	the Internet (1)
الشّابِكة	the Internet (2)
النِّت	the Internet (3) (coll.)
الويب	the web
شَبَكة الإِنْتِرْنِت العالَميّة	World Wide Web (WWW) (1)
الشّبَكة العَنْكَبوتيّة العالَميّة	World Wide Web (WWW) (2)
تِكْنولوجيا المَعْلومات وَالاتِّصالات	information and communication technology (ICT)
عَصْر المَعْلوماتيّة	information age
مُجْتَمَع المَعْرِفة	knowledge society
مُجْتَمَع المَعْلومات	information society
الوَعْي الرَقْميّ\المَعْلوماتيّ	digital literacy
الفَجْوة الإِلِكْتْرونيّة\الرَقْميّة	the digital divide
العَصْر الرَقْميّ	the digital age
فَضاء مَعْلوماتيّ	cyberspace
نادي الإِنْترنت	cyber café
مَوْقِع (ج) مَواقِع	website, site
شَبَكة (ج) -ات	network
شَبَكة رَقْميّة	digital network
اتَّصَل يتصل اتصال	to connect (online)
بَرْمَجَ يُبَرْمِجُ بَرْمَجة	to program
بَرْنامَج حاسوب (ج) بَرامِج حاسوب	software, program
تَطْبيق (ج) -ات	app/applet
تَطْبيق الويب (ج) -ات الويب	web application

نِظام تَشْغيل (ج) أَنْظِمة تَشْغيل	operating system
حَدَّث يُحَدِّث تحديث	to upgrade/to update (system or software)
خَزَّن يُخَزِّن تَخْزين عَلى الإنْتِرْنِت	to store (web)
خادِم\خادوم	server
مُعْطِيات\بَيانات	data
مَعْلومة (ج) -ات	information
حَمَّل	to upload (file)
تَحْميل	uploading (UL)
نَزَّل	to download (file)
تَنْزيل	downloading (DL)
نَصَّب\ثَبَّت	to install
تَثْبيت\تَنْصيب	installation
شَغَّل\حَمَّل	to load (software)
تَشْغيل\تَحْميل	loading
رَقَّم	to digitize
تَرْقيم\رَقْمَنة	digitization/digitalization
رَقْميّ	digital
رُخْصة المَشاع الإبْداعيّ	Creative Commons (CC) licence
مُمْتَلَكات رَقْميّة	digital rights
حُقوق رَقْميّة	digital asset management (DAM)
آداب وأخْلاق الإنْتِرْنِت	netiquette (net etiquette)

البَحْث والتَصَفُّح SEARCHING AND BROWSING

تَجَوَّل	to surf/to navigate (the Internet)	لَوْحة القِيادة	dashboard	
تَجَوُّل	web surfing	خِيارات	options	
الصَفْحة الرَئيسة	homepage (1)	خاصّيّة (ج) خَصائِص	properties/specifications	

الصَّفْحة الأُم	homepage (2)	مُواصَفات	settings
المَدْخَل	homepage (3)	الإعْدادات	tools
اتِّفاقيّة خِدْمة المَوْقِع	terms of use (of site)	واجهة الاسْتِخْدام	graphical user interface (GUI)
شُروط الاسْتِخْدام	conditions of use	خَريطة المَوْقِع	site map
جَميع الحُقوق مَحْفوظة	all rights reserved	آخِر التَّحْديثات	latest additions/ updates
مَرْكَز المُساعَدة	help centre		
الدَّعْم الفَنّي	technical help/ support	نافذة (ج) نَوافِذ	window
		صَفْحة (ج) صَفَحات	page
اسْتِكْشاف الأَخْطاء وَإصْلاحها	troubleshooting		
قائمة (ج) قَوائم	menu	عَلامة تَبْويب	tab
لَوْحة التَّحَكُّم	control panel	أَيْقونة (ج) -ات	icon
مَجال (ج) -ات	domain (web)	إخْتِصار (ج) - ات	shortcut
على الشَّبَكة\مُتَّصِل	online	لِلأَعْلى	skip to top/ back to top
خارج الشَّبْكة\غَيْر مُتَّصِل	offline	المَزيد ...	more ... (content)
		أَقَلّ ...	less ... (content)
عالية الوُضوح	HD (high definition)	تابِع القِراءة	continue reading
مُوافِق	OK	اسْحَب واسْقِط	drag and dro
تَمَّ	done	رابِط (ج) رَوابِط	link (1)
اذْهَب	go	وُصْلة (ج) -ات	link (2)
اسْتِبْعاد	dismiss	ارْتِباط مُتَشَعِّب	hyperlink
تابِع\مُتابَعة	continue/proceed	حفَظ يحْفَظ حِفْظ	to save
السَّابِقة\رُجوع	back	ضَغَطَ يَضْغَط ضَغْط	to click (1)
التالية	next	كَبَس يَكْبِس كَبْس	to click (2)
أَعْلى	top		

نَقْرة (ج) نَقَرات	click	جاري التَّنزيل	downloading
اضْغَطواسْحَب	click and drag	جاري التَّثبيت	installing
ضَرْبة (ج) ضَرَبات	hit (web)	جاري الإرْسال	sending
اقْتراحات وَمُلاحَظات	feedback and suggestions	خِدْمة التَّلقيم	RSS service
يُرجى الانْتظار	please wait	المَقالات\المَواضيع	the articles/ the topics
يُرجى المُحاوَلة مَرّة أخرى	please try again	الأَكْثَر قراءة	most read
		الأَكْثَر تَصَفُّحًا	most browsed
قَيْدَ الإنْتظار\في الإنْتظار	waiting	الأَكْثَر شَعْبيّة	most popular
		الأَكْثَر تَفْضيلاً	most favoured/ bookmarked
جاري الاتِّصال	connecting		
جاري التَحْميل	loading		

البَحْث والتَصَفُّح في الإنْترْنِت SEARCHING THE INTERNET

بَحَث يَبْحَث بَحْث	to search
اسْتِخْدام مُحَرِّك البَحْث جوجْل\غوغْل	to Google, Googling
الباحوث	web search engine (1)
مُحَرِّك البَحْث (ج) -ات البَحْث	web search engine (2)
دَليل البَحْث (ج) دلائل البَحْث	web search engine (3)
عَلامة مَرْجعيّة	bookmark
كَلِمات مِفْتاحيّة\أَساسيّة	keywords

أُعْلومة (ج) -ات	tag (1)
وَسْم (ج) وُسوم	tag (2)
تَوْسيم	tagging
تَصْنيف (ج) -ات	category
أَرْشيف (ج) -ات	archive
أَرْشَفة	archiving
نَتائِج البَحْث	search results
تَفْضيلات\خيارات البَحْث	preferences (search)
تَرْتيب حَسَبَ: الصِلة	sort by: relevance
تَرْتيب حَسَبَ: الثَمَن من أَعْلى إلى أَقَلَّ	sort by: price high to low
تَرْتيب حَسَبَ: الثَمَن من أَقَلَّ إلى أَعْلى	sort by: price low to high
تَرْتيب حَسَبَ: الشَعْبيّة	sort by: popularity

Online communication and social networking التواصل الاجتماعي على الإنترنت

EMAIL COMMUNICATION التَّواصُل بالبَريد الإلِكْترونيّ

بَريد مُزْعِج	spam/junk email (2)	بَريد إلِكْترونيّ	email (electronic mail)
تَمْرير	forward	عُنْوان بَريد إلِكْترونيّ	email address
رَدّ	reply	رِسالة إلِكْترونيّة	email message
رَدّ عَلى الجَميع	reply to all	مُرْسِل (ج) -ون	sender
إرْسال	send	مُرْسَل إلَيْه\مُرْسَل إلَيْهِم	recipient
		سُخام	spam/junk email (1)

INSTANT MESSAGING المُراسَلة الفَوْريّة

مُراسَلة فَوْريّة	instant messaging (IM) (1)
حِوار مُباشِر	instant messaging (IM) (2)

دَرْدَشة إنْترْنِت	chat (1)
خَاطَب/دَرْدَش	to chat
نِقاش حَيّ	chat (2)
شات	chat (3) (coll.)
عامِّية الإنْترْنِت	chatspeak
أَخْلاقِيات دَرْدَشة الإنْترْنِت	chatiquette (chat etiquette)
صاح يَصيح صِياح	to shout (using capital letters)
تَعْبيرات انْفِعالِيّة	emoticons
غُرْفة دَرْدَشة (ج) غُرَف دَرْدَشة	chatroom
الحِوار المُباشِر في الوَقْت الفِعْليّ	real-time chat
قائِمة الأَصْدِقاء	buddy list
صَديق دَرْدَشة	penpal/keypal

التَّواصُل الاجْتِماعيّ ●CIAL NETWORKING

مَوْقِع تَواصُل اجْتِماعيّ	social networking site (SNS)
مَوْقِع تَشْبيك اجْتِماعيّ	social networking site (SNS) (2)
مَوْقِع مَشاهير	celebrity site
شَخْصِيّة الإنْترْنِت (ج) -ات الإنْترْنِت	Internet personality
مَشْهور الإنْترْنِت (ج) مَشاهير الإنْترْنِت	Internet/web celebrity
مَشْهور اجْتِماعيّ (ج) مشاهير اجْتِماعيّ	social celebrity (social networks)
مُنْتَدى إنْترْنِت/مُنْتَدَيات إنْترْنِت	Internet forum, message board

التَّدْوين ●OGGING

مُدَوَّنة (ج) -ات	blog (weblog)	مُدَوَّنة فيدْيو	vlog (video blog)
دَوَّن يدوّن تدوي	to blog	مُدَوَّنة صَوْتِيّة	podcast (audioblog)

مُدَوِّن (ج) - ون	blogger	مُدَوَّنة صُوَرِيّة	phlog (photoblog)
تَدْوينة (ج) -ات	blog post	تَعْليق (ج) -ات	comment
مُدَوَّنة مُصَغَّرة	micro-blog	مُشارِك (ج) - ون	subscriber (blog)
تَدْوين مُصَغَّر	micro-blogging	مُتابِع (ج) - ون	follower (blog)
تَدْوين الضُيوف	guest blogging		

TEXT PROCESSING AND FILE MANAGEMENT
تَحْرير النُصوص وَإدارة المِلفّات

حَرَّرَ يُحَرِّر تَحْرير	to edit (text) (1)	قاعدة بَيانات	database
عَدَّلَ يُعَدِّل تَعْديل	to edit (text) (2)	نَسَخَ يَنْسَخ نَسْخ	to copy (e.g. text)
مُحَرِّر نُصوص	text editor	لَصَقَ يَلْصِق لَصْق	to paste
وَثيقة (ج) وَثائق	document	قَصَّ يقُصّ قَصّ	to cut
مُجَلَّد (ج) -ات	folder	حَذَفَ يَحْذِف حَذْف	to delete
مِلَفّ (ج) -ات	file	خَطّ (ج) خُطوط	font
حَجْم (ج) أحْجام	size	تَدْقيق إمْلائيّ وَنَحْويّ	spelling and grammar
وَثيقة وورْد	word document		
جَدْوَل مُمْتَدّ (ج) جَداوِل مُمْتَدّة	spreadsheet		
عُروض تَقْديميّة	presentations		

MY DIGITAL IDENTITY هُويَّتي الرَقْميّة

ظِلّ رَقْميّ	digital footprint/cyber shadow/digital shadow
بَصْمة رَقْميّة	Internet identity/Internet persona
مُواطِن الإنْتِرنِت	netizen (net citizen)
مُواطِن أَصْليّ رَقْميّ	digital native

مُهاجِر رَقْميّ	digital immigrant
جيل الإنْتِرْنِت	net generation
مَرْهوب مِن التِكْنولوجيا	technophobe
مَهْووس بالتِكْنولوجيا\جيل	technogeek
مُدْمِن الإنْتِرْنِت	Internet addict/mouse potato
إدْمان الإنْتِرْنِت	Internet addiction disorder (IAD)
حِسابي	my account
اسْم المُسْتَخْدِم	username
كَلِمة المُرور\كَلِمة السِّرّ	password
هُويّة صُوَريّة	photo identity (ID)
صَفْحة شَخْصيّة	personal profile
مُفَضّلاتي	my favourites
انْضِمام\انْخِراط	join
تَسْجيل	sign up/register
دُخول\تَسْجيل الدُخول	log in/sign in
خُروج\تَسْجيل الخُروج	log out/log off/sign out
اشْتِراك\مُشارَكة	subscription
مُشْتَرِك (ج) - ون	subscriber
فَعّل يُفَعِّل تَفْعيل	to activate (e.g. account)

19 Languages and spoken Arabic

اللُّغات والعَرَبيّة المَحْكيّة

In this unit you will learn essential vocabulary, organized as follows:

اللُّغات *Languages*

▷ Core vocabulary

▷ World languages لغات العالم

▷ Language varieties of Arabic تَنَوُّعات اللُّغة العَرَبيّة

Essential dialect words المُفْردات الأساسيّة في اللَّهَجات العَرَبيّة

▷ Commonly used expressions for everyday use

عبارات شائعة للمُحادَثة اليَوْميّة

Religious expressions العِبارات الدّينيّة

Languages اللُّغات

CORE VOCABULARY

لُغة (ج) -ات	language	اللُّغة العَرَبيّة	Arabic language
حَرْف (ج) حُروف	letter	لُغة الضّاد	Arabic language (lit. language of the phoneme ض)
كَلِمة (ج) -ات	word	إزْدواجيّة لُغَويّة	diglossia
جُمْلة (ج) جُمَل	sentence	اللِّسان	
سَطْر (ج) أَسْطُر	line	ثُنائيّة لُغَويّة	bilingualism

251

عِبارة (ج) -ات	expression	فَصاحة	eloquence, fluency, purity of language
فَقْرة (ج) -ات	paragraph		
نَصّ (ج) نُصوص	text	فَصيح (ج) فُصَحاء	eloquent, clear, standard
مُفْرَدة (ج) -ات	vocabulary	عامِّيّة\دارِجة\اللَّهْجة	dialect, colloquial language, spoken language
مُرادِف (ج) -ات	synonym		
قاعِدة (ج) قَواعِد	rule/grammar	عَرَّبَ يُعَرِّب تَعْريب	to Arabize
النَّحو والقَواعِد	grammar	عامِّية الإنْتِرْنِت	Internet slang
طَلاقة	fluency	لُغة دَرْدَشة الإنْتِرْنِت	weblish, netspeak
نَبْرة	intonation	تَكَلَّم يتَكَلَّم تَكَلُّم	to talk, speak
تَشْديد	stress	تَحَدَّث يَتَحَدَّث تَحَدُّث	to speak (two or more people)
مَعْنى (ج) مَعانٍ\المَعاني	meaning		

WORLD LANGUAGES لغات العالم

العَرَبيّة	Arabic	اليابانيّة	Japanese
الهولَنْديّة	Dutch	المانْدرين الصينيّة	Mandarin Chinese
الإنْجْليزيّة	English	الفارِسيّة	Persian/Farsi
الفَرْنسيّة	French	البُرْتُغاليّة	Portuguese
الأَلْمانيّة	German	الروسيّة	Russian
اليونانيّة	Greek	الإسْبانيّة	Spanish
العِبْريّة	Hebrew	التُرْكيّة	Turkish
الهِنْديّة	Hindi	الأُرْديّة	Urdu
الإيطاليّة	Italian		

تَنَوُّعات اللُّغة العَرَبِيّة LANGUAGE VARIETIES OF ARABIC

(الفُصْحى العَرَبِيّة اللُّغة)	Modern Standard Arabic (MSA) (lit. the most eloquent language)
اللَّهْجة\الدّارِجة\العامِّيّة العَرَبِيّة	Colloquial Arabic (CA)
العَرَبِيّة التُّراثِيّة\القُرآنِيّة	Classical/Qur'anic Arabic
اللُّغة العَرَبِيّة للنّاطِقين بغَيْرِها	Arabic for non-Arab speakers
عامِّيّة المُثَقَّفين	educated spoken Arabic
عَرَبيزي	Arabizi, Aralish, Arabish
عَرَبِيّة الإنْتِرْنِت	Arabic chat alphabet, Arabic chat speak

A number of linguistic varieties and dialects in Arabic are currently spoken within the Arab world and they are spread out across North Africa, the Levant and the Gulf. There are six regional dialect groups:

(اللَّهْجة المَغارِبِية) North African dialect group			
اللَّهْجة المَغْرِبِيّة	Moroccan dialect	اللَّهْجة التونِسِيّة	Tunisian dialect
اللَّهْجة الجَزائرِيّة	Algerian dialect	اللَّهْجة الصِقِلِيّة العَرَبِيّة	Sicilian Arabic dialect (extinct)
اللَّهْجة الليبِيّة	Libyan dialect	اللَّهْجة المالْطِيّة	Maltese dialect

(اللَّهْجة الشامِيّة) Levantine dialect group			
اللَّهْجة اللُّبْنانِيّة	Lebanese dialect	اللَّهْجة الفِلَسْطينِيّة	Palestinian dialect
اللَّهْجة السّورِيّة	Syrian dialect	اللَّهْجة الأُرْدُنِيّة	Jordanian dialect

(اللَّهْجة الخَليجِيّة) Gulf dialect group			
اللَّهْجة الإماراتِيّة	Emirati dialect	اللَّهْجة الكويْتِيّة	Kuwaiti dialect
اللَّهْجة البَحْرينِيّة	Bahraini dialect	اللَّهْجة الحِجازِيّة\ السَّعودِيّة	Hejazi/Saudi dialect

اللَّهْجة القَطَريّة	Qatari dialect	اللَّهْجة اليَمَنيّة	Yemeni dialect
		اللَّهْجة العُمانيّة	Omani dialect

(اللَّهْجة السودانيّة) Sudanese group

اللَّهْجة السودانيّة	Sudanese Arabic	لَهْجة جوبا	Juba Arabic
اللَّهْجة التْشاديّة	Chadian Arabic		

(اللَّهْجة المِصْريّة) Egyptian group

اللَّهْجة المِصْريّة	Egyptian dialect	اللَّهْجة الصَّعيدية	Sa'idi Arabic

(اللَّهْجة العِراقيّة) Iraqi dialect group

● INSIGHT – MALTESE ARABIC

Hawnekk Nitkellmu Bil-Malti. *Maltese is spoken here.*

You might not be aware of this but Maltese, the national language of Malta, is the only Semitic language derived from Arabic currently spoken in Europe and written in Roman script.

To an Arab ear, Maltese sounds very similar to Arabic! However, Maltese pronunciation and vocabulary have been influenced by many European languages. In fact, nearly half of the Maltese vocabulary is borrowed from Italian, Spanish, Norman-French and English.

Maltese is descended from Sicilian Arabic, which was developed in Sicily, and later in Malta, between the 9th and 12th centuries.

Here are some examples of Maltese words derived from Arabic:

le (لا)	no
merhba (مَرْحبا)	welcome
sahha (صَحّة)	goodbye
omm (أُمّ)	mother
dar (دار)	house
titkellem bl-Ingliz? (تِتْكَلَّم إِنْجْليزي؟)	Do you speak English?

ssential dialect words

مُفْردات أساسيّة في اللَّهَجات العَرَبيّة

he following is a list of the colloquial words and phrases commonly used by abs in day-to-day communication.

فُصْحى	عامّية	English
نَعَم	أَيْوَه	Yes
لا	لأ	No
ماذا	شو	Why
أَيْن	وين	Where (Lev.)
أَيْن	فين	Where (Egy.)
مَتى	اِمْتا	When
لِماذا	ليه	Why (Egy.)
لِماذا	ليش	Why (Lev.)
مَنْ	مين	Who
كَيْف	كيف	How (Lev.)
كَيْف	إزّاي	How (Egy.)

كَمْ	قَدِّيش	How much, how many (Lev.)
ما\ماذا	إيه	What (Egy.)
ما\ماذا	إيش\شو	What (Lev.)
لأن	عَشان	Because
فَقَط	بَس	Only
قَليلاً	شْوَيّ	Little
الآن	هَلأ\هَلَّق	Now (Lev.)
الآن	هَسّه\هَسَّع\هَسّاع	Now (Lev.)
الآن	دِلْوَقْتي	Now (Egy.)
لاحِقًا	بَعْدين	Later
أيْضًا	كَمان	More
يَكْفي	خَلاص	Enough
يَكْفي\كفاية	بِيكْفي	Enough
هذا	هادا	This
هذا	دَه	This (Egy.)
الذي\التي	اللّي	That (demonstrative pron.)
هَيّا بِنا	يلّا\يايا	Let's go
يوجَد	فيه	There is, there are
اليَوْم	اليوم	Today
البارِحة	امْبارَح	Yesterday
غَدًا	بُكْره	Tomorrow
لا بَأْس	مَعْلِش	It doesn't matter, never min
مِثْل	زَيّ	Like

256

صَحيح	صَحّ	Correct
خَطَأ	غَلَط	Wrong
تَمامًا	تَمام	Exactly
لابُدّ	لازِم	Must
هُنا	هون	Here
مِنْ هُنا	مِن هون	From here (Lev.)
مِنْ هُناك	مِنْ هُناك	From there
مَرْحَبًا	مَرْحَبا	Hello
عَفْوًا	عَفْوًا	You're welcome
شُكْرًا	شُكْرًا	Thank you
مُتَأَسِّف	آسِف	Sorry
عَنْ إذْنك	عَن إزْنك	Excuse me
جَميل	حِلْو	Beautiful
شَهِيّ\الَذيذ	زاكي	Delicious (Lev.)
شَهِيّ\الَذيذ	لَزيز	Delicious (Lev.)
سَعيد	مَبْسوط	Happy
نِصْف	نُصّ	Half
جَيِّد	مْنيح	Good (Lev.)
جَيِّد	كْوَيِّس	Good (Egy.)
سَلامَتُك	سَلامْتك	Get well soon
لَدَيَّ لَدَيْه لَدَيْها	عِنْدي عِنده عِنْدها	I have, he has, she has
نُقود\امال	فُلوس\مَصاري	Money (Lev.)
رَأى	شاف	to see

ذهب		راح	to go (Lev.)
يَفْعَل		سَوّي	to do
يُغْلِق		سَكَّر	to close
أُريد		بَدّي	I want (Lev.)
أَرْغَب في\أُريد		لازِمْني	I need (Lev.)
أُريد		عايِز	I need (Egy.)
س\سَوْف		راح	Future marker (Lev.)
س\سَوْف		حَ	Future marker (Egy.)

COMMONLY USED EXPRESSIONS FOR EVERYDAY USE

عِبارات شائِعة لِلمُحادَثة اليَوْمِيّة

فاهِم؟\فِهِمْت؟	Do you understand?
أنا مِشْ فاهِم!	I don't understand
ماعْرَفْشْ	I don't know!
ماشي	OK!
طَبْعًا	Of course, absolutely!
طَيِّب	OK, all right, fine!
شْوَي شْوَي	Bit by bit, slowly
اتْفَضّل\-ي	Please/go ahead/come in/please help yourself! (m./f.)
لَوْ سَمَحْت	Excuse me/If you please (to call attention)
لا مُؤاخْذة	Pardon me, excuse me! (if you bump into (so.))
أَكيد	Surely, definitely
أَيّ خِدْمة؟\شو تُؤَمَر؟	May I help you?
بَسيطة!	That's OK!

ثانِية واحْدة	One second!
حَقيقة\في الحَقيقة	In reality, actually
حَظّ سَعيد\بِالتَّوْفيق\مُوَفَّق	Good luck!
عَلى فِكْرة	By the way!
عَلى كُلِّ حال	Anyhow, anyway
عَنْ إِذْنك	With your permission! (when you excuse yourself before leaving)
لَحْظة مِنْ فَضْلك	One moment please!
ما فيه مانِع	That's all right! (lit. there is no objection)
ما فيه مُشْكِلة\مِشْ مُشْكِلة	Not a problem!
ما يِنْفَعْش	It's useless, it's not beneficial!
مَعَ الأَسَف\لِلأَسَف\لِلأَسَف الشَّديد	Unfortunately, regrettably
مَعْلِهْشْ	Never mind! Don't worry! It doesn't matter
مُسْتَحيل	It's impossible!
مُمْكِنْ\إذا مُمْكِنْ\يُمْكِنْ؟	Maybe, possible, May I..?
بِكُلِّ سُرور!	With pleasure!
مِشْ ضَروري	Not necessary!
مِشْ مُمْكِنْ	It's not possible!
هذا مِنْ لُطْفك	That's very kind of you!
مِشْ مُهِمّ	It's not important
يا سَلام	My goodness! Wow! (to express surprise)
عَنْ إِذْنك! (f) عَنْ إِذْنك! (m)	With your permission! (when you excuse yourself before leaving)
عَلى مَهْلَك!	Slowly! Take it easy! Slow down!
خَلِّي بالَك!	Be careful!

خَلاص!	Done, finished, enough
كِفايَة!	That's enough!
ثانِيَة واحْدَة!	One second!
إنْتَظِرْ\ي دَقيقَة!	Wait a minute!
بِسُرْعَة لَوْ سَمَحْت!	Quickly, if you please!
شوف!	Look!
إسْمَعْ!	Listen!
أشوفَك بَعْدين\بُكْرَة!	See you later/tomorrow!
أرْجوك!	I beg you!

Religious expressions العِبارات الدّينيّة

Arabs, in their day-to-day communication, are well known to use blessings, benedictions and statements of good will, which are like little prayers for good fortune intended to keep things going well.

Here are some of the most common expressions Arabs use in day-to-day conversations:

السَّلامُ عَلَيْكُم
May peace be upon you.
This is a typical and commonly used Islamic greeting, which can b the equivalent of *hello.*

وعَلَيْكُم السَّلام
Peace be upon you too.
Use in reply to the greeting **السَّلامُ عَلَيْكُم**

الحَمْدُ الله
Praise be to God.
Use when you wish to express satisfaction (e.g. after eating), wher someone sneezes or something good happens to someone.

إنْ شاءَ الله
God willing.
Use when you intend to do something in the future.

ما شاءَ الله
Whatever God wills (will come to pass) or it is as God willed.

سُبْحان الله
Glorious is God.
Use for praising God or exclaiming awe at his attributes, bounties or creation. It can also be used as a phrase of exclamation (i.e. Wow

وَاللّٰه وَاللّٰه العَظيم	*I swear to God, Honest to God!*
بِسْمِ اللّٰهِ	*In the name of God.* Use when starting an action (eating, drinking, driving, etc.).
اللّٰهُ أَعْلَمُ	*God only knows.* Use when uncertain about something.
اللّٰه مَعَك	*May God be with you.* Use when you wish safety for someone.
اللّٰهُ أَكْبَر	*God is great.* Use when someone receives good news.
اللّٰه يخَلّيك	
اللّٰه يخَلّيلَك أوْلادك	*May God protect you (and your children).* Use when wishing protection for someone.
اللّٰه يبارك فيك	*God bless you, Thank you.*
اللّٰه يطوِّل في عُمْرك	*May God extend your life.* Use when wishing someone a long life.
اللّٰه يعْطيك العافيِّة	*May God give you health.*
جزاكَ اللّٰه خَيْرًا	*May God reward you.* Use when you wish to thank someone.
رَحْمة اللّٰه عليه\هـ	*God have mercy on him/her.* Use when referring to someone who is deceased.
في أَمانِ اللّٰه	*Go in the protection of God.* Use when wishing someone safety and protection.
لا قَدَّرَ اللّٰه	*God forbid.*

STUDY TIP

Create small paper flashcards for difficult words with the Arabic on one side and English (or your native tongue) on the other side. Carry them with you when you are studying and test yourself regularly. Cover up the English side of the vocabulary list and see if you remember the meaning of the word.

Beyond Arabic vocabulary

In this unit you will learn essential vocabulary, organized as follows:

- The 100 most frequent words in Arabic
- Foreign loanwords in Arabic مُفْرَدات أجْنبيّة مُسْتَعارة
- Arabized words المُفْرَدات المُعَرَّبة
- Arabic homonyms الألْفاظ المُتَجانسة
- Arabic homographs الألْفاظ المُتَجانسة
- Arabic homophones الألْفاظ المُتَجانسة
- Arabic blends الألْفاظ المنحوتة
- Collocations المُتَلازِمات اللَّفْظيّة

As the Arabs say ... كَما قالَتِ العَرَب

دارِهِم مادُمْت في دارِهِم
وأرْضِهِم مادُمْت في أَرْضِهِم
وحَيِّهِم مادُمْت في حَيِّهِم

Please them as long as you are in their land.
Hail them while in their neighbourhood
and grant them the upper hand while in their home.
Arabic proverb

The 100 most frequent words in Arabic

The following vocabulary was compiled by T. Buckwalter and D. Parkinson in their book *A Frequency Dictionary of Arabic: Core Vocabulary for Learners* (Routledge, 2011).

1	الـ	the (definite article)
2	وَ	and, with
3	في	in, inside, on (a date) at (a time), about, among

4	مِن	from, since
5	لِـ	for, to (prep.)
6	بِـ	with, by (prep.)
7	عَلى	on, above (prep.)
8	أَنَّ	that
9	إِلى	to, towards; till, until (prep.)
10	كانَ	to be
11	لا	no, not, non-
12	اللّٰه	God, Allah
13	أَنْ	(with subjunctive) to
14	عَنْ	from, about (prep.)
15	قال	to say
16	هٰذا	this
17	مَعَ	with
18	الَّتي	who, whom; which (rel. pron.) (m.)
19	كُلّ	each, every, all
20	هُوَ	he, it (pron.)
21	فَـ	and, so
22	هٰذِهِ	this (f.)
23	أَو	or
24	الَّذي	who, whom, which (rel. pron.) (f.)
25	أَنا	I
26	يَوْم	day
27	لَمْ	did not
28	ما	not

29	إِنَّ	that
30	مَا	what, whatever, that which
31	بِـ	to indicate continuous or habitual action (Egy. Lev.)
32	بَيْنَ	between, among (prep.)
33	هِيَ	she, it
34	بَعْدَ	after (prep.)
35	يَا	O ... (voc. part.)
36	ذَلِكَ	that (m. sing.)
37	قَدْ	has/have already
38	آخَر	other, another; one more, additional
39	شَيْء	thing, something
40	عِنْدَ	with, next to, at (time, location)
41	أَوَّل	first, best, topmost
42	غَيْر	other (than), different (from)
43	إِذَا	when, if, whenever
44	نَفْس	same, self
45	عَرَبِيّ	Arab, Arabian, Arabic (Dia.)
46	أَيّ	any, what, which, whatever, whoever
47	رَئِيس	president, leader, chief, head, chairman
48	عَمَل	working, work, activity, action
49	عَرَف	to know (st./so.)
50	بَعْض	some, several
51	دَوْلة	state, country
52	كَمَا	and, also, as well
53	إِلَّا	except (for), but (for)

54	أَنْتَ	you (m. sing.)
55	كَثِير	many, much, numerous
56	واحِد	one, single
57	لِأَنّ	because
58	لَكِن	however, but
59	لَيْسَ	not to be (he/it is not)
60	جَدِيد	new, modern
61	إِنْ	if, whether
62	عام	year
63	أَحَد	one (of), someone, anyone, nobody, no one
64	أَكْثَر	more/most, greater/greatest
65	كَبِير	large, great, important, major, adult, senior
66	أَخْ	brother
67	كَيْفَ	how
68	قَبْل	before, prior to
69	سَنة	year
70	أَمْر	matter, issue, concern, affair
71	قُوّة	power, strength, force
72	هَلْ	yes/no question
73	خِلال	during, through
74	مَرّة	time, moment, occasion
75	رَأى	to see (st./so.), to think, to believe
76	أَب	father
77	هُناك	there, over there, there is, there are

78	تَمَّ	to finish, to conclude, to come to an end, to take place
79	حَيْثُ	where, in which
80	ثانٍ	second, additional, next, following
81	حَتَّى	until, up to
82	جَميع	every one (of)
83	مِنْطَقة	region, area, zone, territory
84	حَقّ	truth, (legal) right
85	أَمْريكيّ	American
86	مِثْل	like, similar
87	لَوْ	if
88	عامّ	general, common, public
89	اِسْم	name
90	أَمْكَنَ	to be possible
91	لَكِن	however, but
92	رَجُل	man
93	عالَم	world
94	حَياة	life
95	مَوْضوع	subject, topic, issue, theme
96	وَزير	minister
97	نَحْنُ	we (pron.)
98	وَقْت	time, moment, period
99	بَلَد	country, nation
100	مَن	who, whom (rel. pron.)

Foreign loanwords in Arabic
مُفْرَدات أَجْنَبِيَّة مُسْتَعَارة

Foreign loanwords are words that are incorporated into Arabic directly without translation from other languages, mainly English, French, Persian and Turkish. These are predominantly in circulation among Arabs in day-to-day communication in colloquial Arabic. Here are some few examples:

راديو	radio	مِيلِّيمِتْر	millimetre
سينما	cinema	مَلْيون	million
فيلم\فِلْم	film	بَلْيون	billion
تليفِزيون	TV	بَلَكون	balcony
تلفون	telephone	صالون	salon
جَوّال\مَحْمول\نَقّال	mobile	أَرْشيف	archives
بورتابل	portable	أُستوديو	studio
أتوبيس\باص	bus	إِسْمَنْت	cement
تاكسي	taxi	أوكازيون	d'occasion (Fr.) i.e. used
أوتومبيل	automobile	بَنْطَلون	pantalon (Fr.) i.e. trousers
ماكينة	machine	كورْنيش	corniche (Fr.)
فاكس	fax	أَلْبوم	album
فيديو	video	موضة	mode (Fr.), fashion
رادار	radar	سوسيولوجيا	sociology
كومْبيوتِر	computer	اسْتراتيجيّة	strategy
الإنْتِرْنِت	Internet	أِيديولوجيّة	ideology
الويب	web	إمبرياليّة	imperialism
إلِكْترونيّ	electronic	ديموقراطيّة	democracy
بَنْك	bank	بيروقراطيّة	bureaucracy
سَنَتِمِتْر	centimetre	بوليس	police

ديكتاتوريّة	dictatorship	ساندويتش	sandwich
أرستُقراطيّة	aristocracy	سيجار	cigar
ليبراليّة	liberalism	سباغيتي	spaghetti
امبراطوريّة	empire	مَعْكَرونة	macaroni
كليشّيه (ج) -ات	clichés	تَكْتيك (ج) -ات	tactics
فيدراليّة	federal	بترول	petrol
براجْماتيّ	pragmatist	بِنْزين	gasoline
بَرْلَمان	parliament	غاز	gas
أكاديميّ	academic	مَدام	madam
باكالوريا	baccalaureate	دُكْتور	doctor
بَكالوريوس	bachelor (degree)	كيلومتْر	kilometre
مُناوَرة	manœuvre (Fr.)	كيلوغْرام	kilogram

المُفْرَدات المُعَرَّبة Arabized words

Arabized words are borrowed loanwords from other languages that have been reshaped and transformed through the process of Arabization in an attempt to promote the use of Arabic language, and hence the Arab culture and Arab identity among its people.

Arabized words	Foreign loanwords	English
تِلْفاز\تَلْفَزة	تِلِفِزْيون	television, TV (institution)
إذاعة\مِذْياع	راديو	radio, radio (institution)
الشّابكة	الإنْتِرْنِت	Internet
هاتف	تِلِفون	telephone
سَيّارة	أتوموبيل	automobile, car
جَوّال مَحْمول	موبايل\بورتابل	mobile
حاسِب\حاسوب	كُمْبيوتِر	computer

حافلة	باص	*bus*
آلة	ماكينة	*machine*
سَجّاد	موكيت	*carpet*
مَصرَف	بَنْك	*bank*
سُخام	سبام	*spam*
سَيّارة أُجْرة	تاكسي	*taxi*
لاقِط صَوْت	مَيْكروفون	*microphone*

الأَلْفاظ المُتَجانِسة Arabic homonyms

An Arabic homonym is a word that is spelt the same as another but differing in meaning. They also differ in one or more of the diacritics. Most common homonymes are obvious such the verbs forms I vs. II (e.g. to study دَرَسَ vs. to teach دَرَّسَ), Nisbah adjectives vs. nouns with possessive pronouns (e.g. مَنْزِلي my house vs. مَنْزِلِيَ domestic).

Here are some more essential Arabic homonyms to learn:

مَنْ	*who*	مِنْ	*from*
أَمْ	*or*	أُمّ	*mother*
أَلْف	*thousand*	أَلِف	*letter Alif*
كُتّاب	*authors, Qur'anic school*	كِتاب	*book*
عالَم	*world*	عالِم	*scholar*
مَدْرَسة	*school*	مُدَرِّسة	*teacher (f.)*
سَلَطة	*salad*	سُلْطة	*authority*
كِتاب	*book*	كُتّاب	*Qur'anic school*
ذَهَب	*gold*	ذَهَبَ	*to go (v.)*
جُزُر	*islands*	جَزَر	*carrots*
حَمّام	*bathroom, toilet*	حَمام	*pigeons*
أَسِرّة	*beds*	أُسْرة	*family*
أُذُن	*ear*	إِذَن	*therefore*

تاريخ	date		تاريخ	history
سُلَّم	ladder		سِلْم	peace
جُمَل	phrases		جَمَل	camel
جمال	camels		جَمال	beauty
قِصاص	punishment		قَصّاص	storyteller
شَعْر	hair		شِعْر	poetry
مُلِحّ	insistent		مِلْح	salt
سُلْفة	loan, advance payment		سِلْفة	sister-in-law
قُبْلة	kiss		قِبْلة	direction of prayer
عَمّان	Amman		عُمان	Oman
مُدَوِّنة	blogger (f.)		مُدَوَّنة	blog
مُشَكَّلة	mixed		مُشْكلة	problem
دَخَل	to enter		دَخْل	income
جِنَّة	sprits, ghosts		جَنَّة	paradise
عِقْد	decade		عَقْد	contract
عَقَدَ	to hold, convene		عُقَد	knots

Arabic homographs الألْفاظ المُتَجانِسة

A homograph is defined simply as two words that are spelled and pronounced in exactly the same way but have different meanings, as in:

I **read** today and I **read** yesterday.

The **coach** sat on a **coach**.

writers, authors	كُتّاب	Qur'anic school
liquid	سائل	someone who asks a question
eye	عَيْن	water well, letter 'ayn (ع)
lover	هاوٍ	someone falling
speaker	قائل	someone taking midday nap or siesta (derived from قيلولة)

flying (f. adj.)	طائرة	aeroplane, pilot (f.)
prophetic tradition	حَديث	modern, conversation, speech
example	مَثَل	proverb
criticism	نَقْد	currency
street	الشَّارِع	the legislator (God)
fine, precise	دَقيق	flour
stream	جَدْوَل	programme
neighbourhood	حَيّ	alive

Arabic homophones الأَلْفاظ المُتَجانِسة

A homophone is simply a word that is pronounced the same way as another but differs in spelling and meaning.

تاريخ	date		تاريخ	history
عَلا	to be elevated, raised		عَلى	on, upon (prep.)
لَيْلى	female Arabic name		لَيْلة	night
دَعْوى	lawsuit		دَعْوة	invitation
شَفى	to heal		شَفا	edge
رُؤْية	vision, dream		رُؤْيا	revelation
عَصى	to disobey		عَصا	stick

Arabic blends الألفاظ المنحوتة

In linguistics, a blend is a word made from parts of two or more words. There are many examples in English, for example: *netizen* (a combination of *net* and *citizen*), *infomercial*, *edutainment*, *flexitarian*, etc.

Blending in Arabic has been common since pre-Islamic times. It was particularly useful for summarizing long expressions into one manageable word. While some blends are still popular today, some have fallen out of use.

now	هذه السّاعة	هَسَّع\هَسّاع\السّاع
now	هذا الوَقْت	هَلَّق

General		
etc. (lit. till its end)	إلى آخِرِه	إلخ
about what	عن + ماذا	عَمّاذا
which	مِنْ + ما	مِمّا
capital (finance)	رَأْس + مال	رَأْسْمال\رَأْسْماليّة
petrodollar	بِتْرول + دولار	بِتْرودلار
space–time	زَمان + مَكان	زَمَكان
present case	عَرْض + حال	عَرْضْحال
electromagnetic	كَهْرَبائي + مَغْنَطيسيّ	كَهْرَطيسيّ
photoelectric	كَهْرَباء + ضَوْئيّ	كَهْرَضَوْئيّ
physicochemical	فيزيائيّ + كيميائيّ	فيزيوكيميائيّ
amphibians	بَرّ + ماء	بَرْمائيّ (ج) -ات
hydroelectric	كَهْرَباء + ماء	كَهْرَماء
transliteration	نَقْل + حَرْفيّ	نَقْحَرة

Islamic expressions		
to say the phrase *In the name of God the Most Compassionate*	بِسْم الله الرَّحْمن الرَّحيم	بَسْمَل\بَسْمَلة
to say *God is Greatest*	الله أكْبَر	كَبَّر\تَكْبير

to say *There is no God but Allah*	الحَمْدُ لله	حَمْدَل\حَمْدَلة
to say *There is no God but Allah*	لا إله إلاّ الله	هَلَّل\تَهْليل
to say *There is no power or might except with Allah*	لا حَوْل ولا قُوَّة إلاّ ب الله	حَوْقَل\حَوْقَلة
to say *Come to prayer*	حَيَّ على الصّلاة	حَيْعَل\حَيْعَلة
to say *Glorious is God*	سُبْحان الله	سَبْحَل\سَبْحَلة
to say the expression *What Allah wills*	ما شاء الله	مَشْأَل\مَشْأَلة

Collocations المُتَلازِمات اللَّفْظيّة

In linguistics, a collocation is words that often go together.

Arabic collocations can enhance your writing dramatically and they are usually acquired through regular reading of news articles, novels, etc.

Here is a selection of common Arabic collocations:

الصَّباح الباكِر	*early morning*
رَأس السَّنة	*new year*
اتَّخَذ قَرارًا	*to make a decision*
زَرَع أفْكارًا	*to plant ideas*
شَنَّ الحَرْب على	*to wage war on*
ابْن آدم	*human being (lit. son of Adam)*
ابْن البَلَد	*citizen, native*
ابْن اللَّيْل	*thief, robber*
لُغة الضّاد	*Arabic language (insight)*
لَيْلة الدُّخْلة	*the wedding night*
تَحْت التَّجْرِبة	*on probation*
صِفْر اليَدَيْن	*barehanded*
الجِنْس الخَشِن	*male (the strong sex)*

الجِنْس اللَّطيف	female (the fair sex)
اليَد العامِلة	labour
عَيْش\خُبْز ومِلْح	bread and salt (socializing)
القَضاء والقَدَر	divine decree and fate
الدِّين الحَنيف	religion
حَديث نَبَويّ	prophetic tradition
أسْعار باهِظة	exorbitant prices
بَرْد قارس	freezing cold
بُزوغ الفَجْر	dawn
تَطْهير عِرْقيّ	ethnic cleansing
تَعاوُن مُثْمِر	productive cooperation
حَديث العَهْد	new, recent
سَماء صافية	clear skies
سَفْك الدِّماء	bloodshed
تَغيُّر جَذْريّ	radical change
هُجوم شامِل	full-scale war
مَعْركة دامية	bloody battle
مُقاوَمة عَنيفة\شَرسة	stiff resistance
مَعْلومات سرِّية	classified information
ثَوْرة مُسَلَّحة	armed revolt
ظَلام دامِس	extreme darkness
ثَراء فاحِش	extreme wealth
فَقْر مُدْقِع	extreme poverty
أبْيَض ناصِع	bright white

STUDY TIP

Start with the most frequent words. First and foremost, learn words of high frequency, both in spoken and written Arabic.

Taking it further

Although this book covers a wide variety of themes and includes many useful words and expressions, it is practically impossible to include all the words that you will come across in Arabic. To expand your wordpower beyond the scope of this book, the following are suggestions for some useful publications that deal particularly with vocabulary acquisition.

THEME-BASED VOCABULARY LEARNING TEXTBOOKS

Building Arabic Vocabulary Through Reading: For Advanced Students of MSA by N. Naili Al-Warraki and N. Harb (American University in Cairo Press, 2014)

Practice Makes Perfect Arabic Vocabulary (Practice Makes Perfect), by M. Gaafar & J. Wightwick (McGraw-Hill, 2012)

Arabic Vocabulary Made Easy (Volume 1 & 2): *Using mnemonics to remember a huge list of Arabic* by D. J. Western (2011)

Harrap's Pocket Arabic Vocabulary (Harrap, 2010)

The Concise Arabic–English Lexicon of Verbs in Context by A. Taher, H. K. M. Abdou and D. Abo El Seoud (American University in Cairo Press, 2010)

Chambers Arabic Vocabulary (Chambers, 2009)

Arabic Vocabulary: Reference Guide/Pamphlet (BarCharts Inc., 2007)

Build Your Arabic Vocabulary by H. Shirwani (McGraw-Hill, 2010)

Your First 100 Words in Arabic w/Audio CD by J. Wightwick (McGraw-Hill, 2006)

Modern Standard Arabic Vocab Clinic (American University in Cairo Press, 2005)

Arabic in 10 Minutes a Day by Kristine K. Kershul (Bilingual Books, 2004)

THEME-BASED LEXICONS

The Arabic/English Thematic Lexicon by D. Newman (Routledge, 2007)

GCSE Arabic Essential Vocabulary List: An Arabic–English Vocabulary List, Arranged by topics by Z. Debs Khayat and L. A Al-Waraa (Arab Scientific Publishers, 2004)

SPECIALIZED VOCABULARY LEXICONS

Security Arabic: Essential Middle Eastern Vocabularies by M. Evans (Edinburgh University Press, 2013)

Internet Arabic: Essential Middle Eastern Vocabularies by M. Diouri (Edinburgh University Press, 2012)

Business Arabic: An Essential Vocabulary by J. Mace (Edinburgh University Press, 2008)

Media Arabic: An Essential Vocabulary by E. Kendall (Edinburgh University Press, 2005)

STANDARD DICTIONARIES (IN ALPHABETICAL ORDER)

Collins Pocket Arabic Dictionary (Harper Collins, 2012)

M-W Arabic–English Dictionary (Merriam-Webster, 2010)

Oxford Essential Arabic Dictionary (OUP, 2010)

Arabic–English/English–Arabic Dictionary by N. Awde & K. Smith (Bennett & Bloom, 2003)

Al Mawrid (English–Arabic/Arabic–English Pocket Dictionary) by M. Baalbaki & R. Baalbaki (Dar El Ilm Lilmalayin, 1998)

ROOT-BASED DICTIONARIES

Oxford Arabic Dictionary (Oxford University Press, 2014)

Arabic–English Lexicon by E. W. Lane (Islamic Texts Society, 1984)

A Dictionary of Modern Written Arabic, by H. Wehr, edited by J. Milton Cowan, 4th edn (1976)

VISUAL-BASED DICTIONARIES

My First Bilingual Book – Opposites: English–Arabic (Milet Publishing, 2012)

Arabic–English Visual Bilingual Dictionary (Dorling Kindersley, 2009)

Oxford First Arabic Words (First Words) by D. Melling (OUP, 2009)

Word by Word Picture Dictionary: English/Arabic Edition (Word by Word Picture Dictionaries) by B. Bliss and S. J. Molinsky (Pearson, 2008)

The Oxford Picture Dictionary: English/Arabic Library Binding, by N. Shapiro (Author), J. Adelson-Goldstein (Oxford, 2008)

My Arabic Words Book by S. Juma (Tahrike Tarsile Qur'an, 2007)

First Thousand Words in Arabic (Usborne First 1000 Words) by H. Amery (Usborne, 2001)

SYNONYMS AND FREQUENCY DICTIONARIES

A Frequency Dictionary of Arabic: Core Vocabulary for Learners by T. Buckwalter & D. Parkinson (Routledge, 2011)

Using Arabic Synonyms by D. Parkinson (Cambridge University Press, 2005)

PAPER VOCABULARY FLASHCARD COURSES

Arabic in a Flash Kit Volume 1 by F. Mansouri (Tuttle Publishing, 2014)

Arabic in a Flash Kit Volume 2 by F. Mansouri (Tuttle Publishing, 2014)

Arabic Berlitz Vocabulary Study Cards (Arabic) Cards (Berlitz, 2011)

Flashcards: School and Classroom Vocabulary Sets 1–4 by I. Alawiye (Anglo-Arabic Graphics, 2005–11)

AUDIO-BASED VOCABULARY COURSES

Arabic Vocabulary Builder + (Learn Arabic with the Michel Thomas Method), by J. Wightwick and M. Gaafar (Hodder & Stoughton, 2013)

Earworms Rapid Arabic (Verb and Vocab Booster) (Berlitz, 2011)

Arabic Vocabulary (Flash Forward) (Living Language, 2009)

VocabuLearn: Arabic, Level 1 & 2 (Penton Overseas, 2005)

Vocabulary Builder Arabic: Language fun for all the family – All Ages (Eurotalk, 2000)(PC/Mac)

بالتَّوْفيق والنَّجاح

تَمَّ بِحَمْدِ اللهِ وعَوْنِه